Superbrands

AN INSIGHT INTO SOME OF BRITAIN'S STRONGEST BRANDS 2007/08

www.superbrands.uk.com

Chief Executive
Ben Hudson

Brand Liaison Directors
Fiona Maxwell
Claire Pollock
Liz Silvester

PR & Marketing Manager
Hannah Paul

Administrative Co-ordinator
Heidi Smith

Head of Accounts
Will Carnochan

Managing Editor
Angela Cooper

Assistant Editor
Laura Hill

Authors
Karen Dugdale
Jennifer Small

Other publications from Superbrands (UK) Ltd:
Business Superbrands 2007 ISBN: 978-0-9554784-0-6
CoolBrands 2006/07 ISBN: 1-905652-03-8

To order these books, email brands@superbrands.uk.com
or call 01825 767396.

Published by Superbrands (UK) Ltd.
44 Charlotte Street
London
WIT 2NR

© 2007 Superbrands (UK) Ltd published under licence
from Superbrands Ltd.

www.superbrands.uk.com

Printed in Italy

ISBN: 978-0-9554784-1-3

The paper used for this book
has been independently
certified as coming from well-
managed forests and other
controlled sources according
to the rules of the Forest
Stewardship Council.

FSC
Certificate No.
CQ–COC–000012

This book has been printed and bound in Italy by
Printer Trento S.r.l., an FSC accredited company for
printing books on FSC mixed paper in compliance
with the chain of custody and on-products labelling
standards.

Contents

Endorsements

Superbrands

John Noble
Director
British Brands Group

The brands you will find in this collection of Superbrands are confidence inspiring. They have built a name for themselves for being excellent at what they do and for being consistent in the delivery of that excellence year after year. Some of these brands we may never have used but their reputation precedes them and we may be confident that they will perform.

Behind each brand is a unique and engaging story, not just explaining how they have come to command such confidence and trust but also what makes them different, unique and special. Through these stories comes the personality of each brand, bringing a more engaging dimension to the relationship between product and user.

The British Brands Group is delighted to support this collection of Superbrands. As an organisation we wish to see a climate in the UK in which such brands continue to flourish and new brands are fostered, bringing us choice, diversity and ever-better performance.

Paul Gostick
Chairman
The Chartered Institute
of Marketing

Can you imagine a life without brands? Whilst for some this might seem a glorious idyll, for the rest of us, having to wade our way through countless undifferentiated and indistinguishable products and services, devoid of meaning and emotion, would be a very unsavoury prospect.

Brands form an essential backdrop to our daily lives. We prefer brands not because of what they are but because of how we feel about them. The brand promise builds trust and loyalty and must be delivered consistently day in day out. Ultimately it is the customer who is the judge of whether this has been achieved!

The Superbrands featured in this book enrich lives, entertain, delight and sometimes even make deep emotional connections with consumers, creating value for them and driving value for their organisations and shareholders too.

The Chartered Institute of Marketing is delighted to endorse Superbrands 2007/08. By examining the excellence of others, we can all improve our own efforts, and ensure that the lives of consumers and businesses alike are enriched.

Derek Holder
Managing Director
The Institute of Direct
Marketing

We're extremely pleased to support Superbrands 2007/08. In the last 5-10 years the branding landscape has changed dramatically with new media, new markets, new channels and new challenges.

The industry is not only far more sophisticated but is now more complex and competitive. The Institute of Direct Marketing (IDM) applauds initiatives that contribute to greater recognition of branding and in particular those brands that have elevated themselves above their peers.

The IDM is proud to be involved in the Superbrands project and hopes that the insights and case studies featured within these covers help further our understanding of the hard work and discipline required to build a successful 'Superbrand'.

James Aitchison
Managing Editor
World Advertising
Research Center

We live in an age of ubiquitous brands and ubiquitous branding. And for good reason. These intangible assets are at the heart of economic activity in UK plc, none more so than the many field-leading examples in this latest volume from Superbrands.

As an organisation that's been in the business of promoting brand knowledge for many years now, the World Advertising Research Center applauds the work of Superbrands and we're delighted to feature the special brands that it honours on WARC.com.

This annual showcase goes well beyond paying lip service to the importance of brands in our economy. It spotlights the individual brands that are setting the standards and leading the way.

What's more, these brands are selected by the people who ultimately always make or break them – consumers. We'd all do well to take heed of the ones they've chosen.

About Superbrands

The Superbrands Stamp

The brands that have been awarded Superbrands status and participate in the programme, are given permission to use the Superbrands Stamp. This powerful endorsement provides evidence to existing and potential consumers, media, employees and investors of the exceptional standing that these Superbrands have achieved.

Member brands use the stamp on marketing materials, including product packaging, POS items, advertising, websites and annual reports, as well as other external and internal communication channels.

Superbrands presents expert and consumer opinion on the UK's strongest brands. The organisation promotes the discipline of branding and pays tribute to exceptional brands through a series of specific programmes. Each of these includes a dedicated publication, launch party and presence on www.superbrands.uk.com.

The independent and voluntary Superbrands Council consists of eminent individuals, well qualified to judge which are the nation's strongest brands. Each brand featured in this publication has qualified based on the opinion of this council as well as a dedicated consumer election which is run by YouGov.

A Superbrand is defined as follows:

"A Superbrand has established the finest reputation in its field. It offers customers significant emotional and tangible advantages over other brands, which (consciously or sub-consciously) customers want and recognise."

Through identifying these brands and providing their case histories, the organisation hopes that people will gain a deeper appreciation of the discipline of branding and a greater understanding of the brands themselves.

Superbrands Selection Process

Superbrands

Independent researchers use a wide range of sources to compile a list of the UK's leading brands. From the thousands of brands initially considered, a list of approximately 1,450 brands is forwarded to the Superbrands Council.

The independent and voluntary Superbrands Council considers the list and members individually award each brand a score from 1-10. The score is intuitive, but council members are asked to bear in mind the level of quality, reliability and distinction that each brand offers. Council members are not allowed to score brands with which they have a direct association or are in direct competition to. The lowest-scoring brands (approximately 50 per cent) are eliminated at this stage.

A nationally representative panel of 3,265 consumers is surveyed by YouGov, the UK's most accurate online research agency. These individuals are asked to vote on the surviving 725 brands.

The top 500 highest-ranking brands, based on the consumer scores, are awarded 'Superbrand' status and are invited to join the Superbrands programme.

Superbrands Council 2007/08

Howard Beale
Founder
& Managing Director
The Fish Can Sing

Drayton Bird
Chairman
Drayton Bird Associates

Leslie de Chernatony
Professor, Brand Marketing
& Director, Centre for Research
in Brand Marketing
Birmingham University
Business School

Mark Cridge
Chief Executive
glue London

Tim Duffy
Chief Executive
M&C Saatchi

Vanessa Eke
Managing Director
Language Line Services Ltd

Peter Fisk
Founder
Genius Works

Winston Fletcher
Chairman
Advertising Standards
Board of Finance

Cheryl Giovannoni
Managing Director
Landor Associates, London

David Haigh
Chief Executive
Brand Finance

Graham Hiscott
Consumer Editor
Daily Express

Paul Kemp-Robertson
Editorial Director
& Co-Founder
Contagious

David Magliano
Ex Director of Marketing
London 2012

Mandy Pooler
Director
Kantar

Chris Powell
Co-Founder
BMP

Anna Ronay
Editor
Ethos

Tim Sutton
Chairman
Weber Shandwick, Europe

Suki Thompson
Founding Partner
The Haystack Group

Mark Waugh
Deputy Managing Director
ZenithOptimedia

Stephen Cheliotis
Chairman
Superbrands Councils (UK)

Foreword

Angela Cooper, Managing Editor

How do brands become 'number one' in their sector? In this, the ninth edition of Superbrands, you will find examples of brands that have reached this elusive position – an impressive achievement in the current climate of rapid and significant innovation and change. In the Brands to Watch section, you will find a collection of the potential Superbrands of the future. The forefathers of today's strong brands – John Boot of Boots, Henry Williamson Gossard of Gossard, Ole Kirk Cristiansen of LEGO®, James Pimm of PIMM'S® and alike – would be proud of the pioneering spirit shown by these brands.

The thread that runs throughout the Superbrands case studies is that brands must deliver excellent products whilst interacting effectively with their target audience. Best practice dictates that this should be supported by an awareness and dedication to environmental and social issues; embracing new technologies – both in terms of improving the actual product as well as how it is delivered; a clear USP and brand personality; and of course not forgetting good old fashioned excellent service.

In the articles at the back of the book, written by members of our Council, these issues are discussed in detail, providing fascinating insights into today and tomorrow's branding climate.

I would like to take this opportunity to thank the members of the Superbrands Council, who individually voted on which brands they believe to be worthy of Superbrand status. The Council is comprised of eminent individuals and opinion leaders who are all well qualified to judge which are the nation's strongest brands. You can find details of who these individuals are on page 12.

The Council was tasked with identifying the strongest brands based on their personal perceptions of their strength and quality in the market. When scoring, they kept the following definition in mind:

"A Superbrand has established the finest reputation in its field. It offers consumers significant emotional and tangible advantages over other brands, which (consciously or sub-consciously) customers want and recognise."

We have found that the aggregate perception of experienced market professionals is as valuable a guide to brand excellence as any other supposedly more scientific processes. It enables the brands to be judged against their peers across a diverse range of sectors.

The Superbrands organisation also gathers the consumers' viewpoint on which brands should be awarded Superbrand status, via an online election managed by YouGov. The consumers' opinions are then combined with those of the Council to create an overall score. The top scoring brands, based on the combined weighted rating, are awarded Superbrand status and invited to participate in our programme.

We hope that the following best practice examples from some of Britain's strongest brands help to further the understanding of branding and the work and investment needed to become, let alone remain, one of the Britian's finest.

QUALITY

RELIABILITY

DISTINCTION

The AA is the dominant brand leader in the roadside assistance market. Over the last 100 years, the brand has been built on the quality, expertise and dedication of its patrol force. Their expertise is not only with cars (they fix over 80 per cent of breakdowns at the roadside); but with car owners. This is key to AA's market leading position.

Market

In recent years, the breakdown assistance market has become increasingly competitive with new entrants and dynamics challenging the hegemony of the big two – AA and RAC. Insurance companies and supermarkets now offer cheap alternative protection. Furthermore, online services are making it ever easier to shop around for the best deal.

The AA is the brand leader in breakdown cover with a 42.4 per cent share of the personal market. It also has the largest dedicated, liveried breakdown patrol force in the UK. Other brands in the market include the RAC, with a 27.6 per cent share, who also provide their own dedicated patrol force

and Green Flag, with an 11.5 per cent share, who provide a contracted garage service. The overall market size is approximately 14 million.

Achievements

The AA has won several recent awards spanning the whole business, from branding awards including the Reader's Digest Trusted Brand award 2006 and 2007 and Best Known Co-brand from the National Credit Card Awards 2007, to Best Breakdown Service at the Fleet News Awards 2007 and Best Vehicle Recovery Supplier from the Business Car Awards 2007, for the fifth year in succession. In addition, the AA Team was

recognised with the Grand Prix Award from Revolution Magazine in 2007.

In 2006, AA was awarded the Diamond Award at the Institute of Direct Marketing Business Performance Awards; Overall HR Excellence Award by HR Magazine; as well as the Accountancy Age Business Finance Team of the Year award.

Product

The AA provides breakdown assistance both in the UK and in Europe where it operates a dedicated English speaking call centre. For motorists who have experienced a breakdown and need work carried out on their vehicle the AA offers a unique breakdown repair product which offers help with labour and parts costs. For breakdowns, the AA operates in the corporate as well as the individual market where its offer includes breakdown cover for fleets and specialist vehicles, driver assessment, driver training and accident management.

As well as breakdown assistance products, the AA also provides a wide range of other services for the modern motorist. It is the largest insurance broker in the UK with a range of products that extends beyond motor insurance to include, home, travel, life, pet, golf, classic car and motor cycle insurance as well as legal assistance with personal injury claims. AA publishing is the UK's largest travel publisher and one of the top 10 worldwide. The AA Route Planner found on theAA.com generated over three million routes a week and over 150 million in total during 2006. In addition, the AA Driving School is the second largest driving school in

1905	1910	1912	1920	1930	1967
A group of motoring enthusiasts meet at the Trocedero restaurant in London's West End on 24th June to form the Automobile Association.	The first AA routes are introduced.	The AA begins inspecting and rating hotels.	The AA introduces pre and post purchase repair checks.	Of the two million motorists on the road, AA membership exceeds 750,000.	AA Insurance Services, the largest broker of car and home insurance in the UK, is launched.

the UK and the only one to use fully qualified instructors. The AA also has a Financial Services Business providing loans, credit cards and savings accounts to members and non members alike. AA Signs is the market leader in event road signage and erected over 76,000 temporary road signs across the UK during 2006.

Recent Developments
2006 was a busy year for the AA. The AA Members Club was launched giving AA members access to a range of exclusive discounts on motoring and travel related products, from Airport Parking to family days out, MOT's Car Servicing and Car Hire. Also in 2006 the AA joined the Nectar programme; the largest loyalty scheme in the UK, through this AA members can collect Nectar points for breakdown membership and renewal. AA Insurance Services purchased Direct Choice, an Insurance Broker complimenting its existing portfolio. A number of initiatives have been introduced to the Roadside business. A new Roadside patrol van is being rolled out across the fleet, equipped with new bespoke technology – Vehicle Recovery System – that enables the recovery of the majority of cars by the attending patrol. This facilitates a 'one stop shop' by the AA's own dedicated patrol which research confirms is very important to its members.

In September the AA Academy Apprenticeship Programme was launched in collaboration with the apprenticeship learning division of Carter and Carter Group plc, one of the leading providers of Government funded learning initiatives for the motor industry.

Finally in 2006 a £1 million investment was made in theAA.com/travel web portal, further extending the appeal of the popular Route Planner service.

Promotion
The AA has been responsible for some of Britain's most memorable advertising campaigns, from 'He's a very nice man' to 'The 4th Emergency Service' and the current 'You've Got a Friend'.

From 1987 to 1992 a series of television, press and radio advertisements were produced featuring the AA's 'He's a very nice man', the 'man who can' helping members in a variety of difficult circumstances. The television advertisements were light in tone, using humour to establish a warm and friendly image for the AA. They also created a catchphrase that lives on today.

By 1993 the breakdown market had become increasingly competitive, new entrants were carving out niche positions for themselves and the AA faced a renewed challenge from an invigorated RAC. Consumer insight revealed that for many people breaking down was an emergency situation. In this environment the AA was viewed in a similar way to the Fire, Police and Ambulance Services. Thus 'The 4th Emergency Service' was born, deploying a real life tone of voice with the emphasis on safety and professionalism. The positioning was that of a market leader, setting standards, leading innovation and motivating people to join and remain AA members.

In 2005, under new ownership, the AA needed a new campaign that focused once again on its core breakdown business. Research revealed that the biggest driver in this very mature market was the quality of the patrols. The communication strategy therefore puts the AA patrol at the very heart of the brand, positioning it as the customers' 'friend' – someone who can be relied on to help whenever and wherever they are called upon. With the help of Carole King's classic soul anthem, 'You've Got A Friend', the recent campaign has helped grow both brand consideration and retention to record levels. As well as television, the AA also uses press, cinema, radio and online for brand building and a complete range of direct media channels on and offline for acquisition.

Brand Values
The AA's key brand values are focused around the brand's relationship with its customers. It aims to be warm, friendly, emotional, expert and offer value for money in everything that it does.

www.theaa.com

1973
AA Roadwatch is launched to become Europe's biggest traffic broadcaster.

AA Relay is launched.

1992
AA Driving School is launched and is the only national body to use fully qualified instructors.

2004
The AA is acquired by two leading European Private Equity firms, CVC and Permira, for £1.75 billion.

2006
The AA purchases Direct Choice, an insurance broker.

Things you didn't know about AA

According to AA research, 98 per cent of AA members who've had a breakdown would recommend the AA to a friend.

Throughout its history, the AA has attended over 100 million breakdowns and now attends a breakdown every nine seconds.

The AA takes care of 390,000 flat batteries and 300,000 punctures every year and its vans collectively drive over 55 million miles looking after its 15 million members.

The most popular destination for routes on the AA Route Planner is Heathrow Airport.

Since its launch in 1932, Anadin has become, and remains, an iconic British brand, well loved and trusted by the nation. Seen as 'experts in pain', Anadin delivers substantial consumer confidence. Its product range is regarded as an effective and trustworthy method of pain relief.

Market

Today's busy lifestyles, coupled with an explosion in consumer information about health, are driving factors behind the rise in self-medication and the consequent growth of over the counter (OTC) medicines.

In the year to December 2006, the total adult oral analgesics market was worth £357.8 million (Source: IRI December 2006). This comprised 292.1 million packs made up of 5.7 billion individual pills.

Analgesics remain the most effective remedy for pain. A wide range of analgesics are available OTC, differentiated not only by their active ingredients but also by their formats.

Achievements

A history of innovative product launches has maintained Anadin's position as a leading pain killer brand and today Anadin has the number one selling branded adult painkiller pack with Anadin Extra 16s (Source: IRI December 2006) and is the second biggest branded analgesic in the UK.

Over the years, the brand has led industry innovation and incorporated all the major 'general sales list' (GSL) ingredients (paracetamol, ibuprofen and aspirin) into its portfolio, enabling it to offer a range of targeted and effective solutions to combat

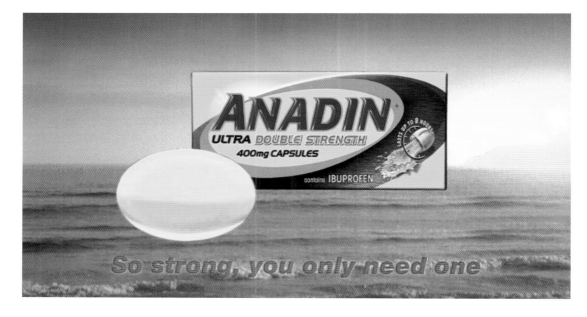

So strong, you only need one

pain. The brand has a solid base of core, loyal users with increasing frequency and weight of purchase. In 2006, the Anadin brand achieved £47.8 million in value sales and sold 26.7 million packs (Source: IRI December 2006).

Product

Anadin understands that most people have hectic and enjoyable lifestyles, and don't want to be interrupted by pain. That's why it has built on years of expertise to create a range of effective and trusted products, designed to let people get on with their lives.

Anadin is the only brand in the UK whose product range covers the three principal GSL analgesics: paracetamol, ibuprofen and aspirin. The brand also offers an extensive choice of products and formulations to meet consumers' pain relief needs.

The most popular Anadin product is Anadin Extra, designed to provide fast, effective relief from all types of pain, from headaches to muscle aches. Its powerful triple action formula contains aspirin, paracetamol and caffeine to target the source of pain, help block pain and speed up relief. This combination is also available as Anadin Extra Soluble tablets which dissolve in water.

Anadin Ultra hits tough pain such as back, joint or muscle ache, hard. Its 200mg capsules contain the most concentrated form of liquid ibuprofen available, making them smaller and easier to swallow, while the liquid formulation gets to work fast.

Anadin Ibuprofen is a sugar-coated tablet designed to target the site of pain and Anadin Paracetamol is gentle on the stomach, suitable for all the family, including children over six years. This is effective for fevers associated with colds and flu. The

1918	**1932**	**1962**	**1981**	**1983**	**1987**
Anacin is launched in the US.	Anacin launches as Anadin in the UK.	Anadin becomes the UK proprietary analgesic brand leader.	Anadin Soluble analgesic tablets are launched.	Anadin Extra launches, followed by Anadin blister packs in 1984.	The Anadin brand is redesigned.

range also includes Anadin Original, with dual action (aspirin and caffeine) tablets coated and shaped for easy swallowing.

Recent Developments

The launch of Anadin Ultra Double Strength took place in 2006. It is the strongest dose of liquid ibuprofen now available to buy in capsule form and is only available from the chemist. Anadin Ultra Double Strength aims to help reduce the need to take multiple doses of ibuprofen. Taking one capsule provides effective pain relief for up to eight hours – a full working day, or night's sleep. It takes effect almost twice as fast as standard ibuprofen tablets, so consumers can experience quicker relief from tough pain.

Promotion

The launch of Anadin Ultra Double Strength is being supported by a national above-the-line campaign worth £4 million across TV, press, radio and outdoor as well as a high profile consumer PR campaign to include sponsorship of charity events, radio promotions and a series of media briefings.

In addition Anadin Extra will be heavily supported throughout the year with national TV and radio campaigns. An emotional stance is being taken to target consumers and reinforce Anadin as the brand 'For people who just get on with it'.

The Anadin Extra advert features a woman who, while juggling her children, husband and mother, suddenly gets an attack of pain and stops to take an Anadin Extra so she can get on with her life.

The Triple Action Formula is also highlighted and emphasis put on the different ingredients and what they do; one targets the point of pain, one helps block pain and one speeds up relief.

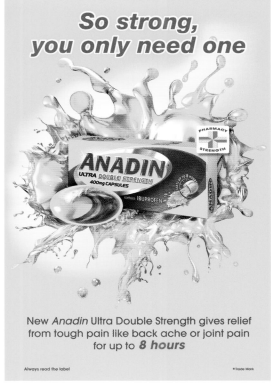

This forms part of an £8 million media spend throughout 2007, designed to drive awareness and volume of purchase, with consumers being exposed to Anadin advertising all year. Meanwhile, all Anadin packaging was redesigned and was relaunched in August 2006. The new packaging was designed to deliver a clear message about what each Anadin sub-brand can offer the consumer, while still carrying the trademark yellow and the Anadin logo.

In line with the relaunch of the Anadin products in new packaging, the Anadin website (www.anadin.co.uk) was also revamped to reflect the brand's new look. The website now plays the role of a 'pain expert' for the consumer, answering pain-related questions, and strengthening the

core brand message: 'For people who just get on with it'. It also educates users about the Anadin range, suitability and healthy lifestyles.

On top of this, Anadin is helping the trade by supporting pharmacists and pharmacy counter assistants by educating them on analgesics and pain. The educational campaign, called 'Ask Anadin', is aimed at answering all their pain related questions, so in turn they can advise their customers.

Brand Values

Anadin aims to understand consumers' pain and how it can affect their enjoyment of everyday life. It hopes to help those who just want to get on with their lives. Its products offer a range of solutions that are designed for effective relief from a wide variety of pains.

www.anadin.co.uk

Always read the label.

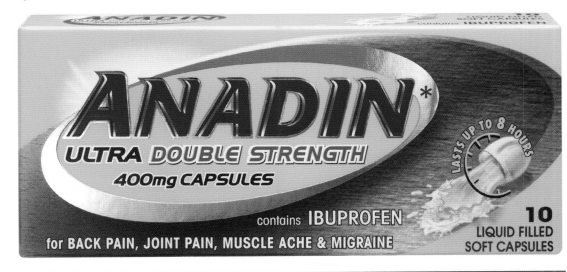

1992	1997	2001	2006
Anadin Extra Soluble tablets are launched.	Anadin Ibuprofen tablets are launched, followed by Anadin Ultra two years later.	The Anadin website goes live.	Anadin packaging is redesigned. Anadin Ultra Double Strength is launched.

Things you didn't know about Anadin

According to Anadin's Pain Nation Pure Profile Consumer Survey in 2006, one in four women think that carrying a pain killer in their handbag is as essential as carrying a mobile phone or their keys.

Anadin was formulated by an American dentist in 1918.

Nearly 27 million Anadin packs were sold last year. If stacked on top of each other, they would reach over 56 times the height of Mount Everest.

Anadin is now 75 years-old.

AUTOGLASS®

Autoglass® is the UK's leading vehicle glass repair and replacement company, serving more than 1.3 million motorists every year. With the widest reaching network in the UK and Ireland, Autoglass® has 121 branches nationwide and 1,300 mobile service units operating 24 hours a day, seven days a week, 365 days a year. Autoglass® is part of the Belron® group, operating in 29 countries with a team of over 10,000 highly skilled technicians serving an average of one customer every four seconds.

Market

Vehicle glass has evolved over the last 20 years to play an integral role in modern automotive design. Today's cars typically use 20 per cent more glass than in the 1980s and often incorporate complex technology such as rain sensors, wire-heating or satellite navigation components. Take the BMW 3 Series, for example; the latest version has 22 variations, 30 if you include compact models. Specialist skill is required to ensure they are repaired and replaced to the highest quality standards and that's where Autoglass® excels. The company is currently the UK's market leading automotive glazing expert.

Achievements

A windscreen accounts for up to 30 per cent of a vehicle's structural strength and

Autoglass® places huge emphasis on training to ensure every screen is fitted to the highest quality standards. It is the only company in its industry to have achieved accredited status from Thatcham and the Institute of the Motor Industry (IMI) for its National Skills Centre in Birmingham and its Startline Induction and Repair training programmes.

Autoglass® has also won a number of independent awards including two National Training Awards, a Glass Training Ltd (GTL) Commitment to Training award and the Insurance Times Training award. In addition, Autoglass® holds the ISO 9001 quality certification and is exclusively recommended by the AA.

As part of its ongoing commitment to caring for customers who have been a victim of car crime, this year Autoglass® announced

a long term partnership with the charity Victim Support. In return, the charity has created a dedicated training programme for Autoglass® employees to help them deal more effectively with distressed customers who may have been a victim of crime.

In addition, the long-standing Autoglass® 'Cracking Car Crime' campaign unites motorists, police forces and local authorities in the battle to beat car crime. The campaign is in its 14th year and is currently focusing on the growing issue of satnav theft, educating motorists to remove them from their vehicles when parked.

Autoglass® is committed to the environment and reprocesses the laminate screens it removes, helping to save the energy and resources involved in the manufacture and distribution of new

1951
F.A. Wilkins & Co Limited is founded. It goes on to become part of the Doulton Group.

1971
Windshields is founded in Bedford and develops the mobile concept, operating across southern England.

1973
The Doulton Group launches Autoglass, and begins operating across northern Britian.

1982
Solaglas International (now Belron®) acquires Autoglass. The following year Autoglass merges with Windshields to create Autoglass Windshields.

1985
Autoglass Windshields rebrands to Autoglass.

1990
The windscreen repair service is launched with the acquisition by Belron® of Glass Medic®.

windscreens. The company also promotes windscreen repair over replacement to help reduce carbon emissions and waste.

Product

Quite simply, Autoglass® fixes broken vehicle glass on any make, model or age of vehicle.

The company operates a 'Repair First' philosophy ensuring that, wherever possible, its technicians will repair a windscreen rather than replace it so that the existing seal doesn't have to be disturbed; a solution that saves time and money.

If the damage is beyond repair, Autoglass® will replace the windscreen. It only uses glass from vehicle manufacturers' suppliers to ensure that each replacement windscreen is a perfect fit for the vehicle. It also uses one of the quickest drying bonding systems for customer convenience.

Appointments can be made by phone or online and customers can choose to take their vehicle into their local branch or arrange for a mobile technician to come to a location of their choice.

Recent Developments

The customer experience is central to Autoglass® and in August 2006, the company opened a purpose built 'drive-in' windscreen repair service at Bluewater shopping centre. This specialist facility offers windscreen chip repairs in a convenient and accessible location. When the customer has finished shopping, they place a call to the Autoglass® branch and arrange to be collected by the Autoglass® buggy and taken back to their repaired car.

Autoglass® recently demonstrated its commitment to raising standards within its sector by becoming the first to introduce the highly regarded Automotive Technician Accreditation (ATA) scheme for the Auto Glazing sector. Under the scheme, technicians can work towards three accreditation levels dependent upon knowledge, skills and experience, ultimately leading to Master Auto Glazing Technician

status. The scheme provides technicians with recognition of their expertise and customers with additional peace of mind.

In 2007, Autoglass® became the first vehicle glass repair and replacement company to offer online booking, through its website www.autoglass.co.uk. Thousands of customers are now using the interactive facility every month to book an appointment at a convenient time for them.

Promotion

Autoglass® became a household name in the 1990s after becoming the main sponsor of Chelsea FC and since then, has invested in a number of high profile brand campaigns to ensure that it remains at the forefront of motorists' minds.

In 2005, Autoglass® launched the 'Heroes' radio campaign, using real Autoglass® technicians to explain the benefits of repairing windscreen chips. The success of the campaign, which airs during drive time shows, lies in the emotional impact of a real Autoglass® technician explaining the importance of chip repair to people who are likely to be sat staring at chipped or damaged glass in their own vehicles. So far, the

campaign has become the most successful in Autoglass® history, helping to boost brand recognition and drive contacts via the call centre and website up by 20 per cent.

The campaign has won two awards – Outstanding Campaign over £250,000 and the 'Grand Prix' for Most Outstanding Radio Planning at the 2007 Radio Planning Awards – and was commended in 2006 for the most effective radio campaign in the GCap Media Radio Planning Awards. The 'Heroes' campaign is currently being used by Belron® subsidiaries in another 15 countries across the world.

In just 24 months Autoglass® has become one of the UK's top five radio advertisers, in terms of spend, and the only advertiser in the top 10 to be 100 per cent focused on radio.

Brand Values

The Autoglass® vision is to be the natural choice through valuing its customers' needs and delivering world-class service. Its brand values are to be caring, expert, professional, innovative and to have integrity.

www.autoglass.co.uk

1994
Autoglass® becomes a registered trademark after a seven year IP registration process.

2002
Carglass in Ireland rebrands to Autoglass®.

2005
Autoglass® launches the 'Heroes' radio campaign, using real Autoglass® technicians to explain the benefits of repairing windscreen chips.

2007
Autoglass® becomes the first vehicle glass repair and replacement company to offer online booking at www.autoglass.co.uk

Things you didn't know about Autoglass®

Autoglass® doesn't just repair chipped windscreens; it has even repaired a chip on the viewing glass at the Tiger compound at Glasgow Zoo.

In 2006 Autoglass® recycled around 8,500 tonnes of glass – that's the weight of 1,700 African elephants.

In 2007 Gavin, the technician featured in the Autoglass® 'Heroes' campaign, beat James Nesbitt from the Yellow Pages adverts to be voted by the listeners of Xfm as the best radio actor of any commercial.

BBC

The BBC is the world's best known broadcasting brand, informing, educating and entertaining the UK. Today's digital BBC plays a key civic role in UK life and aims to be the most creative, trusted organisation in the world and to enrich people's lives with great programmes and services. BBC content is watched, listened to or accessed online via eight national TV channels, 10 national radio stations, 240 websites and 40 local radio stations.

Market

The British broadcasting market is being transformed by digital technology and by 2012 the whole of the UK will be receiving digital television. Already 75 per cent or nearly 19 million households receive digital multi channel television and radio services from Sky, Virgin Media and Freeview. Around 11 million homes and small businesses now have broadband connection.

The original public service broadcasters, BBC, ITV, Channel Four and Five, are now multi-platform, multi-media brands operating 24 hours a day seven days a week with significant online presence. Viewing share of digital only channels is over 30 per cent but the public service broadcasters' new digital channels have helped them hold up overall portfolio share.

The introduction of digital recording and high definition television flat screen sets is helping to drive consumer sales as well as extra services including 'seven day watch again'. A new range of channel operators,

Look into the eyes of the highest predator on earth. Planet Earth. Sundays 9pm.

including BT, are also launching mobile television services aimed at the rapidly growing 3G subscriber base. The total UK television and radio market is estimated to be worth just under £12 billion.

Achievements

In 2006/07 the BBC received 235 programme-related awards across television, radio and new media. These included 32 Baftas (TV, Children's and Craft); 52 RTS awards (Programme, Journalism, Sports, Educational, North West, Craft and Design); 18 Sony Golds for Radio; four Webby awards for online service, as well as three International Emmys for television.

The BBC takes its corporate and environmental responsibilities seriously and works toward bringing added value to the licence fee through non-commercial

partnerships, improving sustainability and minimising adverse impact on natural resources. The Business in the Community Corporate Responsibility Index 2007 awarded the BBC platinum status for work on managing social and environmental impact.

Product

The BBC is primarily thought of as a creator of high quality content and programming, whether on radio, on TV or online. The product offer is a very complex mix, with 21 major television, radio and online public service brands to fulfil the promise of providing something of quality for everyone.

Today's BBC television and radio brands, particularly BBC One and BBC Two and Radio's 1, 2, 3, 4 and Five Live, are hugely popular, attracting large terrestrial audiences. The main channels are complemented by new

1960s

Television goes from black and white to colour. Radio launches its new 'pop' station Radio One, along with Radio's Two, Three and Four.

1970s

A vintage period for television drama includes: I Claudius; Pennies from Heaven; and Last of the Summer Wine.

New comedy includes: Are You Being Served?; The Good Life; and Fawlty Towers. Documentaries include The Ascent of Man and The Family.

1980s

In 1985, in Ethiopia, reporter Michael Buerk alerts the world to a famine of Biblical proportions. This leads to the Live Aid concert which raises more than £60 million.

digital brands, BBC Three and BBC Four on television and BBC Radio 1 Xtra, BBC Five Live Sports Extra, BBC 6 Music, BBC 7 and the Asian Network on digital radio. The online destination, bbc.co.uk is a recognised brand leader in the UK.

The BBC's Nations and Regions services for England, Wales, Northern Ireland and Scotland produce extensive local programming, and, particularly for news, significant audiences. The BBC also runs orchestras and choirs, actively develops new talent and supports training and production skills for the British broadcasting, music, drama and film industries.

The BBC is financed by the TV licence paid by all television households. This means it does not have to serve the interests of advertisers or shareholders and can concentrate on providing high quality programmes and services for everyone, many of which would not otherwise be supported by subscription or advertising.

Recent Developments
The BBC was granted a new 10 year Royal Charter at the end of 2006 which clearly defined what the licence fee payer should expect in a wholly-digital, on-demand world. It set out the BBC's public purposes, defining a unique role for the UK broadcaster over the next decade. A new BBC Trust, which sets the BBC's objectives, defends it from political and commercial pressures and reports on its

performance in its annual report to licence fee payers and Parliament, was set up to regulate it.

The digital revolution is changing the BBC from a one-way, primarily studio based broadcaster of programmes, into an audience focused anytime, anywhere, anyhow, content brand. The BBC plans to launch Freesat – a new national free-to-view satellite service with ITV – which will offer up to 200 channels, full interactivity and high definition broadcasts. iPlayer, an internet delivered seven day catch up service is due later in 2007. BBC radio's 'listen again' and podcasting services already attract millions of regular online users.

The BBC is also required to generate additional revenues by exploiting programme assets that have been paid for by public money. BBC Worldwide sells programmes and footage, and is the UK's number one international television channel broadcaster, with 18 channels, including BBC America. Worldwide produces books, DVDs and other merchandise linked to programmes and is a joint partner in UKTV. The commercial activity is carried out at arms-length and revenues are re-invested in the core public service.

Promotion
The trademark block letters of the BBC master brand are instantly recognisable, understood as standing for quality programmes and services. It appears on everything from channel identities to station literature and commercial magazines as well as buildings, flags, vehicles, huge music and other events, books, DVDs and online around the world.

Today's master brand logo was redesigned in the late 1990s to give a simpler, less

cluttered image. The subsidiary brand identities for channels and services are regularly refreshed and rethought in the light of market changes and audience research. BBC One and BBC Two have both unveiled new looks this year that are more emotionally engaging for the audience.

BBC's marketing, communications and audience research services aim to produce integrated communications campaigns supported by on air trails, posters, print media and live events. The Radio Times also provides invaluable promotion for BBC programmes.

Brand Values
The BBC's core public service purpose to inform, educate and entertain is embedded in the organisation's core values. The BBC has always paid great attention to its audiences' comments and in the digital age they say that as a broadcaster the BBC has to be trusted, entertaining, prepared to take risks and produce stimulating, talked about content and keep people connected. Politically the BBC is constitutionally independent and impartial in all its extensive journalism and factual content.

www.bbc.co.uk

Things you didn't know about BBC

The BBC is a leading global news brand – 233 million people use its combined international television, radio and online services every week.

There have been over 15,000 editions of The Archers radio serial to date.

The BBC was originally formed in 1922 by wireless manufacturers keen to promote the sales of radio sets.

Blue Peter started in 1958 and is the world's longest running children's programme.

1990s

Also in the 1980s, the BBC covers the Falklands War and the miners' strike, as well as launching Eastenders.

BBC Radio 5, the first new network for 23 years, launches in 1990. New comedy shows include Have I Got News for You.

2000s

Costume drama sees Middlemarch and Pride and Prejudice air. Groundbreaking programmes include The Human Body and Walking with Dinosaurs.

Landmark television programmes include: Blue Planet; Planet Earth; and Simon Schama's A History of Britain. Comedies include: The Office; Little Britain; and The Royle Family.

The Berghaus brand is synonymous with adventure and innovation. Founded in 1966, Berghaus has for over four decades pushed the boundaries of what is possible with performance outdoor clothing, rucsacs and footwear. Throughout that time, the company has equipped and supported expeditions to the most demanding environments on the planet and the Berghaus team of sponsored athletes is a mix of iconic names and cutting-edge talent.

Market

The outdoor market was in its infancy in the 1960s, populated by small, enthusiastic businesses. It has since grown into an industry that is worth hundreds of millions of pounds in the UK alone. Starting life as a small business in Newcastle upon Tyne, Berghaus soon established itself as a leading player in this emerging market sector. By the early 1970s, the brand had already delivered a category defining product in Cyclops, the first internal framed load carrying rucsac. With one outstanding piece of kit, Berghaus earned a reputation for innovation that it has continued to enhance to the present day. Now, Berghaus designs and sells a wide range of performance outdoor clothing, footwear, rucsacs and accessories, and the market is getting bigger every year as more people buy into the outdoor lifestyle.

Achievements

The list of Berghaus' significant innovations and awards is too long to print in full here, but includes: launching the first commercially available Gore-Tex jacket in Europe; the Extrem range of technical products for the most demanding mountaineering challenges; the Millennium Product Award winning Nitro sac; the phenomenally successful Extrem Light range of clothing, footwear and rucsacs; and BioFlex, a rucsac system that allows the wearer to flex, twist and pivot at all times – launched in 2005, the system was presented with an innovation award by the outdoor industry and has again redefined the load carrying sector.

Over the years, specialist outdoor magazines have tested hundreds of Berghaus products alongside the competition. The brand's products have won a huge number of 'best in' tests and reader awards, along with plaudits for berghaus.com and the company's advertising. In addition, in 2006 Berghaus was presented with a Queen's Award for Enterprise, for innovation demonstrated throughout the company.

Product

Berghaus designs products for a vast range of outdoor activities. Whether a consumer is climbing the toughest peak, scaling the highest rock face, skiing off piste in deep powder, mountain biking at breakneck speed or strolling through gentle countryside, Berghaus has clothing, footwear, rucsacs and accessories that will meet their needs.

1966	1972	1977	1982	1986	1998
Berghaus is founded in Newcastle upon Tyne.	Cylops, the first internal framed rucsac, is launched.	The first commercially available Gore-Tex jacket is launched into Europe. The following year Berghaus develops the unique Yeti Gaiter.	The original A.B. (Adjustable Back) Carrying System and the unique Occipital Cavity further enhance the company's reputation for rucsac innovation.	Berghaus launches Extrem, a range of serious mountaineering products for serious mountaineers.	The Nitro is introduced. Its unique Limpet carrying and compression system, combined with ultra modern styling, earn it plaudits far and wide including a Millennium Product Award.

We thought you should know their names before you sleep with them.

HealthGuard

Recent Developments

Over the last few years, Berghaus has introduced a raft of new innovations and products. In 2005, the company launched the award winning BioFlex back system and followed it up with Next Generation – Berghaus products for kids. The brand's most technical range, Extrem, continues to develop with the recent addition of mountaineering footwear, while the rest of the footwear range has been given a dramatic and successful makeover.

In 2007, Berghaus introduced the Ator collection – high performance multi-activity outdoor products delivered in a stylish package. Ator has made a strong impact in its first season and will be expanded in 2008, and joined by 365Life, an outdoor inspired lifestyle range that incorporates organic cottons, recycled fabrics, vegetable tanning and other natural materials – a serious step by Berghaus to start reducing the environmental impact of its products.

Promotion

Testing and promoting these innovations and products from across the Berghaus collection are some of the world's leading outdoor adventurers. Sir Chris Bonington has gained legendary status in the world of mountaineering and continues to explore unclimbed peaks into his 70s. At the other end of the generational scale is Leo Houlding; still only in his mid 20s, Leo's achievements have already placed him firmly in the climbing community's elite.

Alex and Thomas Huber from Germany are the

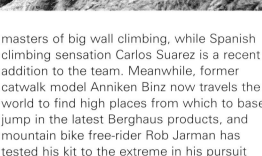

masters of big wall climbing, while Spanish climbing sensation Carlos Suarez is a recent addition to the team. Meanwhile, former catwalk model Anniken Binz now travels the world to find high places from which to base jump in the latest Berghaus products, and mountain bike free-rider Rob Jarman has tested his kit to the extreme in his pursuit of adventure.

The latest addition to the team is Andy Kirkpatrick – climber, journalist, film maker, comedian, lecturer, photographer, gear guru and much more, Andy specialises in 'hard core' expeditions to very cold, very remote places. Everyone in the team not only promotes the Berghaus brand but also works closely with the company's product team to contribute directly to future range developments.

As well as using the exploits of its sponsored team, Berghaus continuously strives to use creative marketing techniques to bring its products to life for the consumer. For a brand that operates in a traditionally specialist market, Berghaus continues to deliver communications support that makes an impression on a much broader audience. Employing print, outdoor and cinema advertising alongside online viral campaigns and proactive PR, the Berghaus brand maintains a very high profile in the UK and abroad. Contemporary images, clever copywriting and standout executions ensure that

Berghaus is a byword for imagination and innovation in promotion as much as in product.

Brand Values

There is a true spirit of adventure that runs through every aspect of the Berghaus brand and its people. Berghaus is as vibrant and restless as ever, constantly innovating and finding new ways to deliver even better products for anyone who lives the outdoor dream or is inspired by what it represents. Products that bear the Berghaus brand ooze quality and high performance and people choose them because they know that they won't let them down.

www.berghaus.com

Things you didn't know about Berghaus

Berghaus is a rough German translation of 'mountain centre', reflecting the name of the shop in which the brand was born – LD Mountain Centre in Newcastle upon Tyne. In 1966, there was a strong demand for quality German or Austrian outdoor products and using the name Berghaus provided the fledgling company with some instant credibility.

When Berghaus launched the legendary Yeti Gaiter in 1978, the rubber rands that enclosed the boot were for a while made out of rubber acquired from a local tyre dump. The product is still recognised as offering the highest level of foot and leg protection available, and continues to be used on major expeditions around the world.

The founders of Berghaus sold the company to the Pentland Group in 1993. Pentland, based in London, has an extensive portfolio of international sports, outdoors and fashion brands.

Born and bred in North East England, Berghaus has always been based in the region and the company is housed in a purpose built headquarters in Sunderland.

2003

Extrem Light is launched. The integrated, lightweight range of clothing, footwear and rucsacs is designed to help people go faster, further and in more comfort.

2005

Berghaus launches the world's most innovative back system to date, BioFlex.

2006

Berghaus footwear reaches new levels of performance with a comprehensive relaunch.

2007

Ator – a stylish high performance outdoor product – is launched.

BLACK&DECKER®

Powerful Solutions™

In 1946 Black & Decker created the world's first portable electric drill for consumers, effectively creating what is now known as the DIY market. The brand has since gone from strength to strength, launching new products and creating new market categories including: consumer power tools, accessories and fixings, outdoor power tools, household cleaning products and more recently a new automotive and electronics range of tools.

Market

Black & Decker has the largest branded share within the categories in which it operates. This is a great achievement as there are many factors that affect the health of the DIY market – from the state of the housing market and the performance of the economy, to weather conditions and the media.

The total DIY market has nearly doubled since 1998 from £4.9 billion to £8.1 billion (Source: GfK Marketing Services). Over the past couple of years, the DIY market has begun to stabilise and recent trends suggest that as DIY tasks become less cosmetic and start to become more like renovations, this trend will generate new growth in the market.

Achievements

Black & Decker has won many awards both for its products and in recognition of its business operations. Most recently, it has been awarded the prestigious 'Best of the Best' Award in the 2007 DIY Industry Awards, highlighting and recognising its achievements over the past 20 years. Black & Decker has also recently been awarded the Good Housekeeping Institute logo for the Dustbuster® Pivot handheld vacuum cleaner – this is a highly regarded division of the Good Housekeeping magazine which independently tests consumer products against competitors.

Furthermore, Black & Decker has been ranked as the number one DIY and household brand by the Superbrands consumer survey.

Product

Black & Decker is a global manufacturer of power tools, accessories, household cleaning products, outdoor tools and more recently automotive tools. Over the 97 years since the company was first established, many other successful global brands have been acquired, expanding the Black & Decker portfolio.

Black & Decker uses the knowledge gained from extensive consumer research to create powerful and practical solutions that make it easier and quicker for people to achieve good DIY results. This process has led the company to being the number one brand in all of its core product groups (Source: GfK Marketing Services).

Black & Decker constantly strives to create everyday power tool solutions for consumers. Products launched over the years include the award-winning Mouse® decorating tool, the Scorpion® powered hand saw, the Workmate®

workbench and more recently the Laserplus™ self levelling laser level.

The launch of a complete range of patented self levelling lasers provided innovation that excited and grew the spirit level market. This created a new market for lasers – in which Black & Decker are the number one branded supplier with 57 per cent share (Source: GfK Marketing Services MAT May 06 – April 07).

Black & Decker leads the market with powerful and innovative tools, most recently the cyclonic action sander, new corded and cordless hammer drills and the Handi Saw™ – a compact and convenient powered saw.

Black & Decker's garden range includes hedge trimmers, grass trimmers, chainsaws, shredders and blower vacuums. Continuing with its innovative culture, Black & Decker launched the award-winning Alligator® powered lopper in 2006, which combines the power and results of a chainsaw with the

1910

Two young Americans, Duncan Black and Alonzo Decker, form their own manufacturing company with US$1200 initial capital.

1914

Black & Decker patents the first handheld power drill with a pistol grip, trigger switch and universal motor.

1946

Black & Decker introduces the world's first portable electric drill for consumers.

1962

The world's first cordless outdoor product, a hedge trimmer, is introduced.

1985

The Automatic Shut-Off™ Electronic Iron sets a new standard for iron performance.

2001

The Scorpion® Powered handsaw hits the market and globally sells 800,000 units in its first year.

safety of a manual lopper. Black & Decker owns the sub-brand Strimmer®, typically used to describe grass trimmers and has released its latest range with an innovative mid-mount design, ensuring balance and maximum comfort for the consumer. The outdoor range continues to expand its cordless offering, with new additions such as the cordless powered hoe, to help with soil maintenance and the powered sprayer which allows an easier application of water or fertilisers to plants.

For household cleaning, Black & Decker's Dustbuster® handheld vacuum cleaner range, invented in 1979, has constantly been upgraded with improved technology, including cyclonic action. In 2006 Black & Decker launched the innovative Dustbuster® Pivot vacuum cleaner with pivoting nose, allowing the consumer to reach into awkward spaces.

Recent Developments

Black & Decker has recently launched a new range of automotive tools, including battery boosters, jump starters, portable power and a selection of leisure products including lighting and travel coolers/warmers. This new range is aimed at people on the go, whether it be by car, boat or motor bike and consumers who enjoy outdoor activities, such as camping and fishing. Continuing with its innovative culture, Black & Decker has launched the first product of its kind: the Simple Start™ battery booster which charges a drained battery from inside the car within 15 minutes so you can re-start the

engine with no assistance required from another vehicle, therefore delivering ultimate safety and security.

Ongoing market research has highlighted that consumers often get frustrated when trying to find the correct setting on their tools for a certain application. This is why Black & Decker has launched a new range of hammer drills and jigsaws which include Autoselect™ technology: the consumer now only needs to select an icon of the application they require and the intelligent technology automatically adjusts the tool into the correct setting, eliminating guesswork.

A new range of innovative bagless cylinder vacuums have recently been developed by Black & Decker. The vacuum cleaners include unique self cleaning filter technology, which cleans the filter after every use, delivering maximum suction power every time. This leading technology has been approved by the British Allergy Foundation.

Promotion

Black & Decker recognises the importance of successful communication plans when launching new products across all categories, therefore continually invests to drive the DIY market forward by focusing on all aspects of the marketing mix from TV, radio and online activity to best-in-class in-store communication driven by a team of Field Marketing Executives. Black & Decker continues to heavily invest in TV and in 2007 will maximise brand exposure and sales through five TV campaigns during key periods.

In 2006 Black & Decker launched its most high performance range of cordless and corded hammer drills which featured on the Talk Sport

Radio breakfast show, targeting over 1.9 million listeners. This campaign also communicated Black & Decker being the official sponsor of the Ferrari Challenge Trofeo Pirelli and the official technical tool supplier to Fiorano Ferrari which continues until the end of 2008.

Brand Values

Black & Decker is a well established brand that aims to help consumers to confidently get the best possible results from the tools they use, acting in a trustworthy way to deliver intelligent products for the home with the power and performance for any task.

www.blackanddecker.eu

Things you didn't know about Black & Decker

Black & Decker invented the first handheld power drill, the first cordless drill, the first consumer finishing sander and jigsaw, the first grass trimmer and hedge trimmer and the first cordless hand held vacuum cleaner.

Black & Decker is a global organisation marketing products in more than 100 countries worldwide.

Black & Decker developed a unique power head for the Apollo Lunar Surface Drill to remove core samples from the moon in the 1968 landing.

In 2005, Black & Decker advertised on television 10 times – the greatest number of times by any power-tool manufacturer.

Black & Decker is an official sponsor of the Ferrari Challenge Trofeo Pirelli and official technical tool supplier to Fiorano Ferrari.

Black & Decker worked with Pierluigi Collina, one of the world's most recognised football referees, to maximise sales during the build-up to the football World Championship.

2003

An innovative range of patented self levelling lasers is launched.

2005

Sales of lasers exceed 150,000 and 160,000 Autotape™ automatic tape measures are sold.

2006

Black & Decker launch the Alligator® powered lopper, winning gold at the 2006 DIY Industry Awards.

2007

Black & Decker receive the 'Best of the Best' Award from the DIY Industry Awards.

Autoselect™ – a new innovation in cordless hammer drills and jigsaws – is launched.

Boots is the UK's leading Health and Beauty retailer and has been trading since the 19th century. With approximately 1,500 stores in the UK and Irish Republic, it serves approximately eight million customers every week. Boots develops and sells own-brand products, a number of which are leaders in their respective markets. The Boots brand is founded on the trust, expertise and heritage, which comes with its longevity in the market.

Market

Boots Group operates three principal businesses: Boots The Chemists (BTC); Boots Opticians (BOL); and Boots Retail International (BRI).

Pharmacy is a fundamentally important part of the brand; representing one quarter of sales, it is the foundation of Boots' authority and credibility.

Boots stores are mostly located on high streets; but, in line with modern shopping trends, its presence in edge of town retail parks is rapidly increasing. Over the last three years 48 such stores have opened, as well as a flagship London store on Oxford Street.

Overseas, Boots is working closely with other major retailers in their local markets, to open Boots branded 'implants' within their stores. There are currently 758 implants in 13 countries. Boots also has 96 stand alone stores in Thailand.

Achievements

Boots has had an illustrious history. From its beginnings in 1849 as an herbalist shop, Boots has continually developed new product ranges, many of which are now household names in their own right.

By the 1930s Boots had more than 1,000 stores selling a wide range of products, including its new cosmetic range, No7. Expansion overseas began as early as 1936 with a store in New Zealand.

Following World War II, Boots continued to grow, expanding its manufacturing and research capabilities, including an agricultural division. The creation of the National Health Service in 1948 led to a vast increase in dispensing, which Boots embraced.

Over the years Boots has successfully introduced brands such as 17 cosmetics, aimed at teenagers, which was introduced in 1968 and new business ventures such as

Boots Opticians – now a major division of the business.

In 1985 the Research Department received the Queen's Award for Technological Achievement for the discovery and development of ibuprofen. The analgesic ibuprofen was introduced in 1969 as a prescription drug, but launched as the over the counter (OTC) brand, Nurofen, in 1983.

Boots' internet business has become increasingly important in the new millennium and a successful part of the brand. Improvements have been made to the online customer experience making navigation easier, resulting in boots.com sales becoming bigger than those of the largest Boots store.

Product

Boots is best known for selling a wide range of products under the Boots brand name across health and beauty. Within this

1849
John Boot opens an herbalist shop in Goose Gate, Nottingham.

1892
A flagship Boots store opens at Pelham Street, Nottingham.

1920
Boots Pure Drug Company Ltd is sold to the United Drug Company of America, however ownership returns to the UK in 1933.

1935
Cosmetics brand No7 launches and beauty parlours are introduced in a number of stores, the first being in London's Regent Street.

1956
The first self-service Boots store opens in London.

1971
The company is renamed The Boots Company Ltd, later changing to The Boots Company plc in 1982.

portfolio, it has the UK's biggest beauty brand in No7, and Soltan, the UK's number one suncare range (Source: TNS Worldpanel). In early 2007, the retailer launched the Boots Expert range; research and development has always been key to Boots, developing new products to improve its own-brands and exclusives ranges.

Boots Advantage Card, which awards customers four points for every pound spent, (with points redeemable for products in-store), is a hugely important part of the business. With almost 15 million active cardholders, Advantage Cards are used in around 70 per cent of BTC sales. Linked to the Advantage Card, in 2005 Boots launched its Parenting Club for expectant and new mothers, and followed it with the Boots Health Club in 2006, giving regular advice and information as well as discounted products to its members.

Installed in 1999, Boots Advantage Card kiosks provide cardholders with personalised offers based on their shopping habits. Boots is now updating its Advantage Card kiosks in 485 of its high street stores with smaller, faster and easier to navigate models. Updated technology will also enable offers to be more targeted.

Recent Developments
The merger between Alliance UniChem plc and Boots Group plc was completed on 31st July 2006, creating an international pharmacy-led health and beauty group operating in more than 15 countries across the world.

The Alliance Boots network will include two retail formats, both under the Boots brand, ranging from approximately 1,500 smaller dispensing pharmacies to approximately 800 larger destination high street and edge of town health and beauty stores. In addition, Alliance Boots will also

operate approximately 300 additional retail outlets, including freestanding Boots Opticians practices.

Boots is also developing in-store 'health zones' in its bigger stores, which will include extended waiting areas for customers collecting prescriptions. Consultation rooms for pharmacists are also being introduced, as part of a Government initiative to alleviate the pressure on GPs' surgeries.

Promotion
Boots uses a wide range of media on an ongoing basis, including TV, press, and direct mailings to its Advantage Card members to highlight new products, offers and services.

Brand Values
Jesse Boot, the son of John Boot, the brand's eponymous founder, took control of the business in the 1870s. He had a business philosophy of buying in bulk and passing the benefit of reduced prices on to his customers. His policy of superior goods

at competitive prices delivered with expert care meant that the Boots name became synonymous with quality, value and service. His earliest marketing was based around the concept of 'Largest, Best and Cheapest – Branches Everywhere'.

This philosophy is still an important part of Boots' today. It aims to treat its customers fairly and to act with integrity in everything it does, which results in the brand regularly being rated as the UK's most trusted brand.

Boots also believes that it has an enormously valuable role to play in promoting the health of the nation. It achieves this by forming innovative, long term partnerships with charities, particularly focusing on women's cancer. Boots has worked with Breast Cancer Care for 11 years, and this year linked with the Eve Appeal to highlight ovarian cancer. Boots also supports the health of the UK everyday through its 15,000 healthcare advisors working in store.

www.boots.com

1987
Boots Opticians Ltd is formed, with the acquisition of Clement Clarke Ltd and Curry & Paxton Ltd. It becomes the UK's second largest retail optics chain.

1997
Boots Advantage Card launches.

2003
The online shopping channel is renamed boots.com.

2006
Boots Group plc merges with Alliance UniChem plc to form Alliance Boots and the sale of Boots Healthcare International (BHI) is completed.

Things you didn't know about Boots The Chemist

In 2001 Boots launched the world's first disposable hearing aid, Songbird.

Eight per cent of Boots customers visit boots.com before going into the stores.

No7 cosmetics have been relaunched six times, most dramatically in 2005 when the entire new range was introduced overnight in all Boots stores.

Boots made a significant contribution to the war effort, producing items such as water sterilisers, vermin powder and anti-fly cream for men at the Front.

During 2005/06 Boots sold 0.8 million pairs of spectacles.

bp

BP has been an international household name for decades. One of the world's largest energy companies, it provides fuels for transport, energy for heat and light, and retail services. It also develops an array of petrochemical products used to create all manner of everyday products. These many products and services are delivered to the public through a range of internationally respected brands. Together, they have made BP the global force it is today.

Market

Every day, millions of BP customers buy fuels, lubricants and a range of other items from more than 25,000 petrol stations worldwide. They clearly trust the company's collection of established brands, including ampm, ARCO, Aral, BP, Castrol, Ultimate and Wild Bean Café.

The second-largest fuels retailer in Europe as a whole, BP is also the largest in Europe's biggest market, Germany. Its 2,500 German outlets are branded as Aral, with a brand link to the corporate BP brand.

In the US, the company markets through the BP retail brand east of the Rocky Mountains and the ARCO masterbrand to the west. BP is the second largest fuels marketer in North America, and BP Ultimate gasoline leads the premium grade market there.

BP has always been a pioneering brand and is growing strongly in developing markets. The company has partnerships with Petrochina and Sinopec in China and TNK in Russia, and is planning to develop its presence with more retail outlets in the developing world.

Achievements

Early in 2007, the readers of Business Car magazine voted BP's 'targetneutral' initiative 'Innovation of the Year'. The first mainstream UK scheme for neutralising CO_2 emissions from cars, targetneutral allows customers to calculate their cars' CO_2 emissions, and then to neutralise these emissions by paying a fee – around £20 for the average driver. This is then used to support projects that reduce an equivalent amount of environmental CO_2. BP also makes its own contribution every time a targetneutral member buys BP fuel and swipes their Nectar card.

Other notable recent achievements have come through BP's Aral brand in Germany, which has been named Reader's Digest 'Most Trusted Brand' in fuels for the sixth consecutive year. It also won 'Best Brand' from a leading German car magazine for the second time running. This is a powerful demonstration of consumers' enduring loyalty to the Aral brand.

Product

The wide choice available at BP's retail sites runs from premium fuels to convenience items, freshly prepared food, cafés and bakeries. In the UK, the company recently completed a 12 month trial that brought Marks & Spencer's Simply Food range onto BP retail forecourts. The results were overwhelmingly positive with 97 per cent of customers rating the combined offer good, very good or excellent.

BP has seen a strong strategic fit between its own brand and Marks & Spencer, and plans to roll the combined offer out over 200 sites. Customers will be able to buy selected items from Mark's & Spencer's range including sandwiches, ready meals, fresh produce, wine, flowers and basic groceries alongside BP's own food service brand, Wild Bean Café.

1909
The Anglo-Persian Oil Company (as BP was first known) is formed.

1940s
After World War II, BP's sales, profits, capital expenditure and employment all rise to record levels as Europe is restructured.

1954
The company name becomes The British Petroleum Company Limited.

1965
BP finds the West Sole gas field – the first offshore hydrocarbons to be found in British waters.

1975
BP pumps ashore the first oil from the North Sea's UK sector when it buys the Forties field on stream. This field development is financed by a bank loan of £370 million – the largest wholly-private bank advance ever arranged at the time.

Wild Bean Café is BP's youngest brand, offering fresh, high-quality food and coffee on the go. In 2006 Wild Bean Café was given a new look which separates it more clearly from the rest of the store, creating a distinctive café environment. Another innovation is BP LPG that has revolutionised the gas bottle market with BP Gas Light, a pioneering new lightweight bottle that was first to market in many European countries.

BP Ultimate was launched as a premium fuel in Russia and South Africa in 2006, reflecting BP's global/local approach to branding. Originally launched in the UK in 2003 after 18 months of extensive research, BP Ultimate is now sold in 15 countries – confirming both BP's commitment to more environmentally friendly products and its ability to deliver premium quality fuels in diverse markets.

The advanced formulation of BP Ultimate is proven to have significantly greater cleaning power than ordinary fuels. A cleaner engine is a more efficient engine and can mean more miles per tank, greater performance and fewer emissions, which can help make a car kinder to the environment.

Recent Developments

At the beginning of 2007, BP opened 'Helios House' in Los Angeles, a unique gas station rooted in sustainability and environmental education. Incorporating a range of environmentally focused innovations, the station is an experiment in exploring ways to make gas stations 'greener' and to improve the customer experience.

'Helios House' aims to help customers care for the environment with small lifestyle tips, which also appear on a new website www.thegreencurve.com. The site offers a range of resources to help people 'move up the greencurve' by making simple changes in their lives. As well as providing a better experience for today's customers, BP hopes these resources will help everyone create a better environment for tomorrow.

Through 'Helios House', the company also aims to explore how customers and communities respond to a variety of environmental initiatives within the gas station, such as innovative green design, education, eco-friendly materials and recycling opportunities. The ideas and lessons gathered here will then be shared with BP facilities around the country.

Promotion

Since 2002 BP's communications strategy has been to give a voice to real people about their energy concerns. BP responds using simple and straightforward language about how it is tackling those issues. BP recognises that it can't solve these issues alone, but is not sitting on the sidelines – this is embodied with BP's 'it's a start' language.

All BP executions aim to demonstrate how the company thinks and goes beyond petroleum, both through its investments in alternatives, and how its policies and actions break with the conventions of the oil industry of the past.

BP has introduced sophisticated psychographic targeting, giving fresh insight into the lifestyle of the consumer and importantly how they consume media. A complete media programme is then developed to engage the right consumer at the right moment with the right message. As a result BP now invests over twice the industry average in new/digital media.

Brand Values

In everything it does, BP aims to be performance driven, innovative, progressive and green.

Being performance driven is about proving BP can be trusted. It aims to set global standards for corporate and financial performance, on everything from the environment to the satisfaction of customers and employees.

BP aims to be innovative in every area of its business. Combining the creativity of its people with cutting-edge technology to deliver 'breakthrough solutions' both to business challenges and to the needs of its customers.

Being progressive means ensuring that BP can be relied upon to be open and accessible, looking for new and better ways to do things. Not simply commercially, but in society as a whole, aiming to help communities develop and to give individuals every chance to fulfil their potential.

Lastly, green refers to BP's vision of environmental leadership. The company aims to lead the way in developing solutions that help overcome the trade-off between protecting the environment and providing heat, light and mobility for millions of customers.

These values combine to make up BP's brand theme of 'beyond petroleum', describing a company that looks to develop new forms of energy and innovative ways of producing oil and gas so as to create sustainable energy for the future.

www.bp.com

Things you didn't know about BP

The original BP mark was created as a result of an employee competition in 1920. The winning design came from Mr A R Saunders of the purchasing department.

The original BP petrol stations in the UK were branded red.

In 1922, Castrol became the first company ever to use the sky for advertising, leaving its name hanging in the air for four minutes.

1990s

BP merges with US giant Amoco, and acquires ARCO, Burmah Castrol and Veba Oil, turning it into one of the world's largest energy companies.

1997

In response to mounting evidence and concern regarding greenhouse gas emissions and the rising temperatures of the earth, BP becomes the first in its industry to state publicly the need for precautionary action on climate change.

2005

BP Alternative Energy is launched, dedicated to the development and wholesale marketing and trading of low-carbon power.

British Gas

British Gas, owned by Centrica, is based in the UK and is a well known energy supplier to homes and businesses, as well as an installer and maintainer of central heating and gas appliances. With a workforce of over 8,000 engineers, British Gas looks after customers' central heating systems, plumbing, drains, home electrics and kitchen appliances. It is committed to providing affordable energy while delivering the highest quality workmanship backed up by expert care.

Lowest CO₂ emissions of any major supplier

house.co.uk British Gas

Market

Since the residential electricity market opened to competition in 1998, British Gas has grown to become a significant player in the supply of electricity to domestic customers.

The past two years have been characterised by unprecedented increases in wholesale energy prices. As a result, price has been a key driver of customer switching and online switching websites have proliferated to become a major competitive force in the market. As the energy market entered a period of decreasing prices British Gas was the first major energy supplier to lower prices and followed up with a second price drop which came into effect towards the end of April this year.

The services market is another key area for British Gas. A number of central heating service offerings are available to suit its customer's differing needs. British Gas provides maintenance and repair contracts which offer a yearly maintenance and safety inspection plus breakdown repair. As well as contracts, it offers a one off fixed price heating repair service and also has an installation service for new central heating systems. Central Heating Care is a lead product with approximately 3.8 million customers.

The nature of the home services market is diverse with energy suppliers, insurers, water companies, outsource service providers and small independents making up the main competitors.

Achievements

British Gas is committed to training its employees. The Engineering Academy was awarded Large Employer of the Year by the Learning & Skills Council 2006 Apprenticeship Awards, and Beacon status which is awarded to exceptional learning providers. British Gas also won an award from Women into Science & Engineering (WISE) for its efforts to attract women into engineering. Furthermore, its commitment to identifying employees' potential, providing development and career opportunities within a supportive culture has helped the British Gas business energy supply and services divisions be placed in the Financial Times Best Workplaces 2007.

Improving the nation's energy efficiency is important to British Gas as is responsibly highlighting wider green issues.

In the first half of 2007, British Gas ran a high profile advertising campaign with a key message that the electricity which British Gas supplied to its customers had the lowest carbon dioxide emissions of any major supplier in Great Britain. It is one of the few UK electricity generators that does not feature on the WWF's 'Dirty 30' list of Europe's biggest polluters. British Gas has teamed up with other leading corporations and the Government to launch a campaign to encourage and enable members of the public to take steps to reduce their individual carbon emissions. British Gas boasts the largest energy efficiency program of any supplier in the UK. In 2006, over 1.5 million households completed a personalised Energy Savers

1948	1996	1997	1998	2000s	2001
The Gas Act is introduced creating a nationalised gas industry throughout England, Scotland and Wales, the organisation 'the gas board' is formed.	The market for the supply of gas to domestic customers is opened up to competition.	Centrica plc is created following the demerger of British Gas plc; British Gas' supply, services and retail businesses combine with the Morecambe gas fields' production.	The electricity market is opened up to competition – British Gas successfully enters the electricity market.	British Gas' product range is extended to include home security, plumbing, drains, electrical servicing, kitchen appliance care and telecommunications service.	British Gas now provides care for over four million heating and kitchen appliances.

Report, which identified an average saving for the customer of £176 a year.

British Gas is the only energy provider to sign up to 'Making a Corporate Commitment' – an initiative promoted by the Department of Environment, Food and Rural Affairs (DEFRA). Under this agreement, British Gas commits to goals, including reducing office waste, vehicle use and energy used in its buildings.

British Gas has won the Business Commitment to the Environment Premier Award; Business in the Community Awards for Excellence – Educational & Lifelong Learning Award; as well as Charity & Business Partnership of the Year for its Help the Aged Partnership. Now in its seventh year, British Gas has invested more than £7 million in practical schemes to help improve the lives of around 1.9 million older people.

In 2006, British Gas contributed more than £6 million and 11,000 hours of employee time in support of community initiatives. It also launched an employee volunteering programme which enables staff to spend up to two working days a year volunteering in their local community.

Product

British Gas has been working to help customers in the face of unpredictable and rising prices over recent years. In a time of wholesale price rises, British Gas offered peace of mind with fixed price products such as Price Protection 2010, and as wholesale prices started to fall in 2007, they cut prices. At 1st June 2007 the online energy product, Click Energy, offered the cheapest dual fuel prices in the market. Within the services market British Gas is keen to develop new, innovative products and services to meet a wider range of consumer needs such as the introduction of HomeCare Flexi, launched in 2006, which is designed specifically for those customers who want peace of mind but at a lower monthly cost and a £50 fixed fee for each completed repair.

For customers who wish to have confidence in high quality boiler repairs without a contract, British Gas also offers one off heating repairs for a fixed price.

Recent Developments

British Gas recently rolled out a new look and feel for the brand focusing on the 'trusted expertise' associated with British Gas. 2007 saw the launch of British Gas New Energy, a business unit committed to educating, engaging and enabling British Gas customers to reduce the impact of their energy use on the environment – for example, it now offers solar panels. British Gas has also made significant investments in developing the latest energy efficient and renewable technologies, for example, highly efficient boilers that produce their own electricity.

Promotion

The animated flame has become an effective creative property for British Gas – it brings strong branding and memorability to communications. In the (not too distant) context of rising wholesale prices, it has also served the brand well in establishing a likeable voice.

In the first half of 2007, the British Gas Services campaign extolled the virtues of the most comprehensive offering on the market; whether the customer wants ongoing central heating care or one off repair, British Gas has expert engineers to rely on. The TV commercial explained this whilst the other channels of poster, press, radio, online and direct marketing focused on one service and carried further details, such as price. Real engineers were used in all marketing material, enabling strong internal motivation as well as external.

The price cut campaign took a simple approach. In the first phase the flames fell to the soundtrack of the Blue Danube as the price cut was announced and the imagery was carried through-the-line. The flames then turned green to dramatise the fact that British Gas electricity has the lowest CO_2 emissions of any major supplier. Finally, at the implementation of the second price drop, a flame firework display, set to the 1812 overture, was rolled out across TV, print and online.

Brand Values

British Gas is committed to excellence and responsible behaviour. Utilising expertise developed over more than 50 years of supplying energy, British Gas aims to be straightforward and forward thinking to be the supplier that people trust to help them to run their homes and businesses.

www.britishgas.co.uk

2003

A new platform is developed to act as a framework to guide the brand's repositioning. The brand promise – 'Doing the right thing' – is manifested both internally and externally.

2005

British Gas creates a new structure with two distinct business units: Residential Energy and Home Services.

Also in 2005, the British Gas flames first appear in television ads.

2007

British Gas launches a new look and feel to the brand and British Gas New Energy – a team specifically to develop energy saving initiatives – is launched.

As well as being one of the best-known companies in Britain, BT is also a brand recognised and understood across the globe. BT's vision is to be dedicated to helping customers thrive within a rapidly changing world – the converged world – where individuals and businesses increasingly need to connect and communicate whenever and wherever they happen to be, using whatever device they choose.

Market

The UK telecoms market is worth tens of billions of pounds and is characterised by intense competition, whether for traditional voice services, mobile telephony or broadband.

The industry is currently in the middle of a sustained period of market consolidation where major communications companies have been joining together so that they can offer customers more than one service.

For example, some offer 'triple-play' (broadband, TV, landline telephony) services, while others provide 'quadruple-play' – where a mobile phone service is added.

A number of powerful brands, including BT, have set their sights on succeeding in this, the quickly developing, increasingly competitive multi-services market.

For BT this means that its brand becomes a critical differentiator and is compelled to work even harder for the company than ever before.

Achievements

BT has successfully transformed itself in recent years. It has evolved from being a supplier of telephony services to become a leading provider of innovative communications products, services and solutions. Its customers range from multinational corporations to residential householders, of which there are more than 20 million in the UK.

The company is the driving force behind the success of 'Broadband Britain' investing millions in a nationwide network providing blanket coverage across the UK. At the end of March 2007, there were nearly eleven million BT wholesale broadband connections in the UK.

In May 2007, BT announced it had become the UK's most popular broadband retailer, by

leapfrogging over the combined customer base of Virgin Media and ntl:Telewest Business into the number one position. BT now has more than 3.66 million broadband customers, equivalent to a 26 per cent share of the overall broadband market.

For the sixth year running, BT has been recognised as the world's top telecommunications company in the Dow Jones Sustainability Index (DJSI).

DJSI assesses companies worldwide on their performance in areas such as corporate governance, environmental management, community investment, human rights, supply chain and risk management.

Product

BT's portfolio offers an extensive range of innovative telephony, broadband and mobility products and services.

The company's developments in products and services for consumers are consistent with its focus on meeting the requirements of today's and tomorrow's customers.

The British consumer's love affair with broadband reached new heights in June 2006 when BT launched BT Total Broadband.

Powered by download speeds of up to 8Mb, BT Total Broadband means BT customers get more for their money through free internet voice calls, free video calls, wireless broadband access and a suite of

1981
British Telecom is created from Post Office Telecommunications and then privatised in 1984.

1991
The company unveils a new trading name, BT, together with the 'piper' brand identity.

2001
BT rebrands its mobile business as O2, prior to its demerger.

2006
Openreach opens for business and is responsible for managing the UK access network on behalf of the communications industry.

BT launches a comprehensive consumer broadband package – BT Total Broadband.

A new brand in digital TV entertainment – BT Vision – is also launched.

2007
BT launches a major new TV ad campaign to promote BT Vision.

security software – all brought together through the revolutionary BT Home Hub.

According to independent broadband service monitors Epitiro, BT Total Broadband provides consumers with the UK's best performing, most comprehensive ADSL broadband service.

Other innovative products include the award-winning BT Fusion, an intelligent mobile service that switches calls to a BT broadband line when the user is at home.

Customers get the convenience of mobile combined with the lower call costs and generally superior call quality advantages associated with a fixed-line phone. Earlier this year BT introduced its BT Fusion WiFi handsets. These use the company's growing network of hotspots and Wireless Cities (where BT is currently rolling out high speed WiFi infrastructures in some of Britain's biggest cities) to offer customers thousands of extra places to get great value on their mobiles.

Meanwhile, BT Home IT Advisor – BT's nationwide home computing help and advice service – boasts more than 40,000 customers and has proven a massive hit with 96 per cent of customers satisfied with the support they receive.

Underpinning BT's range of innovative services is its national network. The company is investing £10 billion to transform the network into an IP-based '21st Century Network'. This transformation is well underway and due for completion in 2011.

The 21st Century Network will carry all voice, video and data traffic on a single, state-of-the-art network giving consumers optimum capabilities to be able to communicate wherever they may be, using whatever device they choose. The first customers went live on the new network in November 2006.

Recent Developments

In December 2006, BT launched its next generation television service, BT Vision.

BT Vision is the first widely available TV service of its kind. It combines the appeal of TV with the interactivity of broadband. Customers can watch what they want, when they want and not be tied to TV schedules.

Delivered through a set-top box, the V-box, BT Vision contains a personal video recorder (PVR) able to store up to 80 hours of content, pause or rewind live TV and record programmes at the touch of a button. The box is also HD ready.

Customers of BT Vision, which is subscription-free, have access to an extensive library of on-demand content via their broadband connection and will also receive more than 40 Freeview channels through their aerial.

Promotion

Since October 2005, BT has been running a major TV and radio advertising campaign pulling together all of BT consumer communications with a consistent theme and tone of voice. The campaign follows a period of running separate campaigns for different BT consumer products. The campaign features a thoroughly modern, albeit everyday family headed by the characters Adam and his partner Jane using BT products to help them navigate through life's ebbs and flows.

The ads are designed to reflect the increasingly converged world of communications we now live in and focus on a range of BT products and services from WiFi to phonebooks, from 118 500 directory enquiries to landline texting.

In May 2007, BT unveiled a new ad campaign designed to position BT Vision as Britain's most flexible digital TV service. The ads develop the story of Adam and Jane as they each rush home from work, anticipating their ideal night of TV via BT Vision.

Brand Values

BT's corporate identity defines the kind of company it is today – and the one it needs to be in the future.

Central to that identity is a commitment to create ways to help customers thrive in a changing world. To do this, BT focuses on 'living' its brand values which are as follows:

Trustworthy – doing what it says it will; Helpful – working as one team; Inspiring – creating new possibilities; Straightforward – making things clear; Heart – believing in what it does.

The BT strapline – Bringing it all together – conveys leadership in the way BT enables global business customers to profit from convergence.

www.bt.com

Things you didn't know about BT

More than a million BT customers have now chosen to switch to paper-free billing.

Engineers from Openreach collectively climb the equivalent of Mount Everest every single day while carrying out maintenance on telegraph poles.

In addition to 300 million telephone calls, 350 million internet connections are also made across the BT network every day.

The use of conference calling by BT staff worldwide has helped reduce BT's carbon footprint by at least 97,000 tonnes of CO_2 and eliminated more than 860,000 face-to-face meetings, in the last year.

Registered Trade Mark

The Coca-Cola Company is the world's largest beverage company and the leading producer and marketer of soft drinks. Coca-Cola is the number one selling soft drinks brand worldwide and in Great Britain, Coca-Cola and sugar-free diet Coke are also the country's two biggest soft drinks. Coca-Cola is also the world's most valuable and iconic brand, heading the 2006 Business Week/Interbrand Top 100 Brands survey with a brand value of US$67.5 billion.

Market

Coca-Cola is by far the biggest soft drinks brand in the UK. Take-home sales in 2006 saw the brand reach £942 million in the UK, compared to £216 million for its nearest rival (Source: ACNielsen). Furthermore, the brand's year-on-year sales have increased by five per cent in the year from December 2005 to 2006, while sales for its nearest rival have decreased by 4.8 per cent (Source: ACNielsen).

In general, the soft drinks category has enjoyed strong growth in the year to December 2006, with data from the same report showing that sales of soft drinks are up eight per cent to more than £5.9 billion. This growth is partly being driven by the health and wellness trend sweeping Britain,

which has seen the soft drinks market innovate and offer consumers more choice in sparkling and still beverages. Diet and light drinks have seen particular innovation and growth, as well as fruit juices, waters, performance and energy drinks. Coca-Cola Great Britain continues to respond to this growing trend and currently more than 40 per cent of its volume for sparkling beverages is from light or low sugar drinks, and by the end of 2009, that figure is expected to reach 50 per cent (Source: Inform).

Achievements

The Coca-Cola brand and its family remains strong. It is a remarkable feat to have sustained its place at the pinnacle of global brand recognition, something The Coca-Cola

Company has achieved through continuous product innovation and through its leadership in marketing. Its iconic, cultural power and unifying global appeal was captured by the artist Andy Warhol, who once said: "A Coke is a Coke and no amount of money can get you a better Coke than the one the bum on the corner is drinking... Liz Taylor knows it, the President knows it, the bum knows it and you know it."

Looking ahead, The Coca-Cola Company aims to continue to give consumers a range of choices and create demand that will maintain the brand's unique position and continue to grow the market for soft drinks.

Product

Being in step with consumer trends and being able to anticipate what lies ahead as well as marketing innovation has always been a hallmark of The Coca-Cola Company, helping the brand evolve with time and keep in step with consumers' changing lifestyles.

Last summer Coca-Cola Great Britain made a bold addition to its brand with the launch of Coca-Cola Zero. The Coca-Cola family now has three core members: Coca-Cola, diet Coke and Coca-Cola Zero.

Complementing these, and meeting consumers' desire for new ways to 'enjoy the great taste of Coke', the company has also introduced brand extensions such as diet Coke with Citrus Zest and diet Coke with Cherry. Limited edition extensions have also added variety and interest. Summer 2007 sees the launch of Coca-Cola with Orange.

1886
Coca-Cola is invented by John Styth Pemberton, a pharmacist in Atlanta, Georgia. Asa Candler acquires the business in 1888.

1893
The famous signature 'flourish' of Coca-Cola is registered as a trademark for the first time. By 1895, Coca-Cola is available in every US state.

1915
The famous Coca-Cola Contour bottle, made from Georgia green glass, makes its first appearance and has a unique 3D trademark to protect Coca-Cola from a growing army of imitators.

1919
The business is sold to Ernest Woodruff. In 1923, his son Robert becomes president of the company, declaring that Coca-Cola 'should always be within an arm's reach of desire'.

1984
The launch of diet Coke takes place – the first brand extension of Coca-Cola in Great Britain.

2006
Coca-Cola Zero becomes the third brand in the Coca-Cola family in Great Britain.

Recent Developments

Coca-Cola Zero, dubbed "Bloke-Coke" by the UK media, the third Coca-Cola brand from Coca-Cola Great Britain, was the most successful new food and beverage launch in the past three years, according to ACNielsen data. In the 16 weeks following its July 2006 launch, Coca-Cola Zero achieved sales of £24.1 million, more than double the size of any other new product.

Coca-Cola Zero was the biggest addition to the Coca-Cola portfolio since diet Coke was launched 22 years ago, and completes the Coca-Cola 'trilogy'. With a similar full-bodied Coke taste but with zero sugar, Coca-Cola Zero is aimed at men in their 20s, who may have enjoyed traditional Coca-Cola when they were younger, but are now looking for a no-sugar option.

Coca-Cola Great Britain took the strategic decision to return diet Coke to its female heartland and focus Coca-Cola Zero to male consumers. The multi-million pound launch campaign encouraged over a million 18-34 year-old men to try the new drink between July and September 2006 (Source: Millward Brown).

Promotion

Coca-Cola has always been renowned for memorable marketing. The 1971 'Hilltop' TV commercial, featuring the song 'I'd like to buy the world a Coke', is not only one of the most famous-ever advertisements, but it also broke new ground for being one of the first truly global advertising campaigns.

Today, Coca-Cola continues to enjoy its iconic and well loved brand status amongst consumers. The Company recently ran its most successful advertising campaign to date when it launched 'The Coke Side of Life', and included the hugely popular 'Happiness Factory' and new Christmas TV ad, 'The Greatest Gift'.

2007 also saw Coca-Cola reinforce its commitment to music, teaming with iTunes for Europe's biggest music promotion ever. The promotion ran across over two billion promotional packs of Coca-Cola, diet Coke and Coke Zero, spanning 17 European countries.

The brand also continued its link with 'the beautiful game', bringing the FIFA World Cup Trophy to British consumers prior to the tournament in 2006. More recently in March 2007 the brand extended its biggest-ever domestic football commitment, The Coca-Cola Championship, with a new three-year deal up until the end of the 2009/10 season. The involvement of Coca-Cola has brought innovation and renewed excitement to the Football League, with its most successful consumer promotion for football to

date – Win a Player. This award-winning prize draw gives fans the chance to win a share of a transfer kitty of £350,000, for their football club to spend on a new player, or players. In 2007 Coca-Cola launched Buy a Player – a promotion that gives all Football League and Scottish Premier League Clubs the chance to win part of a £10 million transfer kitty.

Summer 2006 saw the launch of Coca-Cola Zero with a multi-million pound marketing push, helped by the biggest TV, outdoor and digital campaign ever mounted by the company in Great Britain and a series of male focused advertisements for the brand featuring the England and Manchester United striker Wayne Rooney.

Rooney has been working with Coca-Cola on a number of high-profile projects encouraging young people to enjoy 'the beautiful game'. This has included starring in a pre-Christmas 2006 photoshoot for Coca-Cola Zero with fiancée Coleen McLoughlin, with images featuring on London's World famous Coca-Cola Piccadilly sign. Wayne Rooney also appeared in TV advertising for Coca-Cola Zero which featured the striker showing off his skills in a tongue-in-cheek execution.

For diet Coke, 2007 saw the return of the 'hunk' with a revival of the diet Coke Break TV ad campaign made famous in the 1980s and 1990s. Like its predecessors, the new ad features a hunk alongside a group of young female office workers creating their own diet Coke Break.

Brand Values

The enduring brand values of Coca-Cola have stood the test of time. It has a unique

and engaging point of view on the world, conveying optimism, togetherness and authenticity. Coca-Cola is not political, but aims to brings people together with an uplifting promise of better times and possibilities. These values make Coca-Cola as relevant and appealing to people today as it always has been, and underpin the fierce loyalty, affection and love that generations have felt for the brand and the product. The Coca-Cola Company's reputation for strong marketing ensures that this connection remains as powerful as ever.

www.coca-cola.co.uk

Things you didn't know about Coca-Cola

The Company markets more than 400 brands worldwide, with 20 in the UK alone, providing over one billion servings of sparkling and still beverages every day.

Coca-Cola is thought to be the second most widely understood word in the world, after 'OK'.

Santa celebrated his 75th anniversary in December 2006, with a new TV ad, 'The Greatest Gift', aired in the run-up to Christmas.

The launch of Coca-Cola Zero was Coca-Cola Great Britain's biggest in 23 years since diet Coke.

Coca-Cola has been an official partner of the Olympic Games since 1928 – the longest running sport sponsorship in history.

In UK grocery stores, sales of diet Coke now exceed Coca-Cola.

COSMOPOLITAN

British Cosmopolitan launched in 1972, and has since remained one of the dominant magazine brands in the UK. Having just celebrated its 35th birthday, Cosmo attributes this success to the brand DNA, consistency of its voice and the constant ability to innovate and evolve for its generation. The brand believes that relevance counts for more than heritage because a consumer purchase of a magazine is an act of trust – "You know something I don't".

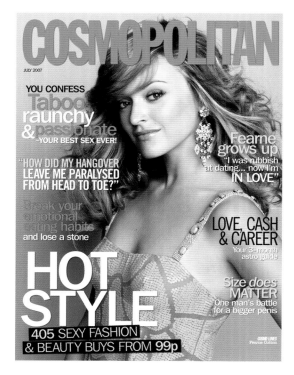

Market

The magazine market has come a long way since Cosmopolitan was launched.

Today, despite the unprecedented levels of competition, Cosmo consistently delivers an average circulation of more than 450,000 every month. Its readership is more than 1.7 million, 38 per cent greater than its nearest competitor (Source: NRS July – December 2006). What's more, 851,000 readers are unique to Cosmo, choosing not to read any other magazine on the market (Source: NRS July – December 2006). The Cosmo reader accounts for £1 in every £11 spent on beauty and £1 in every

£9 spent on fashion in the UK. Furthermore, Cosmo also generates the highest retail sales value of all monthly magazines in the market.

Achievements

In February 2002, Cosmopolitan celebrated its 30th birthday and was praised highly in the comment of the day. In The Times leader column it was said that "Cosmo is bigger than a magazine; it is a brand, an empire, a state of mind."

Since 1972, Cosmo has established an enviable campaigning heritage on a variety of issues, from equal pay and sexual health to

motivating political engagement on the rights for rape victims. For a three-week stretch leading up to the May General Election in 2005, Cosmo was never out of the headlines as being the voice of young women. The strength of the magazine's 'High Heel Vote' campaign saw editor Sam Baker featured on the cover of The Observer, putting the 6.8 million young women in the UK who were unlikely to vote in the spotlight. The campaign was subsequently nominated for a Channel 4 Hansard Society Politics Award.

2005 saw Cosmo launch an anti-fur campaign, 'Smart Girls Fake It'. Banning real fur from its pages, Cosmo was joined by a host of celebrities who signed up in support of the campaign to publicly make a stance against real fur. The campaign was awarded the PETA Humanitarian Award in 2006.

Cosmo has received a number of prestigious awards, including British Society of Magazine Editors (BSME) Innovation of the Year in 2003, for the magazine's Rapestoppers Campaign. The magazine has also been awarded the BSME Women's Magazine Editor of the Year in 1991, 1993, 1999, 2001 and the Periodical Publishers Association Consumer Magazine of the Year in 1992. In addition, Proctor & Gamble awarded Cosmo its Beauty Award in 2004 and 2006 for the magazine that has 'Best supported the Beauty/Grooming Industry'.

Product

For the British reader, Cosmo aims to be her life and relationship bible. Through its pages she is able to observe life and, more importantly, change her life. The USP of

1972	2001	2002	2004	2006	2007
British Cosmopolitan launches with an issue price of 20p. The first issue – supported by Saatchi & Saatchi – sells out in three hours.	CosmoGIRL! and www.cosmogirl.co.uk launch.	Cosmo launches a travel-size format, offering consumers more choice.	Cosmo appoints London ad agency CHI for the first ATL campaign since its launch.	The new cosmopolitan.co.uk launches.	Louise Court is appointed as editor, as Cosmopolitan celebrates 35 years.

Cosmo is to 'Inspire women to be the best they can be'. As a result, readers can feel engaged, empowered and able to achieve anything they want.

Cosmo's core business is the magazine, which now has an extended family including cosmopolitan.co.uk, CosmoGIRL! and Cosmo Bride. Building on the strengths of its magazines, the Cosmopolitan brand has diversified into other areas, such as licensed merchandise carefully selected to fit with the brand's personality. The Cosmopolitan Collection includes soft furnishings, bedding, handbags, swimwear and beauty accessories. Cosmopolitan has also published a significant number of books on relationships, sex, beauty and emotional wellbeing, including 'Was it good for you, too?' – a book celebrating the brand's dominance in the UK.

Recent Developments
The website, www.cosmopolitan.co.uk was launched in 2006 – a new content-rich and community driven site. Representing the key editorial pillars of the magazine, the site also

employs interactive elements that are unique to the site. Users can spill their secrets in the Cosmo confessions booth, put problems to the public vote with Moral Dilemma, upload pictures of boyfriends, exes or single friends for the Cosmo community to judge – alongside the customary mix of fashion and beauty that Cosmo is famous for and, of course, the Naked Male Centrefolds.

In such a dynamic marketplace, a business strategy that keeps the brand fresh, modern and relevant is essential. Recent innovations have included the launch of a new editorial property – the Fun Fearless Female Awards. More than just your average celebrity awards, Cosmo rewards the most fun, fearless females from all walks of life, from celebrities to readers, bound by their inspirational qualities.

The Cosmo Beauty Awards, launched in 2003, have become an ultimate buying guide for the consumer and are used extensively by the trade as a powerful brand endorsement of best in class.

In 2006, Cosmo celebrated the 10th anniversary of the Naked Male Centrefold, a famous editorial and event property that supports Everyman – the testicular and prostrate cancer charity – raising invaluable research funds and awareness.

Louise Court became Cosmo's editor in January 2007 and aims to inject her own brand of humour into the magazine, whilst continuing to do what Cosmo does best – inspiring women to be the best they can be.

Promotion
Cosmopolitan aims to be the industry benchmark in magazine publishing. To its readers, Cosmo is as relevant today as it was in the 1970s, 1980s and 1990s. In the 2000s, Cosmo has developed a travel-size version that offers consumers choice and convenience at newsstand.

In 2005, Cosmo launched its first above-the-line advertising campaign since 1972 to help protect the unique position of the brand. The campaign introduced a new ad line,

'Bring out the Cosmo in you', designed to reinforce Cosmo's 'fun, fearless female' positioning, with posters rolled out regionally. 2006 saw Cosmo back on TV, working with creative agency Clemmow Hornby and Inge.

Now a multi-platform media brand, it can connect with its readers over and above the magazine, through online, events, surveys, reader polls, subscribers, e-subscribers, text and email.

Brand Values
The Cosmopolitan mission is to celebrate fun, glamour and passion for life as well as inspire young women to be the best they can be. A magazine for a 'fun, fearless female', it has eight core editorial pillars: relationships and sex, men, real-life stories, beauty and fashion, careers, emotional health and wellbeing issues and campaigns. The relationships element of the mix is unique to Cosmo and is the crucial element that enables a trusted and more intimate relationship with its readers.

www.cosmopolitan.co.uk

COSTA

The largest and fastest growing coffee brand in the UK and the leading authentic Italian coffee shop chain (Source: Allegra Strategies 2007), Costa Coffee boasts more than 570 UK stores and 175 overseas. Founded in 1971 by Italian brothers Sergio and Bruno Costa, the chain became part of the Whitbread portfolio in 1995, but retains its Italian charisma, with in-store baristas learning the art of coffee-making at the Costa Coffee Academy.

Market

The branded coffee shop market has quickly grown to reach a level of maturity in the UK. The market has undergone consolidation in recent years and there are now three main players, Costa Coffee, Starbucks and Caffè Nero, which are facing the challenges of serving good coffee along with meeting an increased demand for healthy drinks and snacks.

Costa Coffee is the leading branded coffee shop in the UK, with a 23 per cent share of the sector (Source: Mintel 2007). In real terms, this means it has 25 more stores than Starbucks and 277 more stores than Caffè Nero. Going forward, Costa has publicised its intentions to expand to more than 800 UK outlets by 2010, doubling its past expansion rate.

Achievements

Costa attributes much of its success to its traditional Italian coffee-making methods, which have provided the brand with a unique difference. More than three decades ago, the fledgling business was started using a

traditional Italian drum roaster, making only small batches of coffee each time and using a special espresso blend combining seven different beans. The beans were roasted slowly at reduced temperatures to give a fuller, less bitter flavour. Both the special Mocha Italia espresso blend and the slow roasting technique are still used today, continuing to give Costa its distinctive smooth taste.

A further point of difference for Costa is that every in-store barista learns the art of coffee-making at the Costa Coffee Academy,

based at Costa's own roastery in Lambeth. Here, they learn to live by the four 'M's: 'Miscela' (blend) – all Costa's coffee is made using the company's unique espresso blend, Mocha Italia; 'Macinatura' (grind) – Costa coffee is made with beans freshly ground to exactly the right consistency to ensure the perfect extraction of the flavours and aroma; 'Macchina' (machine) – specially designed Italian espresso machines, perfected over the past 20 years to achieve high volumes of high quality espresso and cappuccino; 'Mano' (hand) – the skill of the barista.

1971

Costa is founded by two Italian brothers, Sergio and Bruno Costa. Noticing a demand for high-quality roasted coffee beans, the brothers

start a wholesale operation supplying roasted coffee to caterers and specialist Italian coffee shops in and around the UK.

1978

Elida and Yolanda Costa, the wives of the two brothers, open the first Costa store in London and begin to expand the business at the rate of two stores per year.

1988

Coffee production moves to larger premises at Old Paradise Street, Lambeth, London.

1995

Costa is acquired by Whitbread plc in October, with 41 stores nationwide.

1999

The first overseas Costa store opens in Dubai.

A slice of heaven
Try a tasty Toffee Florentine.

Enjoy a long, cool
Caramel Iced Latte

Golden and delicious.
Try a Caramel Shortbread

Extensive training is given on checking and controlling the correct dose, grind size, tamp (pressure) applied to the coffee grounds, extraction time and cleanliness and maintenance of the equipment.

These distinctive methods have led to Costa winning a series of accolades, including Best Catering Outlet in Scotland at the BAA Food & Beverage Awards, Best Coffee Shop in the City from Durham Life Magazine & Durham Council, and Best Cafe/Restaurant 2007 awarded by the Dubai Mall of the Emirates, the largest shopping mall in the Middle East.

Product
In order to serve the best coffee in the true Italian style, Costa owns its entire coffee production process from bean to cup.

The first stage involves selecting the best beans, so the roastery team ensures that Costa gets only the cream of the world's coffee crop and when the green (unroasted) beans arrive at the roastery they are tested in order to select those with the best flavour characteristics.

The second stage is to create a unique blend, where six different arabica beans and one robusta bean go into creating Costa's

Mocha Italia, an espresso blend that forms the basis of all of Costa's coffee options.

The third stage is roasting: in their raw form the coffee beans are relatively odourless, tasteless and indigestible, so it's the roasting process that is all important, drawing out the aroma and flavour of the bean.

The fourth and final stage in Costa's coffee production process is storage – where the roasted beans are stored in airtight silos or packaged immediately into bags in bean or ground form. Costa is able to pack its beans immediately using a one-way valve that allows gas to escape without letting air in, meaning Costa's coffee is always roastery fresh.

Recent Developments
In 2007 Costa launched a new range of iced blended drinks, designed to provide a refreshing alternative to hot coffee. The Frescato range is available in eight flavours – from fruity 99 per cent fat free variants to creamy indulgent options.

Costa has also recently launched a new range of muffins across its stores – customers can expect real fruit pieces, hearty chocolate chunks and crumble toppings. The range is free of hydrogenated fats, but for those watching their waistlines, a low fat option is also available.

To make it easier and quicker for customers to grab their coffee on the run, Costa was the first coffee shop chain to introduce the prepaid coffee card (the Costa Card) into the UK.

Promotion
Costa's integrated communications strategy is designed to drive customer understanding of Costa's Italian provenance and the quality of its food and drink, as well as highlighting new product innovations.

A new creative style was launched in 2006 for Costa's food and drink offering to

bring to life its Italian heritage. Costa uses in-store marketing, national press, outdoor, retail and media partners, while also using electronic customer relationship management in order to get closer to its customers.

In 2006 Costa hosted the first Costa Book Awards (formerly the Whitbread Book Awards) at Grosvenor House, London. The chair of judges, Armando Iannucci, announced Stef Penney as the winner with her murder mystery 'The Tenderness of Wolves'. The award is one of the most prestigious book prizes in the UK, and was launched 35 years ago, the same year that Costa began trading.

Brand Values
Costa's heritage is firmly rooted in serving coffee the Italian way, from bean to cup and beyond. Although Costa is market leading, at heart it remains a small Italian family business and is as passionate about the welcoming environment it offers customers as it is about making good coffee. It is the interaction between the bean and Costa people that sets it apart.

Costa's mission remains, to be the best coffee shop business wherever it trades.

www.costa.co.uk

Things you didn't know about Costa

Costa's slow roasting technique takes 18 minutes at 230 degrees – compared to the seven to eight minutes of its competitors at 400 degrees.

On average Costa opens a new store every four days.

Costa was the first coffee shop to introduce the prepaid coffee card into the UK.

Costa was named the fastest growing and most popular UK coffee shop brand in a national YouGov survey in 2005.

2001
Costa Coffee makes a £1 million investment in a new roaster at its Lambeth roastery.

2006
The Costa Foundation is founded to implement programmes to improve the social and economic welfare within the countries which Costa sources its coffee beans from.

Also in 2006, Costa opens its 500th UK store, 100th overseas store in Dubai and expands into India, Pakistan and China.

2007
Costa overtakes Starbucks as the largest coffee shop brand in the UK.

Eurostar is the high-speed rail service linking the UK to the Continent, operating up to 17 daily services from London Waterloo International to Paris and up to 10 from London to Brussels. On 14th November 2007 Eurostar will launch services from its new London station, St Pancras International; the completion of High-Speed 1, the UK's first high-speed rail line, will cut Eurostar journey times by an average of 23-25 minutes.

Market

Eurostar has transformed travel between the UK and the Continent, carrying more than 70 million passengers since it began passenger services through the Channel Tunnel in November 1994.

In 2006, 7.85 million people chose Eurostar, up 5.4 per cent on 2005. Leisure traveller numbers rose by 4.5 per cent, while the number of business travellers increased by more than 17 per cent.

The move from Waterloo International to St Pancras International will further improve journey times between the UK, France and Belgium and open Eurostar up to millions of new travellers living to the north of London. Eurostar will minimise disruption by moving overnight.

Achievements

In September 2003 Eurostar took a major leap forward with the opening of the first section of the Channel Tunnel Rail Link – now renamed High-Speed 1 – which shortened journey times: London and Paris are now only two hours and 35 minutes apart; London and Brussels, two hours and 15 minutes; and Lille, one hour and 40 minutes from London.

The high-speed line means trains can travel in Britain at the same speed as they do on the Continent, at a maximum speed of 186mph. Eurostar celebrated this by achieving no less than 208mph with a test run on the new line on 30th July 2003.

In addition, service punctuality in 2006 was a record 91.5 per cent, outstripping airline competitors on the London–Paris and London–Brussels routes.

Eurostar is used by a wide range of people, from royalty and senior politicians to stars of stage and screen to families and backpackers; its passengers come from almost every country in the world and it is an important link in European tours for visitors coming from regions such as North America and the Far East.

Eurostar has received awards for the quality of its service from a range of organisations, including winning the title of World's Leading Rail Service at the World Travel Awards for the last nine years. In addition, awards have been received in categories covering architecture, marketing and the environment.

Product

Eurostar aims to simplify travel – creating a smooth and seamless train journey connecting people from one capital to another.

At 186mph, the high-speed trains provide fast and reliable connections between London, Paris and Brussels. Direct services run daily to the gates of Disneyland® Resort Paris, twice-weekly winter ski services travel direct to the French Alps and a weekly summer Saturday train runs to Avignon in the heart of Provence. Some trains stop en route to the Continent at Ashford in Kent and at Calais and Lille in northern France.

1994
On 14th November, public Eurostar services commence with two services each way to Paris and Brussels.

1996
Services from Ashford International in Kent begin, as do direct services to Disneyland® Resort Paris.

1997
Winter ski train services to the French Alps are introduced.

The introduction of the Belgian high-speed line in December reduces the London–Brussels journey time to two hours and 40 minutes.

1999
The formation of Eurostar Group is announced.

2002
Direct summer services from Waterloo and Ashford to Avignon are introduced.

Eurostar also offers connecting tickets to more than 100 destinations across France, Belgium, the Netherlands and Germany.

In addition to its standard class, Eurostar also offers travellers Leisure Select, which includes a reclining seat, three-course meal, complimentary newspapers and magazines.

Travellers in Eurostar's Business Premier class benefit from a 10 minute check-in and can keep in touch with their offices through WiFi enabled departure lounges. On board, Business Premier offers a full meal and drinks service together with a quiet work-friendly environment, complete with UK and continental plug sockets to charge laptops or mobiles during the journey.

Multilingual sales and customer service staff are a very visible part of the product. Two onboard train managers and a catering crew greet Leisure Select and Business Premier travellers and provide the meal service, while two staffed buffet cars are provided for travellers in standard class. Staff members are also available at all stations to help customers with enquiries and particularly to attend to the needs of any travellers with special requirements. Eurostar aims to be accessible to those travellers with disabilities and assistance can be given to wheelchair users, sight or hearing impaired passengers, elderly travellers and those with children.

Recent Developments

The single most significant event in Eurostar's history will occur in 2007, when it moves on 13th November from its Waterloo home to St Pancras International station where services launch on 14th November. It marks the beginning of a new era in high-speed rail – and a key development in travel between the UK and continental Europe.

St Pancras is in the heart of London and is served by six key Underground lines – Victoria, Northern, Piccadilly, Metropolitan, Hammersmith & City and Circle. In addition, with seven rail companies operating from St Pancras International, King's Cross and nearby Euston, Eurostar will be well connected to the rest of the UK.

The completion of High-Speed 1 will also provide a new intermediate station at Ebbsfleet International near Dartford. Together with the existing station at Ashford, this will increase the number of Eurostar services serving Kent. Journey times from Ebbsfleet International will be 10 minutes quicker than those from St Pancras International. Located near the M25 with parking space for 9,000 cars, it will have a catchment area of 10 million people in South East England, both to the north and south of London.

Promotion

In the highly competitive travel marketplace, stand-out is key, as is delivering communications activity that drives preference for travel with Eurostar. For the business market, it is tasked with driving improved relations with its target markets, namely business travellers and those working within the travel industry.

The development of the service presents new impetus to reinforce Eurostar's position in the market and convert more passengers from among those who still believe short-haul air travel to be more convenient. Significantly faster journey times and the environmental benefits of rail travel to the Continent makes for a powerful argument.

Business communications are more focused with advertising placed in business travel titles or at key business hubs and interchanges. Eurostar also communicates to its most valued business customers through the Frequent Traveller scheme, launched in November 1996.

The brand has a high public relations profile and is regularly featured in films, print and broadcast media. It is frequently used as a tangible visual symbol of Britain's connection to the rest of Europe.

Brand Values

At the heart of the Eurostar brand is a simple but special travel experience, connecting people between the UK and the Continent with a fast and frequent service.

Eurostar's personality embraces an independent spirit, is playful, stylish and cosmopolitan while also being professional and trustworthy.

In its relatively short history, Eurostar has succeeded in appealing to a wide range of travellers, remains highly salient and has established itself as an inspirational brand without being exclusive.

www.eurostar.com

2003

On 30th July, Eurostar sets a new UK rail speed record of 208mph – beating the Advanced Passanger Train's 1979 record of 162.2mph.

In September, Channel Tunnel Rail Link 1 (High-Speed 1) opens on time and on budget. Passenger services on the new line begin on the 28th.

2005

Eurostar launches two new classes, Business Premier and Leisure Select.

2007

Eurostar ends its services from Waterloo on 13th November, launching from St Pancras International the following day.

Fairy was rated as Britain's number one cleaning brand by The Times in February 2007 and has been a regular household feature since the name first appeared in 1898 on a bar of soap. Today the brand represents a range of products renowned for their cleaning ability and caring nature. Over 13 million UK households buy 150 million bottles of Fairy each year, which equates to 57 per cent of the total market.

Market

The dish cleaning market contains sink and dishwasher sectors, with Fairy leading the total category in household penetration, volume and value sales.

The value of the dish washing sector continues to increase three per cent per annum driven by the launch of Premium products such as Fairy Active Bursts and growth of Fairy Antibacterial products which deliver superior performance for the consumer; the future is bright for Fairy with a wealth of new product development in the wings.

Achievements

Fairy has grown in recent years to be in the enviable position of becoming the UK's top selling household brand (Source: Nielsen

May 2007). Following the launch of its dishwasher cleaning tablets, Fairy Active Burst, it is the only national brand to offer a complete range of products in both the sink and dishwasher categories.

This followed Fairy becoming the UK's fastest growing non-food brand in Grocers in 2006, when turnover topped £120 million behind the launch of Fairy Active Bursts for dishwashers (Source: Nielsen).

Further to this, turnover has been driven significantly via adjacencies such as Fairy Powerspray – which provides intense cleaning for dishes with burnt-on food.

Fairy Liquid has always been associated with being kind on skin, so it was an important accolade for the brand to become the only product to be awarded top cleaning results by Which? magazine's Best Buy

survey, whilst remaining mild enough to be certified by the British Skin Foundation.

Product

During the 1950s, most people used powders and crystals to wash dishes. After conducting vigorous tests, Fairy launched a dish washing product, Fairy Liquid. By the end of its first year six out of 10 people in the UK had bought it.

The Fairy brand has stood for 'sparkling performance' for over 100 years. An iconic household emblem, it has maintained market leadership for over 50 years through its unbeatable performance and value; lasting up to 50 per cent longer than the next best selling brand (Source: Independent Laboratory Testing).

Now the Fairy range consists of Fairy Liquid Original which comes in the traditional Original variant as well as four additional scents: Apple Quake, Lemon Twister, Strawberry Flame and Passion Flower Storm.

Fairy Naturals Antibacterial has been specifically created, combining Fairy Liquid's cleaning performance with natural herb and citrus extracts, which provide the additional benefit of controlling the growth of germs on sponges and cloths; the product is endorsed with a gold seal from the Royal Institute of Public Health.

Fairy Naturals with Antibacterial Action is available in Classic with Eucalyptus extracts, Lime and Lemongrass extracts, Pink Grapefruit and Garden Mint extracts.

The Fairy range has also grown to encompass new product areas, such as

1898	1930	1987	1989	1997	2003
Fairy Soap launches through Thomas Hedley & Sons.	Procter & Gamble acquire the brand and Fairy Baby trademark.	Lemon scented Fairy Liquid is introduced alongside Fairy Original.	Fairy's non-bio laundry product launches, for sensitive skin.	Fairy Liquid with antibacterial agents is introduced.	Fairy Powerspray launches, for tough, burnt-on stains, adding £9 million to the category.

As usual Fairy active bursts have cleaned up.
In an independent survey of over 10,000 UK consumers Fairy Active Bursts have been voted Dishwasher Product of the Year. Isn't it time you tried them?

Fairy Active Burst dishwashing tablets, Fairy Powerspray and Fairy non-bio laundry products.

Recent Developments

Fairy has been a familiar face in kitchens for generations, so it was a bold move in 2000 for Fairy to change its signature white bottle to fit in with modern kitchens and times. The new transparent bottle was ergonomically designed, making it easier to control. The formula was also changed to make the product more concentrated.

To maintain the momentum of innovation, 2003 saw the launch of Fairy Powerspray, designed to remove tough, burnt-on food from dishes to make washing up easier.

In 2006 Fairy introduced Fairy Active Bursts for dishwashers, a revolutionary all-in-one detergent plus liquid product, requiring no unwrapping prior to use for unbeatable cleaning and convenience.

The successful launch has seen Fairy Active Bursts within its launch year become the second best selling dishwashing product (Source: Nielsen 2006), with consumers voting it Dishwasher Product of the Year and 90 per cent of independent repairmen recommending the product (Source: GSAT 2006).

Promotion

Fairy Liquid TV advertising campaigns first began in the 1950s. This soon led to a host of celebrity endorsements, including actress Nanette Newman with the much loved and remembered line 'Hands that wash dishes

are as soft as your face with mild green fairy liquid'.

Brand communication now dominates the category, highlighting unbeatable performance through cleaning messages and value due to mileage performance. Fairy aims to put the customer first, with Fairy operating a free phone advice line and money back guarantee. Furthermore, Fairy refuses to produce products for other brands or retailers.

In recent years, Fairy's advertising has seen chefs Ainsley Harriott, Anthony Worrell Thomson and Gary Rhodes front the brand together. TV executions show the chefs in the kitchen, talking about the brand in a light hearted manner. This is backed up with print and outdoor work.

In recent years the use of glamorous spokespeople such as Jodie Kidd, Helena Christiansen and Louise Redknapp has enabled Fairy to talk to a younger audience.

Fairy has also driven a more dynamic brand position in recent years through its False Economy versus Fairy-Conomy campaign, highlighting the value benefits of its longer lasting formula to your pocket and the environment with less bottles required. The campaign has been a success, voted second most memorable by consumers (Source: Adwatch September 2006).

Meanwhile, the brand's Fairy Active Bursts product was launched through its unique 'All in One' positioning with the 'no need to unwrap' benefits. This led ad spend and awareness in the dishwashing detergents category in 2006.

Fairy supports a number of charities and has been the UK's number one fundraiser for the Make A Wish children's charity over the last three years through its 'Helpful Hands' winter campaign, which grants children with life-threatening illnesses special wishes. Its corporate social responsibility policy, means it donates products for use during natural disasters such as the 2007 South Coast oil spillage as it is recognised by RSPB as the best product for cleaning birds following oil spills.

Brand Values

Fairy has always been a family orientated brand with strong links to the kitchen and the role of dinner within families. In 2007 the brand commissioned the 'Fairy Knife & Fork Report'; the Report provides a revealing insight into the heart of the home, the way families are eating together, how parents today understand the importance of regular family meals, and the consequences of abolishing them. The Fairy Knife & Fork Report indicates that parents want to instill strong values in the home first, before they set their children up for the challenges of later life, away from the protection of the home.

The Fairy Knife & Fork Report was conducted by the Future Laboratory and coincided with the Government's 'Respect Zone' initiative. It identified that today parents are being more responsible when it comes to family bonding, and taking the time to serve their children nutritious food in the heart of the home. Importantly it identified families who eat together are more likely to stay together.

Fairy has strong links to environmental and sustainable organisations such as the RSPB, WWF, Energy Saving Trust and Wastewatch. Its products are concentrated to produce less packaging waste and are recyclable.

www.fairy-dish.co.uk

Things you didn't know about Fairy

The Fairy baby that has appeared on all products since the 1930s is called 'Bizzie' and has been produced as a figurine by Royal Doulton.

Since the 1960s the UK has bought over 4.8 billion bottles of Fairy Liquid, enough to circle the earth 2,400 times.

579 bottles of Fairy are produced per minute – over 10 million gallons of Fairy Liquid in a year.

One bottle of Fairy washed 14,763 dirty plates – a world record.

Fairy has strong links with design experts and commissioned work from Celia Birtwell and Linda Barker in 2007.

2006

Fairy Active Bursts launches and sales top £120 million.

2007

Fairy Active Bursts is awarded Dishwasher Product of the Year for a second successive year.

Since its launch in 1960, Galaxy® has seen strong growth that continues to strengthen year-on-year. Such success is built on the consistency of its positioning of magic, femininity and indulgence. Galaxy believes that true chocolate indulgence is about the whole eating experience, which is why everything about Galaxy chocolate, from the taste, to the shape, to the packaging, is designed to make indulging in a Galaxy moment as pleasurable as possible.

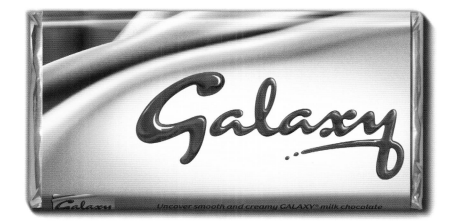

Market

The UK confectionery market, currently valued at an estimated £4.5 billion (Source: IRI Infoscan), has seen a slowing rate of growth. Chocolate confectionery accounts for the bulk of sales in the market, with the remaining share taken up by sugar products. With brands leveraging the indulgent positioning of their products, the premium market has seen considerable development, while occasions such as everyday sharing have also been targeted.

The UK chocolate confectionery market remains dominated by Cadbury, Mars and Nestlé, and new product development (NPD) is firmly centred on brand extension rather than bringing new names to the consumer.

The UK block chocolate market is worth £683 million, with Galaxy block chocolate worth £100.4 million, a 14.7 per cent share of the total market (Source: IRI Infoscan TNS Worldpanel/Usage Panel).

The Galaxy brand represents the largest growth in the block category over the past five years, with this trend accelerating recently to reach an 18 per cent year-on-year growth in 2006 (Source: CAGR IRI 52 w/e 30 Dec 06/IRI 52 w/e 30 Dec 06).

Achievements

If Galaxy were a stand-alone company, it would be the fourth-largest confectionery manufacturer in the UK, behind the current leaders Cadbury, Trebor Basset, Mars Snackfood UK (the brand's parent company) and Nestlé UK.

1960	**1987**	**1987**	**1987**	**1995**	**2000**
Galaxy is launched in the UK and Ireland.	The 'Why have cotton when you can have silk?' Galaxy advertising campaign is launched.	Ripple and Minstrels are rebranded as part of the Galaxy product family.	Galaxy ice cream is launched.	Galaxy Caramel is launched.	The Galaxy Amicelli and Galaxy Silk collections are launched.

The entire Galaxy product portfolio is worth £220 million, with Minstrels worth £51 million and Ripple £26 million (Source: IRI Infoscan Total Market 2006).

The Galaxy brand has grown by 10 per cent in the past three years (Source: CAGR IRI 52 w/e 30 Dec 06/IRI 52 w/e 30 Dec 06).

As part of Mars Snackfood UK, the Galaxy brand is ultimately part of Mars Incorporated, which employs 39,000 people in more than 65 countries. Its products are consumed in more than 100 countries and the company has global annual sales of US$18 billion.

Product
Galaxy offers three main products: Galaxy block chocolate, which is marketed simply as smooth and creamy milk chocolate; Minstrels bite size, which are smooth and creamy pieces of Galaxy milk chocolate encased in crispy shells; and the Ripple bar, smooth and creamy Galaxy milk chocolate with a rippled centre.

There have been many brand extensions to Galaxy, not only in bar format – such as Galaxy Caramel – but other confectionery products such as ice cream and seasonal Christmas and Easter egg variants. In addition to this, the Galaxy range of drinks includes Galaxy chocolate flavoured milk, Galaxy Thick Shake and Galaxy Instant Hot Chocolate Drink.

Recent Developments
Galaxy teams are constantly working to create new and innovative ways with Galaxy chocolate. In 2007, the brand will launch three new large block variants: Smooth Dark; Roasted & Caramelised Hazelnut; and Raisin, Almond & Hazelnut.

These have a new shape and use a new recipe that is designed to create an even smoother taste. The new products will also feature new premium packaging. To support the launch, a large-scale marketing campaign including TV advertising and product sampling is planned.

Promotion
Twenty years ago, Galaxy's 'Why have cotton when you can have silk?' TV communication propelled Galaxy into the hands of consumers. Having provided a strong platform for the Galaxy brand, the chocolate was able to achieve 16 years of strong sales success in

Lose yourself in a good book with Galaxy Minstrels.

the market. In 2003, the brand was refreshed and relaunched to focus on indulgence and women's relationship with chocolate. The relaunch and subsequent consumer activity has aided continued growth for the brand.

These activities included links with a number of key female indulgent occasions such as films or reading.

The first collaboration between Galaxy and films was Down With Love in 2002, followed by the highly successful Bridget Jones partnership in 2004 and another female oriented title, The Devil Wears Prada, in 2006.

The link with reading started in 2005 with different associations with female magazines and bookstore samples. In 2006 Galaxy linked up with the Richard & Judy Summer Book Club and in 2007 Galaxy was the first title sponsor of the British Book Awards with a multimedia campaign, including TV, press, online and PR, to support the link with reading.

Brand Values
With a target audience of women between the ages of 25-45, Galaxy stands for 'me time', indulgence, femininity and sensuousness. The Galaxy brand understands the ritualistic nature of chocolate eating, and as a brand aims to provide an entire Galaxy experience, rather than just chocolate.

www.masterfoods.com

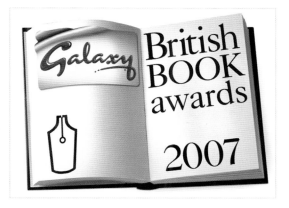

Things you didn't know about Galaxy®

Galaxy was listed at number 26 in Checkout magazine's annual Top 100 Grocery Brands report for 2007, using data from ACNielsen.

Galaxy chocolate has sales which total those of Ferrero, Green & Black's, and Lindt combined (Source: IRI Infoscan, TNS Worldpanel/Usage Panel).

162 bars of Galaxy 150g are purchased every minute across the UK.

6,011 Minstrels are eaten every second somewhere in the UK.

2003
The Galaxy brand is relaunched.

2004
Galaxy sponsors the film Bridget Jones's Diary.

2005
Galaxy's relationship with reading is established.

2006
Galaxy sponsors the film The Devil Wears Prada and launches its Richard & Judy Book Club sponsorship.

Gossard™

Gossard has been at the forefront of lingerie design and innovation since 1901, pioneering new styles and technology that have revolutionised underwear consistently through the decades. The brand has earned an exemplary reputation for quality, comfort and fit and now sells in over 30 countries worldwide. Focusing on fashion-led collections to suit the demands of today's women, Gossard remains one of the most widely recognised and well-loved lingerie brands in the UK.

Market
The lingerie market consists of many brands and is highly competitive. Total lingerie sales in the UK are valued at £1.28 billion, an increase of just under seven per cent in the last four years. Volume sales have grown by eight per cent during the same period, indicating a slight decline in retail prices. Bra sales represent more than half of the market value (Source: TNS FashionTrak September 2006).

Achievements
Gossard Superboost has recently been awarded the UK's 'Best Cleavage Bra'

according to figleaves.com customers. More than 10,000 consumers voted and the Superboost satin range was considered the bra that creates the most attractive cleavage – comfortably.

Product
Gossard's products have evolved in line with both fashion and social acceptance. The 1960s saw the brand pioneer the pantie girdle and bra slip in the UK – both thought to be very daring at the time. Later in the same decade, the company diversified and focused on producing fashionable bras

including the world-famous Wonderbra. As women turned to burning their bras as a sign of liberation and freedom in the 1970s, Gossard responded by developing its Glossies range of sheer, shimmering underwear, providing a very natural look under tight fitting clothes.

Around the same time it was noted that women's figures were starting to change. They were becoming taller and fuller in the bust and, as a result, the demand for larger cup sizes was increasing – a trend that continues today. Still wanting the fashionable styles that their smaller busted friends

1901	1950s		1960s	1970s	1994
Henry Williamson Gossard establishes the H.W. Gossard Company in Chicago and sets about producing corsets and 'top quality merchandise'.	Gossard introduces its first lightweight girdles and takes another innovative step by introducing Silkskin – a lightweight, pre-shrunk girdle featuring an	innovative fibre, Nylon from DuPont. Also in the 1950s, Gossard becomes part of the Courtaulds Textiles Group.	The company diversifies, focusing on producing fashionable bras, including the now world famous Wonderbra.	Responding to bra-burning women's libbers, Gossard develops the sheer glossies range. Noting women's busts becoming fuller, Gossard ups its ranges to DD cups.	Gossard launches the Ultrabra – the first time a cleavage bra is available in larger cup sizes.

THE LOOK

THE FEEL

THE ONLY THING YOU'LL FEEL IS FANTASTIC **Gossard** Super Smooth

were wearing, Gossard developed ranges up to a DD.

Co-ordination was the by-word of the 1980s and with it Gossard introduced its popular Ritz collection of co-ordinates from A-E cup and a basque style.

In the 1990s Gossard's licence to produce Wonderbra expired, and the brand launched the Ultrabra – the first cleavage bra available for larger cup sizes. Superboost followed a few years later with the claim 'Biggest cleavage ever... or your money back!'

In 2002 the trend for low-rise trousers and hipsters emerged and women became more and more concerned about visible panty lines. In response, Gossard launched G-Strings – a collection of decorative G-strings that could be worn everyday or on special occasions. Heavily embellished, they featured diamante shapes on the back and captured the trend of lingerie that was worn to be seen. The innovative launch received fantastic feedback and within two months of launch the diamante T bar sold out across the whole of the UK.

Further innovation followed in 2005 with Gossard SuperSmooth which, as a result of extensive research, was designed to provide invisible support and a comfortable 'second skin' sensation.

2007 sees the launch of the redesigned and much loved Gossard Superboost range.

Still delivering the ultimate cleavage, Superboost Satin has been redesigned for the first time since 1999. The brand's best-selling cleavage bra now features a luxurious satin fabric, satin cup linings, a modern and sexy shape, gold fixtures and fittings and no longer has the tell-tale gate style back often associated with cleavage bras. What's more, it's now available up to a G cup.

Promotion

Over the past few decades Gossard has launched the careers of models such as Kate Groombridge, Emma Griffiths and Sophie Anderton by signing them as the 'face' of the brand. They have all gone on to have successful careers in modelling and television. In 2005, Gossard signed Maria Gregerson to front the new SuperSmooth press and poster campaign created by TBWA, 'SuperSmooth: The only thing you'll feel is fantastic'. The ad was shot by Mary McCartney Donald, breast cancer awareness campaigner, and daughter of Sir Paul McCartney. The campaign bucked the trend for traditional lingerie adverts that focus on the way the product looks, by concentrating on how the bra makes the wearer feel.

Other ground breaking campaigns over the past few decades include 'Wonderbra: Say

goodbye to your feet', 'Superboost: Boob job for £19', and the 'Girl in the grass' campaign, which featured Sophie Anderton, shot by Herb Ritz, with the strapline 'Who said a woman couldn't get pleasure from something soft?'

Brand Values

Gossard is a confident brand for self-assured women – with fashion inspired, pioneering products that meet their needs and desires.

The collections represent contemporary feminine style without compromise – best demonstrated by the award winning, best selling Superboost range.

www.gossard.co.uk

Things you didn't know about Gossard

The average bra uses up to 100 metres of thread, has up to 50 components (including hooks and eyes, wings, cradle, centre gore and wire casing) and can take up to 28 sewing operations.

During World War II the Gossard factory was turned over to assist with Britain's war effort. The workforce produced everything from brassieres for the Wrens, to sails, single-seat fighter dinghies and almost 700,000 parachutes.

Seventy per cent of women wear the wrong size bra. It's important to be professionally measured regularly to ensure the correct support and perfect shape – breast size can fluctuate for many reasons including hormones and diet.

A recent poll highlighted that 65 per cent of women own a cleavage enhancing bra, and one in seven women admit to having stuffed their bra before to give them confidence.

BOOB JOB £19   superboost Gossard

2002
Gossard launches a collection of decorative G-strings that sell out as soon as they hit the shops.

2005
Gossard SuperSmooth proves to be the new 'must-have' – revolutionary no stitching and no seam technology provides invisible support and a comfortable 'second skin'.

2006
DB Apparel is created in February from the acquisition of Sara Lee Branded Apparel Europe by Sun Capital Partners.

2007
The Gossard brand is acquired by Courtaulds (UK) Ltd, this is swiftly followed by the relaunch of Superboost Satin, the brand's best-selling cleavage bra.

The UK bottled water industry is booming. Nearly 60 per cent of the adult population now drinks bottled water, making it the second most popular soft drink and one of the fastest growing sectors in the market. Highland Spring is the UK's leading producer, number one sparkling and kids' bottled water brand (Source: Zenith/ACNielsen). It was the first bottled water in the UK to be granted organic certification from the Soil Association for its protected land in the Ochil Hills, Perthshire.

Market

Bottled water has a 16 per cent share of the UK soft drinks market and is attracting consumers at a faster rate than any other soft drink.

The UK bottled water market is now worth an impressive £1.68 billion, with 2.27 billion litres consumed in 2006 (Source: Zenith 2007). Nevertheless, fewer than one quarter of adults drink the recommended two litres each day, indicating huge potential for sustained growth in the years ahead.

As the number two brand overall in the UK bottled water market, Highland Spring was also one of the fastest growing major brands in 2006, up 12 per cent (Source: Zenith 2007).

Still water is the most popular choice for consumers, with 77 per cent choosing it most often. At the same time, sparkling water has also grown in popularity, with sales up two per cent in 2006 (Source: Zenith 2007).

Highland Spring is the number one sparkling bottled water brand in the UK with 13 per cent share in 2006, contributing 63 per cent of the growth in the take-home sector during the same year (Source: Zenith 2007).

After it was pioneered by Highland Spring in 2001, the kids' bottled water sector has exceeded the 16 million litre mark, continuing to offer significant potential and forecast to reach 40 million litres by 2010. Highland Spring for Kids is the number one kids' bottled water brand in the UK with 26 per cent share.

Achievements

Highland Spring is the UK's leading producer of bottled water, number one in doorstep

deliveries and in the cash and carry sector, exporting to over 50 countries worldwide. The company produces around one million bottles of water a day and in 2006 recorded a sales turnover of £54.2 million.

The entire water catchment area for Highland Spring, extending to 1,260 hectares, is accredited organic by the Soil Association.

As the biggest employer in Blackford, Perthshire, Highland Spring plays a vital role in the local economy and provides an active and supportive role in the local community.

Formed in 1979 Highland Spring has enjoyed sustained growth year-on-year to become a leader in the industry. The

headquarters in Blackford boast one of Europe's most modern bottling plants with four state-of-the-art bottling lines.

Product

Research conducted over the years shows a growing majority of consumers believe Scotland is home to the purest water and the provenance of Highland Spring is certainly core to its continued success.

No farming, agriculture spraying, building or habitation is permitted within 2,000 acres of protected land from which Highland Spring is drawn. The land has been kept free from pesticides and pollution for more than

1979
Highland Spring Ltd is formed.

1993
Highland Spring displaces Perrier from the number one bottled water slot.

The brand wins the contract to supply bottled water to British Airways worldwide.

1998
Highland Spring becomes official water supplier to the World Snooker Association.

2001
Highland Spring becomes the first British brand of bottled water to have its land registered organic by the Soil Association.

The brand continues to innovate, pioneering the children's bottled water market.

Drawn from organic land.

20 years. The water is harvested from naturally renewable sources, constantly replenished by the ample rainfall in the Ochil Hills, Perthshire.

Untouched by human hand, Highland Spring is delivered to consumers exactly as nature intended with nothing added or taken away, apart from the addition of CO_2 for its sparkling range.

The company offers the most comprehensive portfolio of bottled waters in the UK market to meet all needs, from the stylish glass range for fine dining to sports bottles for 'on the go'.

Recent Developments

Created exclusively for the restaurant and licensed trade, Highland Spring's 750ml glass bottle was launched in September 2006 in both still and sparkling as a new addition to the range.

To facilitate increased demand Highland Spring reclassified in April 2007 as a 'spring water', giving the company access to at least another 100 million litres of water a year. The water continues to be pure and natural Highland Spring, sourced from the same organic, protected catchment area.

In addition £3 million is being invested in 2007 in new production facilities to help meet future demand and upgrade existing bottling lines.

Promotion

As advocates of a healthy active lifestyle, Highland Spring is committed to forging the link between active sport and good hydration, as well as encouraging school children to adopt healthier drinking habits.

In 2007, Highland Spring was revealed as exclusive drinks sponsor of Britain's

number one professional tennis player, Andy Murray. The 20 year-old tennis ace, who hails from Dunblane, only 10 miles from the company's bottling plant, displays the brand logo on his shirt sleeve and drinks Highland Spring as part of his dietary regime.

The company also sponsors the world's top three snooker players – Stephen Hendry, Ronnie O'Sullivan and Ken Doherty – and is a major supporter of Glasgow's 2014 Commonwealth Games Bid.

Highland Spring is a long term supporter of major sporting events at a local, national and international level such as: the UCI Mountain Bike World Cup; the renowned Johnnie Walker Golf Championship at Gleneagles; World Bowls Tour; HIHO windsurfing tournament in the British Virgin Islands; and hundreds of running events across the UK. It is also the official bottled water to a number of UK rugby union teams including London Wasps, Saracens, NEC Harlequins, Northampton Saints and Sale Sharks.

To reinforce its organic credentials, Highland Spring has supported a number of initiatives run by the Soil Association including the School Food Awards in 2005 and the Organic Food Awards in 2006.

The company's first ever national TV advertising campaign ran in 2006, promoting the organic credentials of its land. An association with ITV soon followed, seeing Highland Spring as broadcast sponsor of the British Soap Awards, National TV Awards and British Comedy Awards during the same year.

The company has a successful and long standing marketing partnership

with VisitScotland which has now entered its fifth year. Through sampling, advertising and PR, the Scotland Underground campaign promotes Scotland as the ideal destination for a short break, and Highland Spring as the source of the purest, freshest bottled water.

Highland Spring also works closely with Connoisseurs Scotland, an organisation promoting a select, world renowned collection of some of Scotland's most prestigious hotels, including Myers Castle, Gleneagles and The Old Course Hotel Golf Resort & Spa in St Andrew's.

As a corporate sponsor of Scotland's annual showcase event, The Edinburgh Military Tattoo, the brand reaches more than 100 million viewers worldwide through the Edinburgh Tattoo Highland Spring dancers.

In 2004 Highland Spring launched a three-year cause related marketing partnership with Breast Cancer Care. The award winning Pure & Natural campaign saw the famous pink ribbon symbol appear on the majority of the brand's range. A 75 strong 'Team Highland Spring' including GMTV's Lorraine Kelly and Highland Spring employees, ran the 2005 New York marathon. In 2006 the company launched its first pink bottle. Both activities helped to raise upwards of £350,000.

Brand Values

Highland Spring is an iconic Scottish brand. The water is drawn from an underground spring water source in the beautiful Ochil Hills in Perthshire, Scotland.

As guardians of the land, the company goes to great lengths to protect its source, ensuring the water is the purest it can be.

Since many people believe Scotland to be the home of the purest, freshest bottled water, Highland Spring is committed to protecting the environment and developing the business in a sustainable, eco-friendly way.

www.highland-spring.com

Things you didn't know about Highland Spring

Pure water from the Ochil Hills has long been held in high regard. In 1488 King James IV of Scotland ordered his Coronation ale to be made from Blackford water.

Rainwater takes as long as 15 years to reach the source of Highland Spring deep below the Ochil Hills, having collected the minerals which give the water its unique mineral analysis.

Highland Spring was the water of choice at the G8 Summit at the Gleneagles Hotel in July 2005.

2004	2006	2007
Also in 2001, Highland Spring acquires Gleneagles Natural Mineral Water and establishes Watermedia, creating bespoke promotional bottles.	The brand celebrates its 25th anniversary and Highland Spring Dress Tartan is specifically created for the brand.	The first national TV advertising campaign titled 'The Journey' is rolled out.	Highland Spring scoops number two overall brand position from Volvic in the UK.

Imperial Leather has come a long way since it was founded in the 1930s. Today, whilst we're still all familiar with the original Imperial Leather bar of soap and its little metallicised label, the brand has grown to the extent that, at any given minute, thousands of people all over the world use a product from Imperial Leather's expansive range of washing and bathing products.

Market

Imperial Leather is a key player in the UK's personal washing and bathing market. In 2006, this market was worth an estimated £623 million. It is forecast that the total soap, shower and bathing category will have grown a further six per cent in real terms

over the next five years (Source: Mintel November 2006).

With over one in five UK homes now having two or more bathrooms (Source: GB TGI, BMRB Summer 2002 & 2004 & Quarter 3 2006/Mintel) and with UK consumers living busier lives (for example, making more visits to the gym) there has been an increase in shower usage occasions. Coupled with the fact that consumers are demanding more from their shower and bathing experiences – expecting to be pampered and now even using the shower as a chance to unwind – Imperial Leather is well positioned to continue to grow with its prolific portfolio of affordably luxurious, feel good, rich lathering products.

Achievements

Over the last year, one in three people have purchased at least one Imperial Leather product (Source: TNS) – the equivalent of 16.4 million people.

In 1998, Imperial Leather launched the innovative 'Foamburst' shower product range. It was the first shower gel in a can that dispenses as a gel and transforms into a mass of luxuriously rich, creamy lather. This market-leading development has proved to be hugely popular with men, women and children alike.

Imperial Leather has grown to become the leading washing and bathing brand in many key markets across the globe and can be found in countries as diverse as China, Australia, Nigeria, Greece and Indonesia.

Product

Imperial Leather's product range includes shower gels, bathing products, Foamburst shower gels, bath foams, hand washes, deodorants and talcum powder, as well as its famous bars of soap.

Imperial Leather's range is aimed at the whole family to give a trusted feel good, luxurious washing and bathing experience at an affordable price.

1768
Russian nobleman, Count Orlof, challenges perfumers, Bayleys of Bond Street, to create a perfume which embodies the distinctive aroma of the Russian court.

1938
Imperial Leather is brought to the UK by Cussons, introducing the British public to the brand's 'Eau de cologne Imperiale Russe' fragrance.

1940s
Manufacturing operations expand rapidly. Marjorie Cussons, the pioneering daughter of the company's founder, is responsible for energizing public interest in the brand.

Marjorie introduces gift sets at key purchasing periods and later creates several brand extensions such as talcum powder and bath foam.

1942
Imperial Leather advertising suggests that it is the best soap to use during rationing due to its long lasting properties.

1950s/60s
Expansion of production continues, with the addition of manufacturing sites in Manchester and Nottingham.

Recent Developments

In 2005 Imperial Leather was successfully relaunched, making its range more contemporary, feminine and appealing with simplified on-pack communication, premium design enhancements and the introduction of ergonomic curves and improved dispensing mechanisms making it easier to hold and to use.

In 2006, Imperial Leather launched limited edition variants of its shower gel and bath foam; the popular fragrances of Japanese Spa and Indian Spice encouraged new users to the brand. Following this success, Imperial Leather launched further limited editions in 2007 with Thai Fusion and Tahitian Retreat bringing a tropical flavour to the range.

Promotion

Imperial Leather was one of the first brands to recognise the potential and power of advertising.

By 1946, Cussons was spending £100,000 supporting the brand – an enormous sum in those days. Predominantly choosing to advertise in the popular women's magazines of the day, Imperial Leather's advertising campaigns used a series of specially commissioned paintings featuring orchids, tropical fish, miniature gardens and roses.

During the 1950s, cinema's popularity led Cussons to place commercials on the big screen, in advance of the featured presentation, to convey the brand's 'everyday luxury' credentials.

The brand was also one of the first committed to TV advertising. Imperial Leather's first TV commercial aired in 1959 and featured a mother and daughter using Imperial Leather, to create the link between high quality soap and soft clean skin. It is this investment by Imperial Leather and other similar brands that led to the coining of the phrase 'Soaps' in relation to advertiser-funded TV drama.

The famous Imperial Leather 'Family' campaign was launched in the 1970s, and even today triggers fond memories of the brand amongst the British public. Whether travelling across the Russian Steppes in the Imperial Train, or flying high in their Imperial Leather Spaceship, the family always found time to enjoy a luxurious soak in their decadent mobile bathroom.

More recently, the 'Dancing Duck' commercial for Foamburst shower gel and a series of female fantasy based commercials for bath foams (featuring footballer Paolo Di Canio and, separately, a crew of

stripping firefighters) have resulted in the brand, once again, becoming renowned for humorous advertising.

Imperial Leather's most recent TV campaign shows a mum's temporary escape from the rigours of family life – through a hidden door in the shower wall – into a beautiful secret shower room to enjoy 'One of life's little luxuries' under the stars.

Brand Values

Imperial Leather is a leading quality washing and bathing brand aimed at families. The brand understands that luxurious washing experiences are not just for women and aims to give the whole family a luxurious washing experience – every day and at an affordable price.

www.imperialleather.co.uk

Things you didn't know about Imperial Leather

Contrary to many people's belief, the metallicised label featuring the Cussons Imperial Leather logo on each soap bar should face downwards not upwards, to prevent the bar from becoming sodden and waterlogged in the soap dish.

The shape of the Imperial Leather bar has not changed since its inception. Its unique shape was developed to mirror that of saddle soap used by the Russian Imperial household to clean its riding tack.

1970s	1998	2002	2000s
Shower Gel is introduced to the product range.	The innovative Foamburst shower gel range is launched, packaged in a rust-free can rather than a bottle.	Imperial Leather is a main sponsor of the Manchester Commonwealth Games.	Imperial Leather collaborates with The Tussauds Group, with sponsorship of 'The Flume' at Alton Towers and 'Bubbleworks' at Chessington World of Adventures.

The LEGO® Group has come a long way over the past 75 years, from a small carpenter's workshop to a modern, global enterprise that is now one of the world's largest toy manufacturers. The purpose and vision of the LEGO Group is to inspire children to explore and challenge their own creative potential. LEGO products have undergone extensive development over the decades, but the foundation remains the traditional LEGO brick.

Market

Today the founder's grandson, Kjeld Kirk Kristiansen, owns the LEGO Group, which in sales terms is the world's fifth largest toy manufacturer after Mattel, Hasbro, Bandai and MGA Entertainment (Source: NPD).

In the UK, the traditional toy market (excluding video games) was worth £2.2 billion in 2006 – a four per cent growth on the previous year (Source: NPD Consumer Panel). The LEGO brand leads the construction segment of the toy market, which was worth £119 million in 2006 (Source: NPD Consumer Panel).

The LEGO Group has accomplished this by offering a range of quality products centred around its building systems. In the hands of children, the products are designed to inspire fun, creative, engaging and challenging play. This activity develops inventive and structured problem solving, curiosity and imagination, interpersonal skills and physical motor skills, so building with LEGO bricks is about 'learning through play'.

Achievements

With around seven LEGO sets sold each second, it's little surprise that the world's children spend five billion hours a year playing with LEGO products. Indeed, over the years enough LEGO bricks have been manufactured to give each of the world's six billion inhabitants 62 LEGO bricks each. In recognition of this achievement and its longevity, the start of the new millennium saw the LEGO brick twice acclaimed 'Toy of the Century' – first by Fortune Magazine

and later by the British Association of Toy Retailers.

The LEGO Group has also won the title of 'World's Most Respected Company' according to the Reputation Institute's annual report, which surveyed more than 60,000 consumers in 29 countries.

The LEGO Group ended 2006 with net sales 11 per cent higher than the previous year, an increase in sales that was spread evenly across the company's markets, including direct to consumer sales. The LEGO Group is headquartered in Billund, Denmark but has subsidiaries and branches throughout the world and a global workforce of 4,500 people. LEGO products are sold in more than 130 countries.

Product

LEGO products are developed and grouped so that there is something to suit all ages and stages of development. From toddlers, schoolchildren and teenagers to young-at-heart adults.

'Pre-school' products, including DUPLO, are developed to cater for the youngest children, encouraging them through creative play to use their hands and develop their motor skills.

'Creative Building' is the name given to sets or buckets containing traditional LEGO bricks and special parts such as windows, wheels, roof tiles and other items. Creative Building is available in both DUPLO and ordinary LEGO bricks and is produced for builders who like to apply their imagination and think creatively.

'Play themes' are products that are built up around a story, such as a fire station, the police, an airport, a knights' castle or racers. Another example is the BIONICLE deep sea universe, which has its own story. As well as enjoying building, the child can spend many

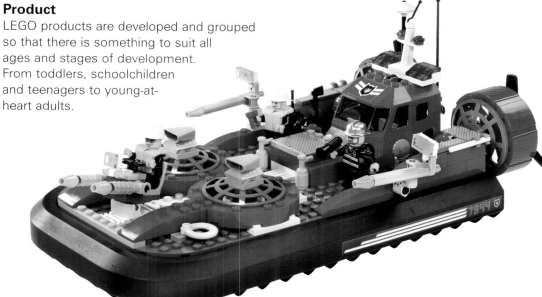

1932
The LEGO Group is founded in Denmark by carpenter and wooden toy maker, Ole Kirk Cristiansen.

1958
The LEGO brick in its present form is launched. The interlocking principle makes it unique and offers unlimited building possibilities.

1966
The first LEGO train – with its own rails and a 4.5v motor – is introduced.

1977
The LEGO TECHNIC series is introduced, including parts such as gears, beams and gearboxes.

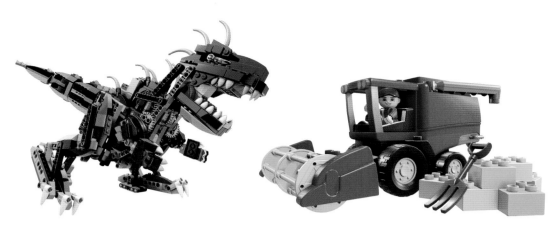

hours playing with the finished models.

'Licensed products' are play themes based on movies or books for which the LEGO Group has acquired the rights, for example Star Wars™ and a Harry Potter range in LEGO bricks.

'LEGO MINDSTORMS NXT' enables the user to design and build real robots. Using the software included in the set, robots can be programmed to perform different operations, reacting to the user's voice or controlled via a mobile phone.

The 'LEGO Factory' website gives children the opportunity to build their own virtual models on the computer using LEGO Digital Designer and then have the bricks to build the physical LEGO model sent by post.

Recent Developments

The LEGO Group's core creative team of 120 designers representing 15 different nationalities works constantly to develop innovative products that promote creativity and fun-packed play.

For 2007, the LEGO Group has launched a raft of new products. One highlight is the Mars Mission collection, which is aimed at children aged seven or over. Launched in August, it includes high-tech mining equipment sets and both ground and airborne assault vehicles packed with special features and futuristic accessories.

Also released in August, the remote control Monster Dino 3-in-1 construction system challenges builders aged nine or over to combine and create the kit into three different build options. Monster Dino

can be re-assembled to make a crocodile and a spider, each powered by remote control and with its own sound effects.

Promotion

It is important to the LEGO Group to have close contact with its consumers throughout the world. To this end, the company engages in many initiatives to strengthen ties between LEGO enthusiasts and the company.

The FIRST LEGO League (FLL) sees LEGO challenge teams of children around the world between the ages of nine and 16 to an international robotics competition. In 2006 more than 80,000 children took part in the competition in 40 countries around the world.

The LEGO Club is for children in the 6-12 age group and has a membership of 2.4 million worldwide, including the US, Canada, Germany, Austria, Switzerland and the Netherlands. Through the LEGO Club special website, members can show each other pictures of their favourite building work and draw inspiration for future play. In the UK, 250,000 LEGO Club members receive the LEGO Club magazine five times per year. In 2006 the main LEGO website had an average of 8,137,062 individual visitors a month – up 29 per cent on 2005 – with each spending an average of 28 minutes at the site.

In addition to these activities, the LEGO Group uses a mix of TV advertising, PR, sponsorship, in-store demonstrators and targeted shows

and events to support its brand image and products.

Brand Values

The LEGO brand is formed by the expectations that people have of the company – towards its products and services – and the accountability that the LEGO Group feels towards the world around it. The brand acts as a guarantee of quality and originality. Children are the role models of the LEGO Group – inquisitive, creative and imaginative – with an innate urge to learn. The LEGO Group sees quality as of key importance, and is striving to be the best and most credible player in the toy business.

It is the LEGO Group's philosophy that 'good play' enriches a child's life – and its subsequent adulthood. With this in mind, the LEGO Group's wide range of products is founded on the same basic philosophy of learning and developing – through play.

www.lego.com

Things you didn't know about LEGO®

The name 'LEGO' is an abbreviation of two Danish words, 'leg godt', meaning 'play well' and also means 'I put together' in Latin.

If you built a column of 40,000,000,000 LEGO bricks, it would reach the moon.

The first LEGO mini-figure appeared on the market nearly 30 years ago. Since then four billion of the little yellow figures have been produced – making it the world's biggest population group.

Nearly 55 million LEGO bricks were used in the building of LEGOLAND Windsor, which opened in 1996.

All LEGO components are fully compatible, irrespective of when they were made or by which factory.

17.8 billion LEGO bricks and other components are made every year – equivalent to two million bricks an hour, or 33,824 a minute.

1986

The LEGO TECHNIC Computer Control is launched, later paving the way for the first computer-controlled LEGO robots.

1994

The LEGO TECHNIC Supercar and LEGO BELVILLE, a product for young girls appear. It has a nuclear family, horses and scenes from everyday life.

2001

The BIONICLE universe is introduced – the first time the LEGO Group develops a complete story from scratch as the basis for a new product range.

2006

LEGO MINDSTORMS NXT is launched, enabling consumers to build and programme a robot that can see, hear, speak, feel and move in just half an hour.

LURPAK is a major player in its category. Driven by growing trends of taste and purity, it continues to go from strength to strength, attracting a new generation of butter lovers 100 years on. A differentiated market position, clear brand positioning, memorable advertising and successful new product development have all contributed to LURPAK's strong growth.

Market
"A little bit of what you fancy does you good". This attitude is driving a return in popularity for butter and butter-blends. Increased household penetration has led to increased sales of LURPAK over recent years. Indeed, over one in three households in the UK buy a LURPAK product every year which rises to one in two households in the north of England and Scotland.

The total Butter, Spreads and Margarine (BSM) market is worth £887 million with LURPAK contributing £173 million to this (Source: IRI Infoscan 52 w/e February 24th 2007). It is a mature market with 99 per cent household penetration, but sales are predicted to decline over the next decade with consumption set to decrease mainly due to a growing interest in health, the decline of host products (such as bread) and the increase in out-of-home eating. Therefore, competition for share of market is tough, with only a handful of brands winning out.

A market driven by taste, health and convenience, LURPAK sits firmly at the taste end of this spectrum and is consistently voted 'best tasting' by consumers. In fact, 'Spreadables' (blends of butter and vegetable oil such as LURPAK Spreadable) are driving the BSM market as the only sector to achieve annual double-digit growth.

Achievements
In a market that is declining in volume, LURPAK grew five per cent in 2006, with LURPAK Spreadable breaking the £90 million brand sales barrier and LURPAK Lighter breaking £50 million. The brand experienced its highest ever level of annual household penetration as a greater number of younger and southern people bought into the brand, driving its value market share to an all time high of almost 20 per cent.

LURPAK Spreadable is the number one brand in the BSM category (Source: IRI Infoscan 52 w/e February 24th 2007), with LURPAK Lighter at number five – an achievement gained only five years since launch.

Consumer loyalty to LURPAK is strong. In fact, over the past two years the brand has accumulated more than 120,000 'LURPAK Lovers' to its customer database.

Product
LURPAK is a lactic butter, giving it a distinct flavour profile that is often described as 'subtle, creamy and pure'. It contains less water than many other butters making it ideal for cooking and baking. Indeed, it was used by Jamie Oliver in the TV series 'Naked Chef'.

From 1911, only dairies participating in a rigorous system of regular blind tastings could use the Lur-mark Danish Butter brand. These quality controls are still practiced today. In fact, to ensure that LURPAK retains its premium credentials, its dairies have to submit samples to a trained panel of independent experts on a weekly basis.

LURPAK's differentiation is visible in the supermarket where its distinct silver packaging sets it apart in a sea of yellow and gold competitor packaging. It is available in slightly salted and unsalted varieties in 250g and 500g sizes.

1901
The 'Lur-mark' is registered on October 23rd. The mark consists of four intertwined 'lurs' and the words 'Danish Butter' and 'Lur Brand'.

1932
In the UK, sales of Lur-marked Danish butter total 130,000 tons per annum – an all-time high.

1957
Individually wrapped packs of Lur-marked Danish butter are launched and the words 'Danish butter' are replaced with 'LURPAK'.

1984
The animated figure Douglas the Butterman is created by Aardman Animations. The people behind Aardman, Nick Park and Peter Lord, will later win Oscars for their popular Wallace & Grommit series.

1997
LURPAK Spreadable – a blend of LURPAK butter and vegetable oil – is launched in the UK.

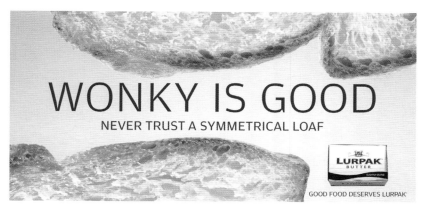

LURPAK Spreadable Slightly Salted – a blend of LURPAK butter and vegetable oil – is available in 250g, 500g, 1kg and 2kg tubs. An unsalted version of LURPAK Spreadable was launched in 2006 and is now available in 250g and 500g pack sizes.

LURPAK Lighter Spreadable – a reduced fat version of LURPAK Spreadable – is available in 250g, 500g and 1kg tubs.

Recent Developments
The most recent development for LURPAK is the introduction of LURPAK Spreadable Unsalted in January 2006. Launched in a 250g pack size in all major supermarkets, the success of this line extension has led to a 500g pack size being launched in January 2007.

Selling more packs than any other BSM launched in 2006 (Source: IRI Infoscan 52 w/e December 2006) and contributing incremental sales to the brand, LURPAK Spreadable Unsalted's success is due to its appeal to people seeking a balanced approach to their diet.

In April 2007, the brand embarked on a £6 million advertising campaign that focuses on communicating to a growing generation of 'foodies' who are willing to pay more for good food.

Promotion
LURPAK's marketing has always been simple and consistent, centred around brand truths that are the same today as they were 100 years ago – namely its distinctive taste and renowned quality.

For almost 20 years, the loveable Douglas the Butterman fronted the brand's advertising, accompanied by Penelope Keith as the voiceover artist. These adverts were hugely popular with a mass audience and helped position LURPAK as an 'everyday luxury'.

However, times move on, and towards the end of the 1990s Douglas was failing to cut-through with TV audiences – especially the younger generations who considered him 'old-fashioned'.

Today, LURPAK has gone back to its roots with a campaign that positions it as an enhancer of good food.

The campaign strapline 'Good food deserves LURPAK' encapsulates the essence of the advertising, encouraging people to think twice about what butter, spread or margarine they use.

Three new TV adverts were created by communications agency Wieden + Kennedy, celebrating simple, wholesome foods such as bread, potatoes and mushrooms, and the benefits that LURPAK brings to them.

Accompanied by eye-catching press and poster work with quirky straplines such as 'Mash – Food of the Gods' and 'Wonky is good – never trust a symmetrical loaf', the advertising creative works through-the-line across a range of media. It creates true impact in what many consider a 'dull' category littered with clichéd advertising and poor consumer recall.

Supporting the new positioning as a 'champion of good food', the brand has launched www.insearchofgoodfood.co.uk – a website providing a haven for foodies to share tips and recipes, read food-related articles and discuss all things culinary via its online forums.

Brand Values
The LURPAK brand values are centred around the product being premium, quality, natural and authentic.

LURPAK believes that good food really matters as one of life's greatest pleasures and is worth taking the time to enjoy, no matter what the occasion.

LURPAK is simply made with pure, natural ingredients to give a subtle and distinctive flavour that brings out the best of food.

The brand's values are firmly established in the minds of consumers and are as relevant today as they were 100 years ago. The fundamentals of the brand have remained unchanged, which is one of the main reasons for LURPAK's continued success.

www.lurpak.co.uk

Things you didn't know about LURPAK

LURPAK is sold in almost 75 countries worldwide.

It is one of the UK's top 20 best-selling grocery brands.

LURPAK butter was first sold in wooden barrels bearing the 'Lur' mark – a 'lur' being an ancient Scandinavian wind instrument.

Old LURPAK merchandise such as butter dishes and toast racks are considered collectors items and can often be found on eBay selling for up to £30 a piece.

More than 20kg of whole milk goes in to making 1kg of LURPAK butter – nothing is wasted though as by-products of the butter-making process, like buttermilk, are used in other products such as soft cheese.

2001
LURPAK Lighter Spreadable – a reduced fat version of LURPAK Spreadable, containing 25 per cent less fat – is launched in the UK.

2002
LURPAK Spreadable becomes the number one sub-brand in the BSM category. It retains this position today (Source: IRI Infoscan 52 w/e February 24th 2007).

2006
LURPAK Spreadable Unsalted is launched in the UK and sells more packs than any other BSM product launched that year.

2007
LURPAK launches its new advertising campaign – 'Good Food Deserves LURPAK'. It is also voted the strongest BSM brand by the Superbrands consumer survey.

Ray Kroc developed his brand vision for McDonald's around a simple but effective consumer-driven premise: great quality, service, cleanliness and value. These values have remained the cornerstones of the company and today McDonald's is the largest food-service company in the world, with more than 30,000 restaurants serving nearly 50 million people each day in 119 countries and territories, from Andorra to The Virgin Islands.

Market

By the end of 2006, McDonald's had over 1,200 restaurants employing more than 67,000 staff in the UK. The chain provides food and drink to over two million Britons per day, and upwards of £460 million is spent annually in its UK supply chain, supporting 17,200 UK and Irish farmers.

Although operating within an increasingly competitive marketplace, McDonald's, through a combination of quality, value, fast and friendly service, clean and pleasant surroundings and insightful marketing, continues to have a strong presence and market share.

Achievements

The strength of the McDonald's brand is recognised by customers, journalists, marketers and analysts. McDonald's Global Stock price is at a record high in 2007.

The company is committed to customer satisfaction and recognises that well-trained and motivated staff are vital to continued success. Training is a continuous process and employees attend courses in the restaurants as well as at the company's six Management Training Centres. In 2006 McDonald's invested £15 million in training their people. The efforts of the brand in developing its people were recognised by several major award schemes including the Great Places to Work

Institute who named McDonald's as one of the top 50 Great Places to Work and the 2007 Working Families Employer Awards.

Recognition of the work carried out within the supply chain came in early 2007 with the Golden Egg Award from Compassion in World Farming for use of free range eggs. The brand's commitment to animal welfare has also been recognised by the RSPCA, with an Alternative Award.

The Work Foundation discovered through research that for an average franchised restaurant in the UK, around £900,000 of turnover stays local and generates a further £2.2 million of local spending power. Aside from all of this, the real achievement of the brand and the foundation of its future

prosperity is in the enjoyment customers take from the food and the experience of visiting a McDonald's.

Product

The McDonald's menu has changed more in the last four years than it did in the preceding 28 years. The menu choice has been extended through the introduction of new permanent ranges, including salads and a new breakfast menu that includes bagels and porridge. Since launch, McDonald's have sold over 15 million salads and 21 million fruit bags. In 2006 alone McDonald's sold 400,000 bags of carrot sticks, 1.6 million portions of Quaker Oatso Simple porridge and used over 81 million free range eggs in its restaurants.

1954
Ray Kroc starts supplying milkshake mixers to Dick and Mac McDonald's restaurant in San Bernardino, California.

1955
Kroc buys a franchise from the brothers and sets up his own McDonald's restaurant in Des Plaines, Chicago.

1959
The chain sells 100 million hamburgers in its first three years of trading and the 100th branch is opened.

1961
Kroc pays US$2.7 million to buy out the McDonald brothers' interests.

1963
The billionth McDonald's hamburger is served live on primetime television.

1965
The McDonald's Corporation goes public and is listed on the New York stock exchange the following year.

The evolution goes on in 2007 which has seen the introduction of Rainforest Alliance coffee, a new range of Toasted Deli Sandwiches, new Chicken Selects and a Chicken Snack Wrap both made from 100 per cent breast meat.

Recent Developments

2006 was characterised by even more ambitious strides to help customers make informed decisions about their whole diet. McDonald's was the first quick service restaurant to provide a complete ingredient listing and detailed nutritional analysis of its menu. In 2006 McDonald's scored another first amongst quick service restaurants with the introduction of nutritional labelling on its packaging. The information is also available on the internet, on tray liners, leaflets and a customer helpline.

Consumers are also offered unprecedented access to the McDonald's business through the Make Up Your Own Mind website which invites questions on any topic the consumer wishes to ask as well as the opportunity to read the questions and answers of thousands of other customers. The site also features the work of 'Quality Scouts' – members of the public who go behind the scenes of the McDonald's supply chain and report back independently on their findings.

McDonald's provides the first job for 25,000 people every year. Another significant innovation in 2006 saw the launch of 'Our Lounge', a website which amongst other features is able to deliver online learning, allowing staff to plug skills gaps in exam

accredited restaurants. Also in 2006, McDonald's launched the Friends and Family Contract, allowing pairs of employees to cover each other's shifts and thus help staff to balance all of the demands of childcare on the modern family.

Promotion

McDonald's promotion continues using the overarching and universally recognised theme of 'I'm lovin' it', first launched globally in 2003. The marketing and communications effort for McDonald's is a significant one, as the brand has positive return on investment for its activity in every conceivable media channel. Careful stewardship of the brand leads to communications which are popular with the target audiences who regard McDonald's as part of the fabric of British life.

McDonald's has demonstrated a strong commitment to sports sponsorship and nowhere is this more evident than in the UK, where the brand has long been successfully linked with football – one of the nation's favourite sports. Besides sponsorship of major international events such as the World or European Cups, McDonald's is proud of a Grassroots sponsorship programme initiated with the four Football Associations of Great Britain. For over a decade McDonald's has supported initiatives to encourage young people into football and in 2006 achieved its ambition of helping to create 10,000 community coaches (including 500 new disability coaches) who, in turn provided a total of 5.6 million coaching opportunities for youngsters

throughout the UK in 2006 alone. To date McDonald's have invested £21 million to support grassroots football and the commitment continues with the aim of creating a further 5,128 coaches by 2010. Hundreds of youth teams play in kit worth over £2 million, donated by McDonald's restaurants across the country.

Brand Values

Ray Kroc was passionate about the business he inspired and his sayings still guide the company today. He once remarked: "If you work just for money, you'll never make it, but if you love what you're doing and you always put the customer first, success will be yours."

McDonald's is committed to providing its customers with food and drinks of the highest quality. To achieve this it is using the best quality raw ingredients, sourced only from approved suppliers and ensuring that food is prepared to a consistently high standard. McDonald's has developed a strong reputation for continually improving the offering in its restaurants and leads the sector by a considerable distance.

www.mcdonalds.co.uk

Things you didn't know about McDonald's

McDonald's is now one of the UK's biggest sellers of pre-prepared fruit.

In 2006 2,300 tonnes of Cheddar cheese from farms in England and Wales were used.

In 2006 McDonald's started a trial where used cooking oil is turned into bio diesel for use in the brand's distribution fleet.

The first drive-thru McDonald's was created in 1975 to serve soldiers from an army base in Sierra Vista, Arizona, who were forbidden to leave their cars while in uniform.

1974	1977	2001	2006
The first McDonald's in the UK opens in Woolwich, South East London.	The 5,000th restaurant opens in Kanagawa, Japan.	McDonald's acquires a minority interest in the UK sandwich chain Pret A Manger.	McDonald's UK turnover is in excess of £1.6 billion a year.

Microsoft®

Microsoft, whose software is widely held to power more than 90 per cent of all the world's personal computers, has been a leader in the wave of personal computing innovation that has created new opportunity, convenience and value over the past three decades. During that time, it has created many new products, added new lines of business, and expanded its operations worldwide.

Market

Microsoft is a worldwide leader in software, services and solutions designed to help people and businesses realise their full potential. It generates revenue by developing, manufacturing, licensing and supporting a wide range of software products for many computing devices. Its software products include: operating systems for servers, personal computers (PCs) and intelligent devices; server applications for distributed computing environments; information worker productivity applications; business solutions; and software development tools.

Microsoft provides consulting and product support services, and trains and certifies system integrators and developers. It sells the Xbox video game console and games, PC games, and peripherals. Online communication services and information services are delivered through its MSN portals and channels around the world. It also researches and develops advanced technologies for future software products.

Achievements

Microsoft now does business almost everywhere in the world. It has offices in more than 90 countries, which are grouped into six corporate regions: North America (the US and Canada); Latin America (LATAM); Europe, the Middle East, and Africa (EMEA); Japan; Asia Pacific (APAC); and Greater China. It also has operational centres in: Dublin, Ireland; Humacao, Puerto Rico; Reno, Nevada, USA; and Singapore. Microsoft believes that over the past few years it has laid the foundations for long term growth by making global

citizenship an integral part of its business, delivering innovative new products, creating opportunity for partners, improving customer satisfaction, putting some of its most significant legal challenges behind it, and improving its internal processes.

Product

Microsoft prides itself on providing software and services that help people communicate, do their work, be entertained, and manage their personal lives. Over the past 32 years of Microsoft's lifetime, innovative technology has transformed how people access and share information, changed the way businesses and institutions operate, and made the world smaller by giving computer users instant access to people and resources everywhere. Microsoft's business continued to grow in 2005, increasing its total revenue by US$2.95 billion, or eight per cent year-on-year, to US$39.79 billion.

Yet Microsoft's mission extends beyond making and selling products for profit. Through its business activities and community support, it aims to leave a lasting and positive impression on the communities and society in which it works. Years ago, it was convinced that its original vision of 'a PC in every home' could change lives. It remains convinced of the broad and positive power of giving people better technology. It takes corporate responsibilities very seriously, and in its interactions with its employees, customers, partners, suppliers and the communities where it works, it aims to reflect its broader awareness and ambitions.

1975
Microsoft is founded in Seattle by two young men, one of whom was a college dropout.

1982
Microsoft opens its first international subsidiary in the UK.

1990
Microsoft becomes the first personal computer software company to exceed US$1 billion in sales in a single year, with revenues of US$1.18 billion.

1995
Microsoft launches Windows 95 and sells more than one million copies in the four days following its launch.

2001
Microsoft launches Xbox – the most powerful gaming system ever built.

2004
Bill Gates delivers Microsoft's vision of 'digital entertainment anywhere'.

Today, Microsoft is the largest contributor in the high-tech industry and the third-largest among all businesses in the US. Annually, Microsoft donates more than US$47 million in cash and US$363 million in software to non-profit organisations throughout the world. In the UK, Microsoft gives to a range of major charity projects both financially and through the donation of software. Charities including NSPCC, Childnet International, Leonard Cheshire, AbilityNet and Age Concern have all benefited from Microsoft's giving programme.

Bill Gates and his wife Melinda, who have three children, are also known for their charitable work. As well as investing millions in research for an AIDs vaccine, their foundation has established a scholarship scheme to enable the brightest students to go to Cambridge University. The Bill and Melinda Gates Foundation is currently working on a global health programme in the developing world.

Recent Developments

Microsoft believes that delivering breakthrough innovation and high-value solutions through its integrated platform is the key to meeting customer needs and to its future growth.

2004 saw Bill Gates deliver Microsoft's vision of digital entertainment anywhere, unveiling Windows XP Media Center Edition 2005, and showcasing a variety of sleek new computer designs, portable media devices, and digital content services.

In a step towards that vision, May 2005 saw the launch of Windows Mobile 5.0, the newest instalment of Microsoft's software for mobile devices, designed to power a new generation of phones, personal digital assistants and media players for people who want to customise devices to fit their needs.

In the same month, Microsoft launched Xbox 360, its 'future-generation' video game and entertainment system designed to place gamers at the centre of the experience. Xbox

With Windows Mobile® in your pocket, when, where and how you work is entirely up to you.

also enables gamers to link up and play against each other through Xbox Live.

Promotion

Microsoft's marketing has come a long way since it kicked off its first television advertising campaign in 1992.

Now no stranger to high profile launches, Microsoft linked up with MTV Europe to showcase the Xbox 360 game system. Elijah Wood, Scarlett Johansson, The Killers and Snow Patrol hosted a half-hour star studded European premiere of the new product with performances from The Killers and Snow Patrol airing exclusively on MTV channels across Europe.

Windows Vista™, the next generation of the Windows® client operating system, was launched at the end of 2006 with the aim of continuing to deliver on Bill Gates' vision of digital entertainment everywhere.

Everyday, millions of people around the globe rely on their Windows-based PCs to manage the increasing amounts of digital information in their lives. While the tools currently used for managing this information are powerful and familiar, Windows Vista aims to cut through all the clutter. Today's digital generation will be able to explore entertainment such as TV and music and stay

connected to people and information on their Windows Vista-based PC safely and easily.

Brand Values

Microsoft aims to provide people as well as businesses from all walks of life, from all around the world with the tools to fulfil their potential. It also takes its role as being a good corporate citizen very seriously and gives back to the communities in which it works.

Microsoft also wants to play its part in developing a safer computing environment, to allow people in the UK to benefit from advances in technology. Microsoft continues to be committed to building software and services that will better protect its customers and the industry. Because there is no one solution, its approach to security reaches beyond technology to public awareness. In technology, Microsoft is focused on improving quality, building in greater resiliency, and working with Government, law enforcement and industry partners to enable them to benefit promptly from developments in this area. In the wider community, it is focused on awareness and education around security and child safety online as well as making a contribution to the public policy debate.

www.microsoft.com

2005

Gates is granted an honorary knighthood by the Queen. Now the world's wealthiest man, Bill Gates is worth an estimated £28 billion.

Also in 2005, Microsoft launches Xbox 360, its 'future generation' video game and entertainment system.

2006

Gates announces that his foundation will donate US$691 million towards life-saving vaccines for millions of children in poor countries.

2007

Microsoft launches Windows Vista and the 2007 Microsoft Office system to consumers worldwide.

Things you didn't know about Microsoft®

The Windows 95 launch was set for August 24th because it had never rained in Redmond, WA during that week in recorded history. It sold more than one million copies in the four days following its launch.

Bill Gates, Microsoft chairman and Steve Ballmer, chief executive, first met at Harvard University.

In December 2004, Microsoft announced a commitment of US$3.5 million in financial support for relief and recovery efforts in response to the Indian Ocean tsunami.

Mr Kipling from Manor Bakeries, part of Premier Foods Group, is the number one cake brand (Source: IRI). Consumed in over half of UK households, the Mr Kipling broad range of cakes has been developed to satisfy cake eating occasions throughout the day. The brand has seen continued growth, most recently demonstrating significant increases of 16 per cent year-on-year due to a focused marketing campaign which included redesign and new product development.

Market

The total UK ambient packaged cake market, currently valued at more than £969 million, growing at three per cent year-on-year (Source: IRI), is a mature market with more than 95 per cent of the UK population consuming products.

Cakes are consumed in the home, and increasingly out of home, throughout the day meeting sweet treat needs from mid-morning, to the afternoon break and to evening indulgence as well as satisfying snacking/sharing occasions.

There are huge opportunities within the ambient cake market, from expanding product lines to driving value growth through high quality innovation.

Achievements

Mr Kipling launched in 1967 and since then has been a driving force in the development of ambient packaged cake in the UK. By 1970 the brand had risen to national status and by 1976 Mr Kipling was a brand leader, a position that has been retained for three decades.

Within a year of going national, there was a huge 89 per cent awareness of the brand and over the following 30 years, Mr Kipling became synonymous with cake. It has been the only consistent advertiser in the ambient cake market, contributing significantly to the creation of a brand with a powerful and longstanding reputation.

Today the Mr Kipling brand is worth more than £155 million in terms of retail sales (Source: IRI). This represents more than 146 million packets of cake being sold per year.

Mr Kipling's share of the cake market is 16 per cent, making it the biggest brand within this market (Source: IRI).

Product

The Mr Kipling strategy is to produce the nation's favourite ambient cakes and the brand prides itself on consistently over-delivering when benchmarked against its competitors.

All Mr Kipling products are free from artificial colours, flavours and have no hydrogenated vegetable oils (HVOs).

Covering a broad range of consumer need states and eating occasions, the Mr Kipling range is split into five main categories and currently includes over 30 different lines of cake.

The 'slices' sector, in which Mr Kipling holds a 90 per cent share, includes favourites such as Lemon Slices, Angel Slices, Victoria Slices and Almond Slices. Meanwhile, 'small cakes' encompasses variants such as French Fancies, Viennese Whirls and Victoria Mini Classics. In 'large cakes' Manor House cake and Battenberg are key performers for the brand. The 'pies and tarts' sector includes Cherry Bakewells, Jam Tarts and Bramley Apple Pies with the newest 'healthier' category introducing Mr Kipling's new Delightful range.

1965	1967	1970	1971	1976	2007
Work begins on a new range of cake – with the same stamp of quality, integrity and expertise as local bakers had provided but in a more modern and convenient format.	In May Mr Kipling is launched in London and the Southern regions in colourful, premium boxes with handles for carrying the product home.	The brand is rolled out throughout the country with an initial range of 20 products based on traditional bakers' fare such as Jam tarts, Almond Slices and Battenberg.	The brand achieves 89 per cent awareness.	Mr Kipling becomes brand leader and remains at the top of its market over the next 30 years.	Mr Kipling becomes part of the Premier Foods Group.

In addition to this, there are more than 15 seasonal products in the portfolio with Mr Kipling being brand leader in mince pies at Christmas time. Further to which, limited edition launches every year bring variety and refreshment to the brand, reflecting the constant drive for innovation.

Recent Developments

The Mr Kipling brand has had considerable recent success, with 16 per cent year-on-year growth which is attributed to a number of key initiatives. Firstly, product packaging has been refreshed with a recent brand redesign. This has made a direct contribution to incremental sales. In addition, a promotional in-store campaign has been undertaken to remind consumers of the Mr Kipling offer. This has also been successful, with penetration rising to over 52 per cent.

In line with the brand's overall strategy of innovation, Mr Kipling launched the

Delightful range in early 2006. The entire range is lower in fat and calories than Mr Kipling standard products. Due to the success of this launch, the range of Apple Slices, Lemon Sponge and Chocolate Slices was followed in 2007 by the introduction of a Blueberry Bar, which contains less than three per cent fat and a Cherry Bakewell with 30 per cent less fat than Mr Kipling standard products.

This introduction into the healthier sector, which is valued at £38 million (Source: IRI) has resulted in Delightful achieving a £5.8 million stake in the market, with a 15 per cent share of this growing sector. It has also driven incremental growth for Mr Kipling, and the category as a whole.

Promotion

The original objective to express the personality of the Mr Kipling brand still remains today, achieving this not only through the products themselves but also through the brand name, packaging, pricing, above and below-the-line promotional campaigns, display and merchandising.

Television was chosen as the primary launch medium, partly for its impact and immediacy and partly for its ability to express the intended warmth and friendliness of the Mr Kipling character. TV has continued as a major medium for the brand over the past 30 years and the phrase 'exceedingly good cakes' has become one of the best-known slogans in advertising. Although Mr Kipling himself is a fictitious character, Manor Bakeries has developed and cultivated his warm image among consumers.

Mr Kipling TV campaigns have evolved over the years, reflecting the changing nature of the brand as well as bringing it more up-to-date.

In recent years the focus has been on other activities with investment being channelled into poster ads outside major supermarket chains and heavyweight PR and print campaigns targeting the women's and lifestyle press. The advertising has been supported with strong in-store

promotional activity, new point of sale material and merchandising.

The new Delighful brand was recently supported with a fully integrated campaign, which included posters and radio, aimed at raising awareness and generating brand trial.

Brand Values

The essence of the Mr Kipling brand has always been to produce highly desirable cakes finished with the care and attention to detail required to create little treats. This is designed to generate a feeling of happiness from a baking brand that strives to be seen as warm, friendly and personable, rather than simply a food.

The brand values have evolved to reflect a product range that can be eaten any time, any place, with modern convenient packaging to appeal to today's consumers.

www.mrkipling.co.uk

Things you didn't know about Mr Kipling

1.7 million Mr Kipling cakes are eaten every day.

The most popular variant is Angel Slices – more than 10 million packs are sold per year.

Mr Kipling uses 770 tonnes of marzipan each year to make its Battenberg cakes and uses 5,250 tonnes of icing every year.

Mr Kipling uses 60 million English Bramley apples in its individual apple pies every year.

A whopping 1,900 tonnes of mincemeat goes into Mr Kipling mince pies each year. That's the equivalent weight of 317 adult elephants.

Müller® is one of the UK's largest grocery brands and the leading manufacturer of short life dairy products with Müller® Corner® being the market's best selling brand (Source: IRI). In 2007, Müller® is encouraging consumers to 'Lick the Lid of Life™' through all major communications including a new TV advert featuring 100 members of the general public, aged 1-100 years.

100 real people
The Lid Lickers
of all ages 1-100

Market

The short life dairy products (SLDP) market encompasses drinking yogurt, fromage frais, adult desserts as well as yogurt which dominates the category, accounting for 47 per cent of sales (Source: IRI).

Müller® is the market leader with a 23 per cent volume market share (Source: IRI), with Müller® Corner® and Müllerlight® between them accounting for more than 15 per cent of the total market value. Other major manufacturers include Danone and Yoplait, with further competition coming from smaller brands and supermarket own label products.

Consumer concern over health issues, coupled with a continued desire for convenience, has driven the SLDP category forward as the products have become an integral part of the everyday diet.

In 2006, the total SLDP market was worth more than £1.8 billion, an increase on 2005 of almost £50 million, accounting for almost a quarter of total dairy sales. Over 96 per cent of households bought from this category last year (Source: TNS).

Achievements

Müller® Corner® continues to be the UK's best-selling yogurt brand, maintaining this position with a strong innovation agenda. Fruit® Corner® has been made fruitier, whilst the Müller® Corner® Healthy Balance™ range was relaunched in 2007, marking a move to these products becoming 100 per cent natural.

Further to this, The Grocer magazine named Müller® Vitality®'s advertising creative, which communicated the benefits of Omega 3,

as its Top Campaign in their 2006 Top Products Survey.

Müller® is keen to support healthy eating initiatives in the local area around its Shropshire base. In recent years The Müller Community Trust has worked with the North Shropshire Pre-School Alliance to promote food education to both parents and children. In addition, The Alliance supports toddler groups in the North Shropshire area, and is keen to develop extra resource packs to be used within these groups to promote both healthy eating and active, physical lifestyles.

The Trust has also supported the Community Council of Shropshire to back a pilot project set up by the North Shropshire Rural Transport Partnership. This project provides a minibus service for members of the local community who don't have transport alternatives.

1896

The Müller® company is established in Germany by Ludwig Müller, grandfather of the present owner.

1970

Theo Müller takes control and recognises the opportunity to expand the products from small popular regional brands to those with nationwide appeal.

1988

Müller® launches in the UK with a test market of three Müller® Corner® flavours. Müller® Corner® has gone on to become a £169 million brand.

1989

Müller® Rice is launched in the UK.

1990

Müller® launches Müllerlight®, now the UK's leading healthy yogurt brand with a value of £109 million.

1991

Construction begins on a state-of-the-art production facility in Market Drayton, Shropshire.

Product

Müller's uniquely diverse portfolio caters for all consumer needs, from functional products through to an indulgent offering and a range specifically developed with children in mind.

Müller® continues to build its healthy offering with the Müller® Corner® Healthy Balance™ range, while Müller® Vitality®, currently number two in the dynamic drinking yogurt market, focuses its communication of this range on 'the goodness of 3 in 1' (prebiotic, probiotic and Omega 3) found in these products. At the beginning of 2007, the Müller® Vitality® range was also expanded with a Red Berry drink being added to its 0.1 per cent fat/no added sugar range. In addition, the communication of the range that Müllerlight® offers has been simplified and clarified into four distinct sub ranges: Layers, Smooth, Dessert and Fruity – catering for a wide range of tastes and all virtually fat free.

The Müller® Little Stars™ children's range offers parents peace of mind with its 100 per cent natural ingredients credentials in addition to the products being made with as little as

five ingredients. The range of fromage frais, smooth yogurts and yogurt drinks, which is supported by distinctive advertising, has proven to be very successful, achieving more than a 10 per cent volume share of the children's SLDP market in their first eight months (Source: Müller® four w/e 24th March 2007).

Meanwhile, Müller's luxury yogurt brand Müller® Amoré® has seen exceptional growth as consumers, while acting increasingly healthily, still seek an indulgent treat or reward.

Recent Developments

The UK's leading healthy yogurt brand, Müllerlight®, saw the introduction of Müllerlight® Layers, consisting of Müller® yogurt above a layer of fruit compote, in 2007. The Müllerlight® sub-categories, as well as flavour specific colours and category icons on-pack, aim to make it clearer and easier for consumers to identify their choices on shelf.

The start of 2007 also saw Müller® introduce a new range – Simply Desserts™, a combination of fruit compote, covered in thick and creamy Greek style yogurt with a crunchy topping kept in a separate 'top hat' compartment, with less than five per cent fat. The range is aimed at those wanting the indulgent pleasure of a dessert without the accompanying guilt that a high fat content gives.

Promotion

Müller® has recently launched new advertising intended to take the very successful 'Lead a Müller Life®' campaign a step further in terms of how it engages with consumers. The new campaign is designed to capture the positive nature and love of life (and yogurt) of 100 everyday people in a warm and energetic way. The ads feature one person of every age

from a one year-old to 100 years-old and aims to encourage more people to share in their simple passion for yogurt.

First aired at the beginning of May 2007, the 'Lick the Lid of Life' TV campaign aims to further establish the fun and positive nature of the Müller® brand through the unique personalities of 100 everyday people, collectively known as 'Lid Lickers' due to their love of yogurt and zest for life. These volunteers love the taste of Müller® yogurt so much that they lick the lid – and then apply this same love-of-life philosophy to everything they do.

Müller® has developed a new website which profiles all 100 people and gives visitors the opportunity to find out more about them.

Brand Values

Innovation is at the heart of the Müller® brand, driving it forward in this dynamic and energetic category.

The brand has a love-of-life philosophy and aims to be warm and friendly towards its customers, promoting a healthy way of life.

www.müller.co.uk

1992	2000	2006	2007
Müller® becomes UK market leader – a remarkable feat that took the brand just five years to achieve.	The launch of Vitality®, takes Müller® into the probiotic market with its Feel Good Bacteria™.	Müller® Little Stars™ launches.	Müller® launches Simply Desserts™ and Müllerlight® introduces the Layers range.

NationalExpress

National Express has been part of the fabric of the UK since the 1970s, linking people and places up and down the country with the iconic coaches emblazoned with their red, white and blue livery. Ever committed to offering affordable travel, the National Express brand balances its value proposition with a high level of customer service. Unmistakably British, the National Express name evokes strong feelings of decency, honesty, reliability and trustworthiness.

Market

National Express provides Britain's only national scheduled coach network and serves more than 1,000 destinations, providing approximately 19 million customer journeys each year. National Express has an 80 per cent market share of the scheduled coach market in the UK and is a major force within the wider surface travel market. The National Express airport services provide premier, high frequency scheduled coach services to the major UK airports.

Brand tracking research shows that of all the surface travel brands in the UK, the National Express brand holds the most equity. Brand familiarity is at a near unbeatable 99 per cent, with 22 per cent of the population having an affinity to the business (Source: Millward Brown, Brand Tracking October 2006).

National Express is part of the leading transport provider, National Express Group, which delivers services in the UK, North America and Spain and employs over 40,000 people. The Group carries more than one billion passengers a year worldwide through its, bus, train, light rail and express coach operations.

Achievements

Revenue for 2006 was £207.3 million (compared to £200.5 million in 2005) with a normalised profit of £23.7 million (up on the 2005 figure of £21.5 million). Furthermore, passenger growth of over four per cent was achieved during the same period. Within the core scheduled coaching business, the success of yield-managed fares, which ensure greater efficiency and utilisation of available coach seats drove growth. 'Funfares' starting from £1 are offered on 32 popular routes.

National Express is working closely with its 1,700 employees to raise skill qualifications and consequently the level of customer service. As a result the requirements of the new European driver training, which is scheduled to commence in September 2008, has already been exceeded. By increasing salary, benefits and training levels employee turnover has dropped by 20 per cent in 12 months. Opportunities such as Home Working are available for members of the Customer Call Centre, improving the work/life balance for employees.

In 2005, the Disability Discrimination Act came into effect for coach services; however, there wasn't a solution to provide wheelchair access that suited the needs of National Express' customers, so a bespoke, award wining solution was developed. Working in partnership with coach manufacturer Caetano, an easy access vehicle was developed and has been described as the 'holy grail' of wheelchair transport by a leading transport trade magazine. National Express will invest some £100 million in making the network fully accessible in time for the 2012 Olympics.

1968
The National Bus Company is formed to bring greater structure and organisation to a host of independently operated bus and coach companies.

1974
The National Bus Company adopts a sales and marketing focus and the National Express brand name is introduced to offer a uniformed consistency.

1988
The de-regulation of the National Bus Company leads to a management buy-out of National Express; a new company, National Express Holdings Ltd is formed.

1992
National Express is floated on the London Stock Exchange.

Recent awards include the National Customer Service Award 2005 for Transport Team of the Year and in 2006 a second award for the Best Use of Technology was received. In addition to this, the business is now a three time gold winner of the Royal Society for the Prevention of Accidents (RoSPA) Occupational Safety Awards and in 2007 a major award will be given to the business. In 2007 the business became a finalist in the Employee Benefits Awards.

Product
National Express has a fleet of more than 600 coaches running between a total of 1,000 nationwide locations. Its services are split between scheduled and non scheduled operations: the inter-city and cross country coach network; the Airport coach network; Eurolines, operating coaches to 500 European destinations; Airlinks, providing contract bus/coach services for airlines; Rail replacement, offering planned and emergency bus and coach services to the major UK train operating companies; and the event coach network, specialising in direct services to major events such as Glastonbury as well as the G8 Summit in Gleneagles.

Recent Developments
At the beginning of 2007, National Express signed up to become an Official Supporter of the England Team and The FA Cup, as well as the Official Travel Provider to Wembley Stadium. These two sponsorship deals signify the ambition of the brand to raise its profile and become a relevant travel choice to a wider UK audience. The business has also signed up to become a member of The Climate Group's 'We're in this Together' campaign, joining other leading businesses in making it easier for consumers to access products and ideas that can reduce their impact on the climate.

Promotion
National Express has always understood the role that advertising plays in delivering a high volume of sales. It utilises all available channels when communicating to its target audience, from digital escalator panels on the London Underground, to washroom panels in student bars. Looking forward, communications will also leverage the brand's sponsorship properties.

For over a decade pricing has been at the heart of the brand's consumer messaging, ever stimulating demand for great value travel. However, price is now only one aspect of the brand's offering and the task at hand over the upcoming years is to develop marketing strategies that deliver sales through direct response channels, as well as build brand equity.

Brand Values
National Express is a leading transport provider with the aim of making travel simple. Its honest marketing approach sees simplified pricing, an increase in sales channels as well as greater access to travel information as an essential part of its consumer offering.

The brand strives to put the customer at the heart of everything it does, to take the initiative and lead the way for the transport industry. National Express is aiming for constant improvement and to show that it cares about what it does by understanding and developing the contribution it makes in the political, social, economic, safety and environmental arenas.

www.nationalexpress.com

2003
A major rebrand takes place as a multitude of acquired businesses come under the National Express umbrella and adopt its identity.

2007
National Express becomes a sponsor of The FA and Wembley Stadium.

NOKIA

Since launching the first hand-held mobile phone in 1987, Nokia has continually pushed the boundaries of design and technology to become a global leader in mobile communications. Nokia uses innovative technology to create cutting-edge, easy to use products and services that meet the changing needs of its customers. As part of its ongoing evolution, Nokia offers experiences that enrich the lives of consumers.

Product

Nokia's devices were the first to feature text messaging, integrated cameras and MP3 players as well as access internet-based information services. Today, Nokia continues to lead the way in convergence with its Nseries range of high performance multimedia computers, which include the Nokia N95 – the first device with in-built GPS – and its Eseries devices that offer optimised solutions to business users. 2006 saw Nokia sell more than 140 million camera phones and over 70 million devices with music capabilities, making it the world's largest manufacture of cameras and digital music players.

In Nokia's next evolution, the company will increasingly provide consumers with experiences in music, navigation, video, television, imaging, games, business mobility and the internet through its devices. With an estimated 850 million users, Nokia is positioned to connect more people to the internet than any other company.

Market

The mobile phone market is heavily competitive; established mobile phone manufacturers such as Motorola, Samsung, Sony Ericsson and LG continue to bring competitive products to market and new entrants, such as Apple, have elevated that competition to a higher level.

However Nokia continues to build on its leading position with its trusted brand, diverse product portfolio and global manufacturing and distribution networks. Nokia continues to achieve record-breaking device volumes and net sales, with over 77 million sales of mobile phones during the first quarter of 2007 and a 36 per cent UK market share (Source: Strategy Analytics Ltd).

Achievements

Nokia has successfully won over consumers, insiders and journalists, consistently winning highly coveted industry and consumer choice awards. The company has also won various awards for its flagship devices such as the EISA (European Imaging and Sound Association) 'European Media Phone' for the Nokia N90, a prestigious TIPA (Technical Image Press Association) Award for 'Best Mobile Imaging Device in Europe' for the Nokia N95 and Mobile Choice's 'Best Camera Phone Award 2006' for the Nokia N93. In addition Nokia has won numerous awards for its promotional campaigns, for example the Marketing Week Effectiveness Award for the Nokia Fashion Collection.

1987	1994	2000	2001	2004	2005
The first and original hand-held mobile phone – the Nokia Mobira Cityman 900 – is launched.	The Nokia 2100 series are the first digital hand portable phones to support data, fax and SMS (short message service).	Nokia's first dust, water and shock resistant handset – the Nokia 6250 – is introduced.	The Nokia 7650 – the first Nokia camera phone with MMS picture messaging – is launched.	Nokia introduces its first Fashion Collection of three handsets.	Nokia brings its first 3G device, the Nokia 6630, to market. In addition, the Nokia NSeries sub brand is launched – showcasing cutting-edge technology.

Recent Developments

Design remains a fundamental building block of the Nokia brand, as is its strategy to provide mobile devices for all. Recent developments have seen Nokia push the boundaries of convergence with the launch of the Nokia N95. With in-built GPS, five mega pixel camera, HSDPA offering broadband download speeds, navigation and music player – the Nokia N95 is not one thing but many. The company's reputation for iconic design has continued with its Fashion Collections which complement the latest catwalk trends and this year's Nokia 6300 combines a contemporary edge with classic elegance in a uniquely affordable package.

Promotion

The brand's enduring success is not only down to its products, but also its efforts to help people get close to their passions – whether that's fashion, music, photography or film.

Nokia was one of the first technology brands to work with the fashion industry, sponsoring London Fashion Week from 1999 to 2004 and working with leading fashion designers including Kenzo, Donatella Versace, Cath Kidston and Giambattista Valli. In the past three years Nokia has developed the company's fashionable side even further by launching three collections of fashion inspired mobile phones – the Nokia Fashion Collection, the Nokia L'Amour Collection and the Nokia L'Amour II Collection. Nokia has

also sponsored the Glamour Women of the Year Awards since 2006.

Music is a key passion of Nokia customers and the brand aims to 'bring people closer to the music they love' through a range of innovative music-led projects. In 2006, Nokia launched www.MusicRecommenders.com – a unique music download service which enables music fans to explore new music personally recommended by 40 of the world's most influential independent record stores. Music fans can browse and buy tracks plus get an insight into new music through city music guides and artist interviews. Music legend David Bowie also regularly contributes exclusive features, podcasts, commentary and recommendations.

In 2006, Nokia also launched its own mobile ticketing service, www.ticketrush.co.uk, which is a free service that gives registered users the chance to buy tickets before the general public, as well as being kept up-to-date by text message of any last minute tickets for sold-out gigs.

Nokia continues to support grassroots music through the third year of its Rock Up & Play initiative. Rock Up & Play gives people the chance to explore and celebrate their passion for music through providing the opportunity to simply 'rock up and play' at Nokia hosted gigs. Rock Up & Play also featured at the Carling Weekend Festivals which included Q&A sessions that gave festival-goers the chance to interact with their favourite bands.

Brand Values

Nokia is about connecting people – to the people that matter to them and the things they find important. Whether a music lover, photographer, fashionista, business professional, or budding film-maker – Nokia develops mobile devices that support nearly everyone's lifestyle. Nokia is dedicated to enhancing people's lives and productivity by providing easy to use, secure products – from entry level handsets, to iconic design-driven mobile devices, to sophisticated multimedia computers encompassing cutting-edge technologies such as digital music, print and DVD quality cameras, in-built GPS and mobile TV.

At the heart of Nokia's handset design is usability: product interfaces are styled to be easy to navigate, keypads are pleasant to the touch and the size and shape is comfortable and appropriate – all adding to the consumer's trusting of Nokia as a brand.

www.nokia.co.uk

Things you didn't know about Nokia

Nokia is named after the river Nokia in Finland.

When Nokia was founded in 1865, it initially manufactured paper, then card, then moved on to rubber.

The world's first transportable phone, the Nokia Mobira Talkman came with a 10kg charging box the size of a suitcase.

Nokia was the first handset manufacturer to introduce coloured covers to its mobile phones in 1994 – before this, all mobile phones were black.

2006

Also in 2005, the Nokia N90 – the world's first multimedia computer with superior Carl Zeiss optics – is launched.

Mobile TV trials also take place, using Nokia devices, and the first mobile devices to allow DVBH are launched.

The Nokia N91 – the first mobile device with a hard drive allowing space to store up to 3,000 songs – goes on sale in the UK.

2007

The Nokia N95 is launched – it is the first mobile device to combine integrated GPS, a five mega pixel camera with Carl Zeiss optics and HSDPA connectivity offering broadband download speeds.

P&O Ferries

P&O Ferries is more than 170 years old and offers a choice of four routes sailing from the UK to the Continent. Its service offering is based on the company ethos of an affordable and hassle free travel experience that is simple, flexible and focused. With no hidden or excess baggage charges, the fleet of cruise style ships offers a viable alternative to European airline and train travel.

Market

The cross channel market has become increasingly competitive in recent years with customers focused on both price as well as service levels – a trend which looks set to continue.

Low cost airlines which offer cut priced fares on flights to the Continent have grown in popularity. In addition, the chunnel and Eurostar services offer another alternative. This is an increasingly important factor with the launch of Eurostar services from Kings Cross St Pancras in late 2007.

As a result of this level of choice, customers have become less loyal, shopping around for the best deal.

Achievements

The Peninsular Steam Navigation Company started regular paddle steamer mail services between England, Spain and Portugal in 1837. After this route expansion saw the company become The Peninsular and Oriental Steam Navigation Company – P&O. Now, more than 170 years after its services began, P&O Ferries is still sailing strong and receiving recognition for its high standards of service. Named Cruise/Ferry Travel Retailer of the Year at the 2007 Raven Fox Global Travel Retail Awards, the company was voted Best Ferry Operator as well as Favourite Ferry Company at the British Travel Awards 2006. Furthermore, it won the Travel Weekly Globe Award in 2005 and was chosen as Best Ferry Operator by Group Leisure in 2005.

Alongside such awards the company has also been recognised for excellence in

customer service and staff training, winning at the National Training Awards UK 2006 and named as Leisure & Tourism Customer Service Team of the Year at the National Customer Services Awards 2005.

P&O Ferries has one of the largest fleets of ships in the UK, offering a wide range

of services and facilities as well as a comprehensive and frequent route network.

Product

Connecting the UK to European gateways in France, Spain, Belgium and Holland, P&O Ferries operates four routes: Dover–Calais;

1837	1840	1914	1987	1998	2000
The Peninsular Steam Navigation Company starts regular paddle steamer mail services between England, Spain and Portugal.	The company is granted The Royal Charter of Incorporation by Queen Victoria and by the middle of the decade is pioneering deep sea cruising.	P&O and British India shipping lines merge, creating a combined fleet of 201 ships.	The company acquires the European Ferries Group which includes the Townsend Thoresen brand and the Townsend Car Ferries operation based at Dover.	The company joins forces with Stena Line of Sweden at Dover, to form P&O Stena Line. P&O later buys out Stena's interest in the joint venture.	P&O demerges its cruise business; the P&O Cruises brand continues but is no longer part of the P&O Group's portfolio.

Portsmouth–Bilbao; Hull–Zeebrugge; and Hull–Rotterdam.

Targeting a wide range of prospective customers, from regular ferry travellers and families to the ferry novice, the product portfolio includes daytrips, short breaks, longer stays and minicruises. Money-saving season tickets are available for frequent travellers, who benefit from fixed price tickets and increased flexibility, able to amend bookings right up to the day before their departure.

On board, passengers are presented with a spacious environment and the flexibility to do as much, or as little, as they want. A choice of restaurants and bars ensures that a wide range of tastes are catered for, while onboard shopping areas provide hundreds of products at competitive prices offering passengers everything they might need or want – from

the latest Perfume House or the most fashionable sunglasses brand, to vintage champagnes and wines.

On overnight ferries – which see passengers arrive at their destination at a civilised time – cabins are equipped with an en suite shower room and toilet, towels and bed linen.

Recent Developments

P&O Ferries has recently undergone a major review of products, services and marketing, before effectively relaunching the brand. The aim was to introduce dynamic airline-style pricing together with a simplified product offer.

In addition, in 2007 P&O Ferries has announced plans for two new ships to replace the Pride of Dover and Pride of Calais – first introduced to service in 1987.

Promotion

The P&O flag, a central part of the brand's logo, provides an easily identifiable and powerful icon for the brand. To increase awareness of P&O Ferries, a variety of above-the-line promotion, including radio, national and regional press, specialist magazines and outdoor advertising is used, as well as TV sponsorship of Meridian weather and Hull FC. Below-the-line activities include direct mail, email, online advertising and dynamic content.

In 2005 a multi-million pound award-winning advertising campaign, P&Ople, was launched. Aiming to change the way people view ferry travel and competing head-on with low cost airlines, P&Ople stressed the importance of the company's most valuable assets – its employees and its customers.

P&O Ferries also seized an opportunity to target a younger male audience, using a viral campaign – entitled 'fan van' – to promote ferry travel to the 2006 Germany World Cup.

Brand Values

From clear pricing and value for money, frequent services and easy loading, to onboard entertainment or peace and quiet, the P&O Ferries brand is governed by the desire to create an affordable and hassle free experience.

Simple, flexible and focused, the brand believes its customers deserve to sit back and relax, to enjoy the sea views and to get in to the holiday spirit.

www.poferries.com

Things you didn't know about P&O Ferries

In February 2000, P&O Ferries carried the first pet to travel under the UK Government's Pet Passport Scheme; Frodo Baggins, a five year-old Pug dog travelled on the Dover–Calais route. The company now carries more than 10,000 pets each year.

Scientists from the Biscay Dolphin Research Programme have travelled with P&O Ferries for more than a decade, recording sightings of whales and dolphins. Nearly 40,000 individual animals, from 21 different species, have been logged.

The annual service and MOT test for a family car can be over in a couple of hours, but the maritime equivalent for a ship in the P&O Ferries fleet takes two weeks.

It's commonly misquoted that a ship's captain is qualified to perform marriage ceremonies at sea, but P&O Ferries regularly hosts wedding receptions on board.

P&O Ferries is one of the world's top 10 offshore retailers; the company sells a bottle of wine every nine seconds.

Created in 1837 for The Peninsular Steam Navigation Company, P&O's house flag incorporates the Royal colours of Spain and Portugal.

2001

P&O North Sea Ferries launches the two largest cruise ferries sailing from the UK – the Pride of Hull and Pride of Rotterdam – at a cost of almost £100 million each.

2003

Separate ferry divisions operating on the North Sea, Western Channel and Dover Strait combine, now trading as P&O Ferries.

Services to Ireland remain under sister company P&O Irish Sea.

2006

Dubai-based DP World acquires P&O Group. P&O's international port operations rebrand to reflect the new ownership but the P&O name is retained in the Ferries division.

PIMM'S®

From the City gents in James Pimm's 1840s Oyster Bar, to the discriminating palates of the 21st century, PIMM'S® has shown itself to have both longevity and universal appeal. Through a long-standing association with outdoor summer events, the gin-based drink – flavoured with a blend of fruit and herbs – encapsulates a quintessential British charm, that has contributed to its reputation as one of the UK's most popular summer drinks; anyone for PIMM'S®?

Market

PIMM'S® currently commands a 20 per cent share of the 'speciality' drinks market and within this sector is the biggest selling brand, ahead of other leading competitors such as Malibu and Southern Comfort (Source: ACNielsen 2007). The underlying growth of the brand – 20 per cent over the last three years – is almost 10 times greater than other speciality brands; within the UK, its lead market, PIMM'S® currently sells more than 275,000 cases each year making it one of the highest selling speciality spirits. In addition to the speciality spirits market PIMM'S® also commands a strong presence in the 'occasional drinks' or 'seasonal' sector with its main competitors in this category – white wine and beer – being the two alternative drinks most strongly affiliated, by target consumers, with the outdoor summer market.

Achievements

Global recognition of PIMM'S® as the number one summer speciality spirit in the grocer's channel (Source: ACNielsen 2006) counts as a major brand achievement and serves to reinforce its lead position in the UK market. Wimbledon is just one of several notable outdoor events the brand has a significant promotional presence at and each year an average of 250,000 glasses of PIMM'S No.1 CUP® are sold at the tournament.

Further to this, PIMM'S® and the 'ANYONE FOR PIMM'S®?' campaign has been recognised by Marketing Communications Consultants Association (MCCA), being awarded the most prestigious BEST awards for 'Best and most effective long term marketing communication campaign 2003-2007'.

Product

PIMM'S No.1 CUP®, a gin-based drink which dates back to 1841, is still made in strict compliance with the original recipe – the precise ingredients of which remain, even today, a closely guarded secret. The 'Classic PIMM'S®' – one part PIMM'S® to three parts quality lemonade, topped with half a slice of orange and lemon, a slice of cucumber, strawberries and a sprig of mint – has become synonymous with the 'great British summertime', and is consumed, by the pitcher-full, at many outdoor events including The Henley Regatta and Royal Ascot.

In addition to the more traditional one litre bottles, PIMM'S No.1 CUP® (from which the pitchers are made up) also comes ready mixed with lemonade in a picnic sized 250ml can and a 'Ready to Drink' one litre bottle. These brand extensions illustrate the growing adaptability of PIMM'S® with market forces, without compromising the product itself.

Recent Developments

PIMM'S No.1 CUP® was the first in the series of what would ultimately become a range of

1823
PIMM'S® Spirit Drink is created by James Pimm as an accompaniment to oysters, a favoured dish amongst City gents of the time.

1841
James Pimm invents a unique blend of gin, liquors and fruit and names it PIMM'S No.1 CUP® – the first in what will become a series of six cups.

1887
MP and Lord Mayor of London Sir Horatio Davies, becomes the new owner of PIMM'S®, expanding the original 'Oyster Bar' concept to five PIMM'S® Spirit Drink restaurants.

1913
PIMM'S® Spirit Drink becomes a registered trademark.

1937/38
The first major advertising campaign for the brand runs, playing on the theme 'I could do with a PIMM'S No.1®'.

six cups. Created during Queen Victoria's heyday – when there were no swizzle sticks or branded glasses – sophisticated drinking vessels of the time were restricted to pint mugs or tankards, hence the aptly named 'CUP'. The third of these cups to be created (No.3) was brandy based and in 2004, after a lengthy absence on the UK market, it was relaunched as PIMM'S WINTER®. The idea behind the UK centric relaunch was to offer a warming winter alternative to the popular summer-centric PIMM'S No.1 CUP®. PIMM'S WINTER®, a brandy based liquor, is marketed with distinctive orange packaging (to denote a warming glow) instead of the familiar PIMM'S No.1 CUP® red. When it comes to mixing PIMM'S WINTER® the recommended mixer is warm apple juice, not lemonade. However, in line with the PIMM'S® brand, PIMM'S WINTER® should still be served, ideally, with fruit on top.

Promotion

The high profile 'ANYONE FOR PIMM'S®?' campaign, featuring British comedian Alexander Armstrong as the jocular, outdoorsy 'Harry' (complete with either a barbie and PIMM'S® or picnic hamper and PIMM'S®) has been running for the past five years. The main focus of the campaign is to democratise the brand; opening it up to a wider audience to demonstrate that

PIMM'S® is not – as has been thought in the past – elitist, but a drink that everybody can enjoy. Deformalising PIMM'S® in this way has increased the brand relevance outside the traditionally accepted PIMM'S® drinking occasions. In keeping with this spirit, the campaign appears through a wide range of mediums including television, the national press, radio and digital upload which serves to increase accessibility and brand awareness.

Over the past two years PIMM'S® has run an experiential campaign involving two traditional Routemaster buses. The customised buses – which travel between various festivals throughout the summer months – come complete with quirky extras such as chrome alloys, grilles and an electric roof that, when pulled back, exposes a top floor decked out like a Gentleman's Club. Epitomising the PIMM'S® brand essence – British with a twist – the buses aim to simultaneously tap into the sociability of the product through the natural optimism associated with summer.

PIMM'S® has one of the UK's largest alcohol sampling campaigns; sampling more consumers than any other alcohol brand. High profile visibility at major outdoor events serves to raise consumer awareness of the brand even further – especially early in the summer season.

Brand Values

The essence of PIMM'S® is that perfect summer feeling: the sun on your face, sharing time with friends and spending as much time as possible outdoors. Its personality is young and optimistic with a view that life is made for celebrating and every day should be marked as an occasion. Throughout a long and colourful history, PIMM'S® has remained true to its British heritage while still creating a contemporary freshness that has expanded its modern day appeal and increased the brand awareness. Its target audience now covers a wide range of ages and backgrounds, not a definitive 'type' or social class.

www.anyoneforpimms.com

Things you didn't know about PIMM'S®

PIMM'S No.1 CUP® was created to improve the bitter taste of gin (popular amongst 19th century drinkers) by adding a selection of carefully chosen herbs and spices.

PIMM'S No.1 CUP® is still made to its original recipe, a closely guarded secret known only to six people called 'The Secret Six'.

The significance of fruit in PIMM'S® is historical. It was originally drunk by the upper classes at a time when fresh fruit was a luxury; to put it in an alcoholic drink was the ultimate sign of opulence.

Around 15,000 ready mixed PIMM'S® and lemonade convenience cans are sold every day throughout the summer in the UK.

PIMM'S No.1 CUP® was originally delivered by bicycle around London, this delivery method is to be re-instated from 2007 – to help aid sample distribution.

1991

The first PIMM'S No.1 CUP® Spirit Drink can is marketed in 33cl cans – later reduced in size to a more manageable 25cl and sold ready mixed with lemonade.

2001

The 'ANYONE FOR PIMM'S®?' campaign launches, introducing the cheerful character of Harry, played by British comedian, Alexander Armstrong.

2004

PIMM'S WINTER® is launched in the UK. Based on the previous No.3 cup it has a brandy liquor base.

2007

PIMM'S® receives the BEST award for its long term marketing communications, from the Marketing Communications Consultants Association.

RAC has been meeting the needs of the motorist since the beginning of motoring itself in the late 19th century. Today's RAC aims to satisfy all consumer needs throughout the motoring lifecycle – including financing, inspecting, purchasing, insuring, protecting and repairing cars. A people-centric business, RAC is committed to leveraging its motoring knowledge to come to the rescue of its customers.

Market

It is a fact of life that cars break down. Most drivers will find themselves let down by their vehicle at some time or other; new cars may be becoming increasingly reliable from a mechanical perspective, but the incidence of simple faults such as flat batteries and tyres remains stubbornly high – supplemented by a host of modern electronics-related incidents.

For most drivers, the answer to these problems is to call for assistance from a breakdown recovery organisation. There are 27.5 million cars on the road in the UK and 30.6 million licensed drivers (Source: RAC Report on Motoring 2006). Of these, some 75 per cent have membership of a motoring breakdown organisation, either personally or as part of a corporate scheme (Source: RAC Report on Motoring 2006). RAC's share of the total market is approximately 30 per cent (Source: RAC Report on Motoring 2006).

Achievements

RAC strives to offer its customers the best service possible. In the UK Roadside Assistance Study in 2006 – an annual survey undertaken by consumer research company, J.D. Power and Associates – RAC ranked the highest in satisfying emergency roadside assistance customers.

The survey of nearly 3,000 UK motorists showed that RAC received the highest ratings for all three of the factors, which are driving customer satisfaction – timing, quality of service from operators/dispatchers as well as mechanics/vehicle drivers.

The study highlighted that the use of subcontractors by RAC is significantly lower than most other providers, which is also a key element of satisfaction for the motorist.

RAC has also been shown to be one of the country's most progressive motoring organisations. At the 2006 Greenfleet Awards it won the Breakdown/Recovery Company of the Year award for its efforts to provide environmentally friendly roadside patrols.

In addition, RAC Auto Windscreens' company-wide policy was also praised. This encourages customers to seek windscreen repairs before replacement, making significant saving on glass waste

disposal. RAC works proactively with its fleet customers to help achieve this.

Product

In the early days of motoring, most drivers joined RAC, which became the arbiter of matters relating to cars and driving. It promoted and enhanced the new 'motoring movement' by teaching driving, issuing road maps, approving garages and hotels, organising insurance and eventually establishing road patrols to help its members.

The core of RAC's offering continues to be its breakdown service and this is the main benefit for the organisation's 6.5 million

members. However, today's RAC offers a broad range of services dedicated to the needs of motorists, from traffic information to driving tuition through BSM, the driving school of RAC. It is UK's largest driving school with over 3,400 driving instructors and is one of the largest driving instructor training providers. Indeed, someone passes their driving test with BSM approximately every two minutes.

Other services include windscreen repair (through RAC Auto Windscreens) as well as car finance. RAC Direct Insurance offers car, van, motorbike, home and travel insurance. Meanwhile, RAC Loans offers up to £25,000 for any purpose; they are available to everyone, not just RAC members. RAC also offers a courier service on all personal loans and can deliver a cheque within 24 hours of applicants being accepted.

RAC Vehicle Checks and Examinations help give customers peace of mind when buying a used car. The vehicle check will show whether the car has been stolen, written-off, has outstanding finance or previous plates, is at risk of being sold illegally, and that its number plate and chassis number correspond. With RAC Examinations, qualified inspectors will conduct up to 166 physical checks on the car to make sure it is mechanically and structurally sound.

Another element of RAC's total offer is its legal services which provides expert advice and representation to customers involved in personal injury claims.

RAC has become one of the leaders in developing in-car telematics, working with TrafficMaster to provide traffic and travel information using communications and satellite location technology.

RAC also helps drivers travelling at home and abroad through its provision of travel insurance, route planning, European breakdown assistance and travel accessories. Fully qualified RAC engineers conduct vehicle checks for individual motorists, manufacturers and garages.

The rac.co.uk website provides further online services to members and the general public from live traffic news, through car

purchasing advice to downloadable children's games.

For corporate customers, including the leading passenger car, truck and motorcycle manufacturers, contract hire and leasing companies, RAC offers bespoke solutions. In addition to breakdown and recovery, the services offered to business customers include accident management, warranties, commercial training, risk management and journey management.

To maintain the tradition of RAC as a campaigning body on behalf of the motorist, RAC Foundation was established in 1991 to take on the role of protecting the interests of the motorist. It is now run as an independent charity to promote the environmental, economic, mobility and safety issues relating to use of motor vehicles.

For a second season, RAC are sponsoring a professional race team – Team RAC in the Dunlop MSA British Touring Car Championship (BTCC). Managed by West Surrey Racing (WSR), Team RAC are entering the 10 race event this year with two new RAC branded BMW 320si E90 cars driven by Colin Turkington and Tom Onslow-Cole.

Recent Developments
In March 2005, Aviva plc acquired RAC for around £1.1 billion. The acquisition brought together RAC's brand and customer base with the expertise and leading position in motor insurance of Norwich Union Insurance (part of Aviva).

Promotion
RAC has a considerable history as a television advertiser, with campaigns that have, for the most part, focused on roadside rescues.

The challenge facing RAC has therefore been to create an advertising platform true to this breakdown heritage, yet equally applicable to its other key business divisions such as direct insurance, car buying and corporate partnerships.

Following a period of extensive research and planning in autumn 2006, it became apparent this could be achieved through a focus on the motoring expertise upon which each part of the business can draw. This expertise, when applied to the needs of the RAC customer, translates into an 'RAC standard' of customer care. So whether the RAC is rescuing a stricken motorist at the roadside, providing a car insurance quote or undertaking a vehicle history check for a first time buyer, its motoring expertise comes to the aid of motorists through the care it delivers to them.

This thought is summarised in the latest RAC advertising as 'RAC to the rescue', something since widely adopted across the business and permeating from top to bottom.

Brand Values
RAC's vision is to be the UK's first choice provider of motoring solutions. RAC aims to provide a comprehensive range of services for its customers and act as a caring organisation, with the environment being of key concern.

www.rac.co.uk

Things you didn't know about RAC

RAC has more patrols per member than any other rescue organisation (Source: Quarterly market share report complied from Taylor Nelson Consumer Omnibus Report March 2007).

RAC's 1,500 expert Patrols fix almost 80 per cent of breakdowns at the roadside, excludes accidents and extreme failures (Source: RAC 1st January – 31st December 2006).

RAC never sleeps, providing round the clock cover, 365 days a year.

RAC can find customers fast, with the help of their mobile phone signal.

ROTARY

Established in Switzerland 1895

Established in La Chaux-de-Fonds, Switzerland in 1895 by Moise Dreyfuss, Rotary Watches is a fourth generation, family run company offering contemporary classic dress watches. Rotary is proud of its reputation for offering quality and innovation combined with value for money. In the UK, Rotary is the brand leader in the mid-market, defined as watches that retail between £100 and £200.

Market

According to GFK's UK consumer panel, the watch market is worth £706 million and the average price paid for a watch is £45. Growth in the market is being driven by an increasing incidence of multiple ownership as accessorising for both men and women becomes more and more important. The most significant growth is being seen in the higher price brackets, notably £100+ as consumers become more aware of the benefits of investing in a watch that will last a lifetime rather than a lower priced more disposable

model. In keeping with this, classic styling is also seeing a return to popularity as consumers move away from short-lived high-fashion designs. Rotary's key competitors in the mid-market are Seiko and Tissot.

Achievements

The annual UK Jewellery Awards, which are administered by Retail Jeweller Magazine, are the leading trade title for the watch and jewellery industry. Rotary has been a consistent victor, winning the Volume Watch Brand of the Year title in 1998, the Watch

Supplier of the Year award for two consecutive years in 2002 and 2003 and was a finalist for the Watch Brand of the Year award in both 2004 and 2006. In addition, Rotary Revelation™ was voted 'Watch of the Year' by the duty free title TFWA in 2004.

In 2000 Rotary's heavy investment in its standards of supply and service also led to the launch of the trade's first and only business-to-business (B2B) trade website, allowing retailers to order online with guaranteed delivery the following day. Setting new standards of customer service, it provides transparency in the form of online stock availability, updating in real-time via data links to the company's management information system, online statements and invoices, service and repair tracking as well as spare parts ordering.

Product

From diamond set watches with matching bracelets to the hugely popular Limited Edition series of Swiss automatics – presented in distinctive watch winding boxes with production limited to 500 watches worldwide – all Rotary models are produced to a high specification, guaranteeing longevity and reliability but at prices that are affordable.

In 2007 Rotary launched the 'Rocks' range of Dolphin Standard waterproof diamond watches. The collection consists of 20 ladies' strap and bracelet watches in PVD gold plate, stainless steel and bi-colour metal and each model is set with 12 brilliant cut diamonds on the bezel.

1895
Moise Dreyfuss begins making timepieces in a small workshop in the Swiss town of La Chaux-de-Fonds.

1907
Georges and Sylvain Dreyfuss, two of Moise Dreyfuss's three sons, open an office in Britain to import the family's watches.

1925
The now-famous Rotary logo, the 'winged wheel', is introduced.

1940s
Rotary is appointed as official watch supplier to the British army.

1985
The Swiss business and its trademarks, with the exception of the rights for the UK and Gibraltar, are sold to the Hirsch Group.

Rotary 'Vintage' is a collection of strap and bracelet watches for men, combining designs inspired by historic Rotary watches with advances in manufacturing, thanks to their Dolphin Standard waterproof properties. The collection focuses on key features such as luminous dial markers, domed bezels and retrograde dial designs.

Recent Developments
The launch of the Dolphin Standard in 2005 as an innovative waterproof standard marked one of the most important technological breakthroughs in watch-making for the last decade. For consumers the new standard offers peace of mind thanks to a simple promise: "Swim and Dive all Day". The standard marks a move away from the complex and confusing system of water resistance criteria to which the rest of industry subscribes. Unlike most competitor brands, which reserve water-resistance features for a limited number of chunky sporty models, Rotary has applied the Dolphin Standard to virtually its entire range.

The award winning Rotary Revelation™ collection of rotating timepieces will be further developed during 2007 as a result of the success of the innovative Round Revelation™ launched in 2006; the first of its kind, it offered the wearer a round rotating case encompassing two distinctive dials and the ability to keep two different times, ideal for frequent travellers.

Rotary is already present in some 35 countries worldwide via a distributor network. The brand's future plans include the development of a portfolio of sister brands for Rotary's holding company, the Dreyfuss Group, via differentiated propositions. Each with their own unique selling point, these are designed to sit alongside Rotary while targeting a different audience.

Promotion
Rotary does not sell direct to consumers. Rather, the company supplies the trade and as such is committed to a major programme of trade marketing encompassing teams of field trainers who use state-of-the-art multimedia training CDs with the aim of making staff training fun and interactive.

Rotary's trade programme – 'Business Builder' – revolutionises the way the watch and jewellery industry works. Launched in 2003, it is a new approach to managing and ordering stock and is recommended by Rotary's sales team to increase turnover and profit, improve cash flow and reduce levels of working capital.

The programme encourages independent retailers to carry a core range – viewable on Rotary's B2B website – and order little and often so that sales follow demand. In return, Rotary guarantees stock the following day, right up until Christmas Eve. On average, retailers on the programme have seen growth 10 per cent higher than those who have remained true to the industry norm of placing large orders just two or three times throughout the year.

In terms of above-the-line activity, Rotary uses a combination of press advertising and PR to communicate to its target audience, choosing to focus creative executions on anchor products such as 'Rotary Revelation™' and 'Rotary Vintage', with the latter featuring in Rotary's 2007 advertising campaign as a trademark collection of affordable stylish dress watches.

Brand Values
Rotary aims to cater for all ages and all tastes in mid-market watches by offering consumers a wide choice of dress watches with a range of 200 models. It also keeps abreast of technological developments, with innovations such as the Dolphin Standard.

In its position as a household brand name, Rotary engenders trust and confidence in consumers and retailers alike.

www.rotarywatches.com

Things you didn't know about Rotary Watches

Rotary Watches is one of the few remaining family owned watch houses, with chairman Robert Dreyfuss succeeding his father Teddy Dreyfuss to become the fourth generation of the founding family.

In the 1950s a Rotary watch was towed behind the QE2 as it crossed the Atlantic; another was strapped to the Flying Scotsman; and a further watch was dropped from the top of Big Ben. All three watches survived intact.

Rotary regularly receives testimonials from customers who've had their Rotary watch since they were 18 and it's still keeping perfect time – in some cases despite going through both World Wars.

The company's Service and Repair department guarantees to return a customer's watch within seven days, door-to-door.

The Limited Edition series of watches comes complete with a complimentary watch winding box and is limited to just 500 pieces worldwide, all individually numbered on the case back.

1992
Rotary UK buys the trademarks back and now owns the right to use the trademark worldwide.

2005
Rotary invests heavily in product development; the Dolphin Standard is launched.

2006
Further development takes place with the launch of the Rotary Round Revelation™.

2007
Rotary launches the Vintage collection of men's watches, all based on original 1920s and 1930s designs.

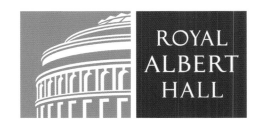

ROYAL ALBERT HALL

The Royal Albert Hall is one of the UK's most treasured and distinctive buildings, recognisable the world over. The world's leading artists from every kind of performance genre have appeared on its stage. This shared experience of the best of live performance is now enjoyed by well over a million people each year at the Hall and by many millions more around the world through broadcasts, recordings and new media channels.

Market
The Royal Albert Hall operates in the highly competitive entertainment, leisure and tourism sectors. It is a registered charity and receives no public funding. Its competitors are the other leading UK performing arts and entertainment venues and organisations, many of whom receive central or local government funding, and more general competition for a customer's leisure time and leisure pound, especially in the fast growing age of digital media and home entertainment.

Achievements
In 2006, the Royal Albert Hall was recognised by the music industry when it once again won International Theatre of the Year at the 18th Pollstar Concert Industry Awards in America – for the fourth year in succession.

The Hall's Box Office also received an award for Outstanding Customer Service at the Visit London Awards in 2006.

The Hall's founding Charter requires it to maintain the building and through it to promote the understanding, appreciation

and enjoyment of the Arts and Sciences. As part of this vision, the Hall launched an extensive education programme in 2004. This has now enabled over 75,000 young people to participate in and learn more about the performing arts, science and the cultural industries. As part of its education programme, the Hall works especially closely with 12 partner schools based in Westminster, Kensington and Chelsea, whose pupils speak more than 75 different languages between them. Key events during the last two years included a concert for young people by Jamie Cullum, which allowed 4,500 teenagers to experience jazz for the first time, and the Madam Butterfly Fashion Show in March (pictured above right). This enabled pupils from secondary schools in London and the South East to create their own live fashion event on the set of the production.

The Hall also supports other registered charities in their fundraising activities, and offers the Hall free of charge to one charity each year. Over the last two years, events held at the Hall have raised over £10 million.

Since 2000, the Hall has been host to a week of concerts in support of the Teenage Cancer Trust, spearheaded by Roger Daltry. In 2003, the Hall held the first Fashion Rocks event for the Prince's Trust. This spectacle encompassed 17 of the world's top designers and models who teamed up with stars including Robbie Williams, Beyoncé and David Bowie.

Product
The Royal Albert Hall hosts and celebrates live performance by artists from around the world and promotes, with partners, productions of opera, ballet, musicals and organ music. From Verdi, Wagner and Elgar conducting UK premieres of their works to performances by Bob Dylan, Jimi Hendrix, Frank Sinatra and The Beatles, the Hall has an unparalleled history of exceptional performances by the world's leading artists.

Each year, over 350 events are held in the Hall's auditorium, including performances of classical music, jazz, folk and world music, circus, rock and pop concerts, ballet and

1871
The Royal Albert Hall is opened by Queen Victoria in March.

1909
A full indoor Marathon is run at the Hall – a total of 524 circuits of the Arena.

1912
The Titanic Band Memorial Concert takes place encompassing 500 performers, with conductors Sir Edward Elgar, Henry Wood, Thomas Beecham and Landon Ronald.

1941
The first BBC Proms season at the Hall takes place.

1963
The Beatles and The Rolling Stones appear on the same bill on 15th September.

opera, dance, comedy, tennis matches, charity concerts, film premieres, corporate dinners, award ceremonies and occasions of national importance such as the Royal British Legion Festival of Remembrance.

Recent Developments

In 2004, following an extensive building development programme, the Hall launched a series of daytime tours of the building, based on the performance and Victorian history of this iconic building.

This was followed in 2005 by 'ignite', a series of free lively lunchtime concerts in the Café Consort each Friday, which feature talented young world music and jazz artists. The success of this series resulted in the Hall launching 'ignite brunch' on Sundays in April 2007. These combine a lazy Sunday afternoon listening to live jazz and world music with a Sunday brunch menu and have been sold out since the launch.

In 2006, the Hall also launched 'reflect', an engaging free photography exhibition series on the Hall's ground floor corridor. Highlights of this series have included the prestigious World Press Photo exhibition, celebrating the best in photojournalism from around the world, and exhibitions highlighting culture in Tibet and the UNHCR initiatives in the Democratic Republic of Congo.

As a result of these initiatives, 24,000 people attended daytime events during 2006. The Hall is continuing its ambition to make good use of areas of the Hall outside of the main auditorium with a new initiative to reach

the youth market and promote young talent, due to launch in autumn 2007.

Promotion

The Royal Albert Hall markets its own programming initiatives and works with its event promoters to assist them with the ticket sales for their events through the Hall's marketing channels. Over the last three years, the Hall's average attendance figures across the year have been strong at around 80 per cent of capacity.

As the result of a recent brand research and positioning project, the Hall is currently launching a new visual language for the brand and extending its distribution channels, especially its online and new media channels, to improve the services that it is able to offer to its promoters and increase audience attendance at the Hall still further.

The Royal Albert Hall is a brand known around the world through extensive PR coverage and through broadcasts as well as DVD releases, which in 2005 and 2006 included the broadcast or recording of over 245 performances. The Hall is working with business partners, such as iTunes, to extend the reach of the Hall and its event profile beyond the building itself, allowing the brand to reach a much wider audience.

The Hall has also toured its co-promoted productions to Hong Kong and Australia and there are plans to tour these productions to China, Germany and America and to develop this area of the business further.

Brand Values

The Hall's brand values are encompassed in the positioning statement – entertaining the world. It is the Hall's ambition that everyone, young and old, and from every nation and culture should feel welcome at the Hall and be able to enjoy the shared experience and excitement of live performance from the very best of today's global artists.

Built as part of Prince Albert's vision for a centre for the Arts and Sciences in South Kensington, the Royal Albert Hall is proud of the building and its heritage. It remains true to his founding ambitions to maintain and develop this magical building for future generations and to continue to promote the appreciation and enjoyment of the Arts and Sciences.

www.royalalberthall.com

Things you didn't know about Royal Albert Hall

There are over 13,500 letter A's in the Royal Albert Hall – featuring on the banisters and in the terracotta and stonework throughout the building.

It took six million bricks and 80,000 terracotta bricks to build the Royal Albert Hall, as well as 11,000 gas burners (which lit in 10 seconds) and five miles of steam pipes.

The first public display of electric lighting was given at the Royal Albert Hall in 1879.

The Hall has hosted many world statesmen including Sir Winston Churchill, President F W de Klerk, Nelson Mandela, His Holiness the Dalai Lama and President Bill Clinton.

1970	**1996**	**2004**	**2006**
Tennis is first played at the Hall.	Work begins on the Royal Albert Hall's eight-year major building development programme.	The official 're-opening' of the Hall by Her Majesty The Queen, to celebrate the completion of the Hall's major building development programme, takes place.	President Bill Clinton speaks at the Hall about his vision for leadership in the 21st Century.
	Cirque du Soleil premieres Saltimbanco at the Hall.		

ROYAL DOULTON

ENGLAND

Having earned a reputation for excellence, creativity, skilled craftsmanship and distinctiveness of design, Royal Doulton is valued for its sense of heritage and quality. Prized by collectors the world over, Royal Doulton has an international reach extending way beyond its English roots.

Market

Withstanding market fragmentation, ceramic giftware has seen considerable growth – gift-giving, home decoration and investment being the main motivations. Despite the introduction of many alternative forms of gifts, ceramics are sought after as offering true qualities of heritage, craftsmanship, and long-lasting value for money.

Royal Doulton is a market leader within the ceramics and chinaware markets, with a large proportion of all English bone china being supplied by Royal Doulton, as well as almost half of the UK's ceramic sculptures.

The key markets worldwide for premium ceramic tableware and giftware are the UK and Europe, North America, Asia Pacific and Australasia. In total the global market is estimated to be worth more than £1.6 billion.

Achievements

Royal Doulton is one of the world's largest manufacturers and distributors in the premium ceramic tableware and giftware market. With 200 years of heritage, Royal Doulton is a thriving global organisation, with around £95 million annual turnover, employing approximately 2,500 people across its production sites and numerous distribution operations worldwide. The company currently operates in more than 80 different markets and has distribution companies in the US, Canada, Australia and Japan. Indeed, approximately half of all sales are generated outside the UK.

Each of the company's principal brands – Royal Doulton, Minton, and Royal Albert – have a long association of royal patronage, and hold at least one Royal Warrant. They are also trademark registered.

Product

Royal Doulton may be one of the oldest chinaware companies in the world, but it is also one of the most up-to-date; focusing on the customer, understanding its buyers, and creating products that suit individual tastes and needs, it aims to stay ahead of contemporary trends.

When drawing up new product design, Royal Doulton's Design Studio studies the market, analyses consumer research, and often refers to Royal Doulton's own museum and archives – dating from 1815 to the present day – for inspiration.

Today, Royal Doulton provides a wide selection of domestic tableware manufactured in bone china and fine china. The brand is also featured in an extensive range of crystal stemware and giftware. Royal Doulton lists among its products extensive giftware offerings, character jugs, china flowers, and an array of collectable figurines often known as the Royal Doulton 'pretty ladies'.

Keeping abreast of the latest lifestyle trends has also seen the brand work with award winning fashion designer Julien Macdonald, producing exclusive ranges of contemporary tableware, giftware and glassware. In addition, the collaboration with celebrated chef Gordon Ramsay saw his Michelin-starred expertise bring a new professionalism to home dining products.

1815	1875	1884	1901	1930s	1960
John Doulton begins producing practical and decorative stoneware from a small pottery in Lambeth, South London.	John Doulton's son, Henry, relocates the business to Stoke-on-Trent.	Following the introduction of new techniques, production of bone china begins.	King Edward VII, permits the company to prefix its name with 'Royal', and the company is awarded the Royal Warrant.	Royal Doulton is involved in the manufacture of figurines and giftware.	A new product, English Translucent China is introduced. Offering the translucent quality of bone china without the expense, this will later become known as Royal Doulton Fine China.

Royal Albert, which traces its origins back to 1896, has also become an internationally recognised brand, offering domestic tableware and gift items. Equally famous, with an illustrious heritage dating back to its inception in 1793 is the Minton range, best known for its most popular pattern Haddon Hall, which is particularly favoured by the Japanese market.

Recent Developments
Spring 2007 saw the launch of both a number of new figurines and gifts as well as additions to current ranges. In particular, a collaboration with Sir Terence Conran – who recently celebrated 50 years in design – sees his expertise brought to the brand with a very 'English' collection for Royal Doulton. Inspired by Conran's passion for traditional English

cooking, the collection has been thoughtfully designed for easy, versatile use and includes practical, classic items such as pudding bowls, pie dishes and a whole family of jugs whose sweeping curves are inspired by birds. The collection combines quality materials with an earthy colour palette and simple designs, to create timeless products that aim to appeal to a wide range of customers.

Promotion
Royal Doulton is undergoing an important period of change in its long history as it implements a three-brand master strategy as a first step in developing the company's brands. New global merchandising systems, an e-commerce website, product packaging, point of sale and designer endorsement have all been identified as key to the brand development.

The Licensing Division, created in the mid 1990s to propel the three brands into new product sectors, has achieved considerable success, not least with the launch of Bunnykins Clothing and Silverware, as well as its Children's Furniture product range. In the UK, licensed products include home textiles, jewellery, candles, stationery, child/baby gifts and accessories.

Royal Doulton's promotional and marketing activities have been central to the development and rationalisation of the brand and its communication. The introduction of everything from new logos to in-store promotional material and branded fixtures has demanded that the focus of activity be centred on the communication

and effective introduction of the recent significant changes.

Brand Values
Royal Doulton is a quintessentially British brand with a strong commitment to craftsmanship and artistic innovation. Excellence and distinctiveness of design are values that it intends to build on in order to take the brand forward.

www.royaldoulton.com

Things you didn't know about Royal Doulton

Royal Doulton ceramics are included in a time capsule inside the base of Cleopatra's Needle on the Thames Embankment in London.

Royal Doulton's largest and most expensive figure takes more than 160 hours to hand paint and costs more than £15,000.

Royal Doulton was the first china to enter space. China plates were carried on the inaugural flight of the space shuttle Discovery in 1984.

Royal Doulton's Royal Albert design 'Old Country Roses' bone china tableware pattern has sold more than 150 million pieces since its introduction in 1962.

During the reign of Queen Victoria, the Doulton family business established the world's first stoneware pipe factory and went on to become Britain's top Victorian manufacturer of sanitary ware.

Royal Doulton's archives give the business and its designers access to some 10,000 watercolours dating as far back as 1815.

1966
The company becomes the first china manufacturer to be awarded the Queen's Award for Technical Achievement, for its contribution to china manufacturing.

1972
Royal Doulton is bought by Pearson and merged with Allied English Potteries – encompassing the Royal Albert and Minton brands.

1993
Royal Doulton separates from Pearson and becomes a publicly quoted company listed on the London Stock Exchange.

2006
Royal Doulton becomes part of the Waterford Wedgwood Group.

Samsung is now one of the world's most recognised brands operating in a range of sectors across the world. At the forefront of this well known brand is Samsung Electronics, part of the wider Samsung Group and currently the world's leading consumer electronics brand. Employing approximately 138,000 people in 124 operations in 56 countries, Samsung Electronics is a leading producer of digital TVs, memory chips, mobile phones and TFT-LCDs.

Market

Over the last decade, Samsung Electronics has grown from a smaller-scale manufacturer with a comparatively lesser known brand, to become one of the world's strongest and most powerful technology companies. With a vast product portfolio, Samsung's success can be largely attributed to its strength in three areas – memory chips, liquid crystal displays and handheld phones. Samsung is a leader in all these areas, holding the number one position in the memory chip, LCD TV and monitor and TFT-LCD markets and the number three position in the handset market.

Achievements

Samsung has evolved into a group of companies spanning multiple industries with widespread success. Well structured and globally-focused but responsive to the needs of local markets, in 2006 Samsung Electronics delivered consolidated sales of US$85.3 billion.

Building on this success, the last 12 months have been a year of milestone product

imagine bringing life to your living room with full HD Blu-ray

Samsung **Blu-ray** BD-P1000 Player

imagine an LCD TV that's as brilliant off as it is on

Samsung R7

launches for Samsung which has seen its efforts recognised by a number of awards. Over 100 Samsung products have received the industry's most influential design awards. This total is the best ever annual showing for Samsung. The prestigious International Forum Design (iF) organisation bestowed 25 iF Design Awards on Samsung products in 2006, over twice the 12 awards given to Samsung the previous year.

Samsung has measured its success by brand value for a number of years and has focused its marketing strategy around raising

brand perception with the public. This focus has resulted in Samsung being ranked the 20th most influential brand in the world by BusinessWeek and Interbrand with a value of US$16.2 billion, making Samsung the most valuable consumer electronics brand in the world.

Product

Samsung is widely respected for the quality of its technology and the design of its products. With an ever increasing portfolio, including the world's slimmest mobile phone,

1938	1950s	1960s	1970s	1993	2000s
Samsung General Store is opened in North Kyungsang Province, Korea.	Samsung becomes a producer of basic commodities such as sugar and wool.	Samsung expands overseas – one of the first Korean companies to do so. The company also successfully establishes a newspaper and broadcasting company.	This crucial period lays the foundations for the present day Samsung. Its strength in the semiconductor, information and telecommunications industries grows.	Chairman Kun-Hee Lee's vision and introduction of 'New Management' acknowledges the need to transform Samsung to keep pace with the global economy.	A 'Digital Management' approach is adopted to ensure that Samsung maintains a leading position in the Information Age.

the world's first 82 inch full HDTV TFT-LCD and the world's first designer home appliances, Samsung is able to provide its customers with a series of products that play a key role in their everyday lives.

As Europe's number one manufacturer of LCD TVs (Source: GfK), Samsung has sold over four million units of the phenomenally successful R7/8 LCD TV series worldwide. This range took its inspiration from the Bordeaux wine glass and has been widely recognised as an iconic consumer product that had a huge impact in raising Samsung's brand value.

Recent Developments

2006 has been another momentous year for Samsung in terms of innovation. Samsung's continued investment in research and development has long been a hallmark of the company. This focus, involving an investment in 2006 of US$6.1 billion, is housed in 16 research centres located in eight countries worldwide. Some 27,000 researchers work to ensure that Samsung remains on the cutting-edge of innovation.

The fruits of Samsung's research and development process resulted in a number of world firsts in design and technical

innovation during 2006. The launch of the Ultra Edition range of mobile phones saw Samsung introduce the world's slimmest ever phone with a profile of just 6.9mm. The introduction of the Ultra Edition 8.4 3G handset, also the slimmest of its kind, dispelled the myth that 3G handsets have to sacrifice design for functionality.

Innovation is not, of course, exclusive to mobile phone handsets. Samsung built on its reputation to be first to market with cutting-edge technologies with the launch of the first ever Blu-ray disc player available to consumers. The launch of the player responded to growing consumer demand for playing and recording high definition content, which far surpasses the video quality DVD can handle. Samsung's focus on research and development allowed it to answer a market need faster than any of its competitors.

Other innovations include the arrival of the K5 MP3 player which combined Samsung's lauded MP3 designs with those of a mini-boom box by incorporating built-in speakers. Despite being a fraction of the size of the smallest stereo system, the speaker design delivers the same quality of sound.

Promotion

Samsung's unique approach to product design has had dramatic results in recent years. The company's development has been supported by an aggressive marketing strategy. Five years ago, Samsung pledged to re-position its brand, aligning itself with premium products – a goal it has achieved through launches such as the R7/8 range of LCD TVs, the Ultra range of mobile phones and the J-Series range of home appliances.

Sponsorship has played a large part in increasing the visibility of the brand, notably the high profile sponsorship of Chelsea Football Club in the UK. Samsung became the club's official sponsor in a five-year partnership which marked the biggest ever sponsorship deal signed by Chelsea and

the second largest by Samsung after its sponsorship of the Olympic Games. Samsung has aligned its brand with the success of Chelsea who have recorded no fewer than six major trophies in the last three years.

Football has always been an important vehicle for Samsung to reach its audience. The 2006 World Cup marked a key milestone for Samsung, building a marketing campaign for the R7 range of LCD TVs around this global sporting event. The R7 has subsequently become the number one LCD TV choice for the UK and Europe (Source: GfK). All of this adds up to a stellar performance by the Samsung brand. From the prestigious Olympic partnership to its compelling product offerings, Samsung is one of the world's fastest moving and most innovative companies.

Brand Values

Samsung's brand is built around the values of technology, design and innovation and is recognised for providing premium products to its customers. Samsung is striving to use its brand to continually position itself as a leader in digital technology and an innovative provider of consumer electronics that people instantly recognise and desire.

www.samsung.co.uk

Things you didn't know about Samsung

Collaborations with some of the world's leading designers, including a prestigious partnership with Bang & Olufsen, have resulted in a unique mobile phone offering.

Samsung has held the number one position in the global monitor market for a staggering 18 years (Source: Internal sales figures).

Over four million homes worldwide house an R7/8 LCD TV.

In 2006, Samsung launched the world's first: 10 mega pixel, 8GB HDD; 82 inch Full HDTV TFT-LCD; and the first ultra mobile PC.

There has never been a time when energy has been such an important world topic, or more in the public eye, and Shell is playing a significant role in meeting growing energy demand in a responsible way. Energy supply to meet growing energy demand, and its effects, are key global issues.

Market

Shell's approach to its global business operations demonstrates its understanding that people want energy that is as clean, convenient and as cheap as possible, and that it shares their concerns about the consequences of energy use. Shell is helping to secure a responsible energy future, built on the breadth of its portfolio, the value of its technology and the quality of its people.

Shell defines responsibility as working safely to achieve a balance between supply, price, and environmental and social consequences, while recognising that it is difficult to optimise all at the same time.

Shell operates in more than 140 countries across a broad spectrum of the energy business from oil and natural gas, to renewables such as solar, wind and hydrogen.

Achievements

For motorists, Shell's focus on stretching energy resources to deliver products designed to improve engine reliability, and to help take them further, has high public visibility. It uses motor sport at the highest level as part of an extensive R&D programme to test, develop, and promote the benefits of its leading edge Shell V-Power fuel and Shell Helix motor oil technologies.

In 2007 Shell celebrates 60 years of shared passion for performance with Ferrari, dating back to the days of Enzo Ferrari himself and the birth of Formula One racing in the 1950s. Over this period there have been many successes and exciting developments with the results of this shared passion benefiting motorists, such as the development of the current generation of Shell performance fuels and lubricants.

Last year for the first time, more new diesel cars than gasoline cars were sold in Europe (Source: J.D. Power and Associates). Shell has responded to this huge growth with Shell V-Power Diesel, a new performance diesel fuel designed to help today's generation of diesel cars deliver more power for longer. One major component of Shell V-Power Diesel in many countries is Gas to Liquids (GTL) Fuel, which is a synthetic product derived from natural gas. Shell GTL's cleaner burning properties, due to its high cetane number, is designed to give it emissions benefits. Shell and Audi proved how far their technical relationship and resultant diesel technologies had come, by winning the legendary 2006 Le Mans 24-hour race. Fuelled by Shell V-Power Diesel race fuel, the Audi R10 TDI set the fastest lap of the race and a new distance record on the way to an historic victory – the first ever Le Mans won by a diesel race car.

The ultimate road test to refine a new fuel designed for extra miles at no extra cost, in some markets, saw Shell set a new Guinness World Record in 2006 for the most fuel efficient circumnavigation of the

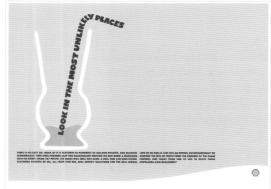

world ever undertaken in a standard car (VW Golf FSI1.6). Over a 78-day period, and crossing 25 countries, only 24 tanks-full of gasoline containing the new Shell Fuel Economy Formula were used – a tribute to the principles of fuel efficient driving and product technology.

Product

All automotive fuels and lubricants are not the same and Shell's extensive R&D programmes continually strive to develop new and better fuels and lubricants to satisfy growing customer requirements for improved engine and environmental performance.

In the retail business its innovation stems from its desire to enhance mobility for its customers through performance fuels such as Shell V-Power, through to its Fuel Stretch tips and fuel economy formulas, as well as 'pay at the pump' technology which reduces re-fuelling times and keeps people on the move.

Its technical partnerships with Ferrari and Audi Sport ensure that it tests its fuels in the most extreme and demanding conditions.

1833
Marcus Samuel opens a small shop in London dealing in antiques, curios and oriental sea shells. He goes on to set up regular shipments to the Far East.

1890
Marcus Samuel Jnr starts exporting Kerosene to the Far East, sending the world's first oil tanker through the Suez Canal. He brands the kerosene 'Shell'.

1907
Shell forms a close alliance with Royal Dutch Petroleum, also active in the Far East. Rapid growth follows with the onset of the new motorcar age.

1950s
Supply and demand both boom and during this period, Shell supplies almost one seventh of the world's oil products.

1970s
Major oil fields are discovered in the North Sea and Shell becomes a major player in this area.

2007
Shell celebrates the centenary of one of the longest Anglo-Dutch partnerships in history, now one company; Royal Dutch Shell plc.

Recent Developments

All oil companies tend to be seen as being the same, so Shell's brand communications tell people what it stands for, and what makes it special and different. The stakeholder audiences are those who care about the energy challenge and want to be part of the solution.

Each stakeholder has their own relationship with Shell and their own needs, such as economy or performance fuels for motorists, reliable plant operations for businesses, responsible exploitation of natural resources and skills transfer for governments. The Shell brand umbrella communications programme focuses on 'real energy solutions for the real world', with real life examples of the Shell attitude applied in practice.

Individual communications tell true stories of how Shell is dealing with the huge energy challenges the world is facing. They bring to life who Shell is, what it does, and why and how it does it. They show the creativity and persistence of its people solving problems for its customers using all kinds of innovation, but especially technology.

The communications programme includes unconventional mini-feature films in docu-drama style, significant digital presence with online interactive films and brain challenges, DVDs distributed through publications, and a challenging print campaign.

The first film is a real life story about a Shell engineer who has a 'eureka' moment, told with two parallel storylines: his struggles as a father and his struggles as an engineer.

The aim is to get people to think differently about energy issues, about Shell and the role that it plays: 'Shell cares about what we all care about – getting energy that is convenient, cheap and clean.'

The communications programme has been launched in 14 markets to date, from the USA through Europe to China, including emerging markets such as Russia and India. Opinion leaders are engaged through supporting

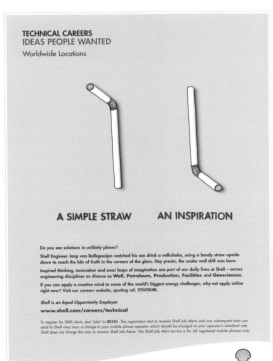

initiatives resulting from global media partnerships forged with key media channels.

Common threads in the brand and product communications are: a passion for improvement – 'good is not good enough'; creative thinking and the application of technology to create customer benefits; persistence to overcome seemingly impossible challenges; the importance of people; and long term relationships.

Promotion

Retail communications focus on what's in it for motorists on a day-to-day level, and why they should choose Shell. Enhanced mobility has always been at the heart of its retail business and Shell believes that it is how things move that makes the difference, with a fundamental customer commitment: 'Shell fuels are made to move people.'

In 2007, Shell launched a fuel economy initiative in 11 countries. It goes beyond the traditional 'tell approach' of conventional advertising, actively involving drivers in seeing how they can achieve fuel economy with Shell products through its educational and training programme. It builds on the 2006 Guinness World Record achievement for fuel efficiency and extends to a global promotion to win free fuel. It aims to help motorists to save 10 per cent or more fuel while driving, by a combination of Shell Fuel Economy diesel or mogas and by following the Fuel Stretch tips developed by Shell. As part of a global study into fuel economy it is also asking professional drivers in several countries to show what fuel savings can be achieved while pursuing their everyday work. It will cover four continents and will include the expansion of availability of the Shell fuel economy formula in gasoline and diesel fuels.

The long term relationship with Ferrari is celebrated with the consumer through collector card promotions, and in some

countries through Ferrari model car promotions. These are supported with PR initiatives topped off with a TV ad featuring different Ferrari Formula One cars from 1952-2007, undertaking a 'dream circuit' around the world fuelled by Shell V-Power.

Human Resources communications focus on the innovative technologies, the creative problem-solving and the solutions delivered by Shell people. Genuine, factual stories celebrate the breadth of thinking found at Shell, and actively encourage target audiences to react to the advertising message – 'ideas people wanted'.

Brand Values

Shell aims to be positive about the benefits of energy, guided by creative thinking and persistent in problem-solving to secure a responsible energy future.

www.shell.com

Things you didn't know about Shell

Shell's retail network serves millions of customers every day, from more than 45,000 service stations, in more than 90 countries and territories.

Approximately 2.5 per cent of the world's oil and around three per cent of the world's gas is produced by Shell companies.

The Shell emblem was first registered as a trademark in 1901, when it resembled a mussel shell. The current stylised scallop shape was created in 1971 by Raymond Loewy and since then only minor updates to the colours have been made.

(Silver Cross logo)

Silver Cross is passionate about offering parents the highest levels of quality, baby comfort and safety with chic, contemporary design. A great British brand celebrating 130 years of heritage, Silver Cross now operates distribution channels in China, Australia, America, Canada and Europe, offering not only fashionably designed wheeled goods, but also making its mark in the home with the launch of its Home Collection.

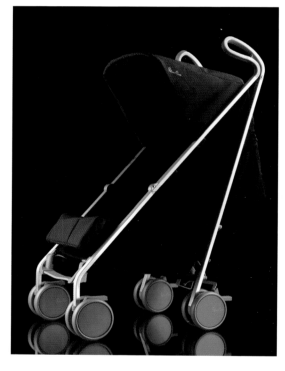

Market

The UK baby market, which is defined as households with babies and children under the age of four years old, is currently worth £916.6 million (Source: The Grocer, year to November 2006).

Already a world leader in the design, development and production of high-quality prams and pushchairs, in the next five years Silver Cross is aiming for an increased share in sales of all nursery products in both its domestic and international markets. Indeed, the particular focus for Silver Cross in 2007/08 will be to offer new parents across the globe a truly international selection of quality nursery products.

Achievements

Silver Cross's leading British design and high manufacturing quality has been put through its paces by parents across the country in 2006 and 2007. The brand's Lifestyle range has won 16 high profile parenting magazine awards in just one year, which stands as proof of what parents really think about Silver Cross.

The brand's recent global expansion has come as a result of global demand for its quality goods. The growing recognition across the globe of this British brand, based in North Yorkshire, has been aided by the popularity of its products in the UK, while celebrity endorsement has also been a key driver in launching Silver Cross worldwide.

Silver Cross's strong celebrity following now includes Heidi Klum, Maggie Gyllenhall, Rachel Hunter, Britney Spears, Gwyneth Paltrow, Sarah Jessica-Parker, Kate Hudson, Courteney Cox, Penny Lancaster, Jennifer Garner, Angelina Jolie, Liz Hurley and of course the British Royal Family.

1877
Silver Cross is founded by William Wilson, a prolific inventor of baby carriages who built a reputation for producing the world's finest carriages.

1920s/30s
Silver Cross is crowned the number one baby carriage for royals, supplying its first baby carriage to George VI and Queen Elizabeth, The Queen Mother.

1951
Silver Cross launches a new pram body shape; the forefather of the iconic Balmoral, now synonymous with the name 'pram'.

1977
Silver Cross celebrates its centenary by flying customers and buyers around the world in its new centenary aircraft, and by presenting a baby carriage to Princess Anne.

Product

Silver Cross products are all created by in-house designers and product development specialists in the UK to make mums' and dads' lives as simple as possible. Along with new products launched in 2007, the Silver Cross brand is famous for its Lifestyle and Heritage Collections.

The Lifestyle Collection was launched in 2003 with the Classic Sleepover and now in 2007 the range includes: the highly acclaimed 3D, which is a fully lie-flat luxuriously lined pram, stroller and travel system in one; an updated Classic Sleepover which has received worldwide acclaim – it comprises a pram, pushchair and carrycot; the Linear Freeway, which is the sleekest, lightest, combination pushchair Silver Cross has ever made; and the S4, a three-wheeler that has been designed with a double-swivel front wheel for extra stability and manoeuvrability for urban living. The Collection also includes four car seats: the multi-award winning Ventura Infant Carrier; the Explorer Sport, a two-stage car seat that grows with your child with a unique seatbelt adjustment system; the Explorofix, using a push click ISOFIX installation; and the Navigator, a group 2-3 car seat.

The Heritage Collection includes two traditional iconic Silver Cross coach-style prams for newborns. The Balmoral has star status with many celebrities wanting a pram that is highly favoured by the British Royal Family, while the Kensington, defined by a sweeping, curved, hand-painted steel body and highly polished chrome chassis, is a practical classic with a detachable body and wheels as well as fully folding chassis. Today the handmade coach prams are still made to the same high standards employed in the early 19th century.

The Silver Cross children's toy range includes The Oberon, a carriage-built doll's pram designed as a miniature version of the Balmoral.

Recent Developments

In 2007, Silver Cross has taken the opportunity to celebrate its 130 years in the business by launching a range of new products. Spearheading this activity is the combination stroller, Dazzle, which is ultra-lightweight and minimalist by design. Created to satisfy the most über-stylish city mums, it was researched on the streets of the world's style capitals: London, Paris, Tokyo and New York.

Silver Cross has also launched a home collection in 2007, which includes two highchairs, a toddler's booster seat and a combined bathing and changing station. Not only is this a major move forward for Silver Cross, but the brand has also exclusively partnered with Microban™ to build its antibacterial protection properties into all home products, setting an industry benchmark for safety and hygiene standards.

These new products are a long way from the traditional image the brand used to conjure up. While still incredibly proud of its heritage, Silver Cross also strives to provide top quality wheeled and home goods designed with the 21st century parent in mind.

Promotion

The Silver Cross global communication strategy is designed to maximise brand potential and to drive profitability. It is built on four key principles: ensuring the customer is central to decision making; producing high quality, fashionable and innovative British product designs; delivering consistency; and constantly strengthening and widening the appeal of the brand.

The Silver Cross global marketing strategy will see further investment into consumer advertising in lifestyle and parenting titles, a strong presence at international trade and consumer events, point of sale promotion within stores, and online promotion. A new website is launching in summer 2007, aimed at building valued online relationships, while substantial investment is planned in advertising, promotions and building strong customer experiences in 2008 and beyond. Silver Cross aims to communicate in a straightforward, frank and honest way about its products. It is passionate

about parenting and aims to make it an even more enjoyable experience. Indeed, Silver Cross's strongest marketing communication tool has always been word of mouth. From trendsetters in the film and music world to British mums on the street, the brand is endorsed by those who have first-hand experience of Silver Cross products.

Brand Values

Silver Cross is one of the UK's most established brands. In 2007, 130 years after its launch, Silver Cross still stands for elegance, fashion and cutting-edge British design. It is known worldwide for its experience and passion in producing stylish and innovative products that deliver genuine value for money while meeting the needs of modern parents.

www.silvercross.co.uk

Things you didn't know about Silver Cross

Founded in 1877, Silver Cross is the oldest nursery brand in the UK.

Over 1,000 individual hand operations are required to make a Balmoral pram.

Silver Cross prams have been the choice of royalty for nearly 100 years.

During World War II the Silver Cross factory was requisitioned by the air ministry to manufacture aircraft machine parts. This experience was later applied to production methods, revolutionising pram design from the traditional plywood into aluminium.

Silver Cross sells prams in more than 20 countries worldwide.

1988	2002	2006	2007
The Wayfarer is launched, later becoming Britain's best-selling pushchair for a decade, selling over 3,000 a week.	Entrepreneur and businessman Alan Halsall purchases Silver Cross and relaunches the famous Balmoral at Harrods.	Silver Cross goes global, forging partnerships with distributors in Europe, America, Canada and Japan.	Silver Cross launches its Home Collection and the combination stroller, Dazzle.

In 1989 there were four terrestrial TV channels in the UK. Sky challenged that and gave Britain choice. Today, Sky's about quality TV, superfast broadband and value phonecalls. Sky's in 8.5 million homes in the UK. A third of families choose Sky for the latest, most talked about shows, ways to watch that fit around their lives and the contribution it makes to big issues like learning and the environment.

Market

It's not just about broadcasting anymore. Telecommunications and entertainment are converging, and consumption patterns are changing. It's a two-way thing now. Entertainment goes beyond TV. It's the internet. It's people exploring, communicating, expressing themselves through digital media. It's MySpace, YouTube, Facebook. It's video on-demand. Mobile TV. Hungry for bandwidth with everything digital on tap.

People want more value, choice, flexibility and quality. So Sky looks for newer, better ways to enrich people's lives with quality entertainment and high-speed communications.

Achievements

Sky has set industry standards, broken records, won awards and brought a new world of entertainment and communications to millions. Its achievements aren't just about shaking up the entertainment industry, and giving people choice, aiming to constantly innovate.

Sky is a challenger brand and the UK's first major media company, as well as being the second company in the FTSE 100 to go carbon neutral. Sky helps consumers reduce the energy they use, with its new Sky+ and Sky HD boxes that power down when not in use.

Sky was the first broadcaster to offer audio description for blind and visually impaired people as standard. Furthermore, Sky is the only broadcaster to offer a remote control that makes life easier for people with manual dexterity problems.

Sky has also pioneered ways for parents to control the programmes their children watch.

Sky aims to help students get A-grades with Sky Learning by bringing the national curriculum to life, on-screen.

Sky pioneered Sky+ technology which can pause, rewind and replay live TV. Since then it has become the UK's first mass market PVR. One in four Sky TV customers now have Sky+.

Sky HD offers the UK's broadest range of high definition content including sport, movies, drama,

documentaries and entertainment. Meanwhile, Sky Sports secured the first deal to screen the Premiership, and it's the UK's most popular sports service, screening almost every sport you can play.

1989

Only four channels exist in the UK. Sky changes all that.

In the same year, Sky launches the UK's first 24:7 news service.

1990

Sky brings the Simpsons to Britain.

1998

Sky becomes the first TV company in the UK to go digital.

2001

Sky launches Sky+, its multi award winning PVR.

2005

Sky launches Britain's first commercial mobile TV channels.

Sky reaches eight million homes.

2006

Sky launches HD, broadband and telephony.

Sky's on demand TV service Sky Anytime is also launched.

Sky's programming is also award winning. Its two part TV series of Terry Pratchett's 'Hogfather' won a double BAFTA. And Sky News was again named RTS Channel of the Year.

Product

Sky offers TV, broadband and phone services.

Sky TV has six entertainment mixes (different groups of channels). These mixes focus on certain types of programmes (Kids, Music, Style and Culture, Knowledge and Variety) so Sky customers can choose the mixes they like. On top of that, customers can add Sky Sports and Sky Movies, and watch the most up-to-date entertainment.

Sky believes entertainment should fit around peoples lives and not vice vera. That's why Sky's award-winning personal video recorder, Sky+, stores hours of TV. It lets people pause, rewind and replay live TV, and record an entire series at the touch of a button. Furthermore, RemoteRecord allows Sky+ boxes to be set to record using a text message so customers don't need to be at home to record a programme.

Sky Anytime is Sky's on-demand service. It gives customers what they want to watch, when they want it on a PC, TV or mobile. Sky HD offers four times more picture clarity and with a compatible home cinema system, Dolby Digital surround sound on many programmes.

Sky Broadband is offered to Sky TV customers as part of Sky's invitation to 'upload, download and save loads'.

Sky Talk, the third key element of Sky, offers great value packages for Sky TV customers for as long as they want, on calls to landlines in evenings and at weekends.

Recent Developments

In the last 18 months, Sky has completely changed its business. It has broadened into digital entertainment and communications, to offer broadband, telecoms and TV on the move. In early 2007, Sky was Britain's fastest growing broadband provider.

Promotion

The 2007 See Surf Speak campaign was the first time Sky offered TV, broadband and phone at 'one great price', and that was the message. It produced the highest number of new customers for six years. Around 340,000 new people joined Sky from January to March, and a record number of existing customers (1.2 million) upgraded or bought new products.

Brand Values

An irrepressible spirit runs through Sky, aiming to challenge the status quo and to make things better for everyone.

Sky aims to be tuned-in to people and their lives. Inviting people in, making them feel at home, keeping things simple.

Most of all Sky is about fun, providing more ways than ever to entertain, connect and experience the world.

www.sky.com

Things you didn't know about Sky

Jeremy Clarkson said Sky+ is the single best invention for the last 20 years. Porsche, eat your heart out.

Sky screens over 4,000 hours of High Definition TV a month.

Sky Sports has screened over 1,000 live premiership matches.

Sky produces the sports magazine with the largest circulation in the world.

The first person in Britain to win £1 million on live TV was Tony Jones, on Sky Sports' Poker Million, just 24 hours before Judith Keppel won the top prize on ITV's 'Who Wants To Be A Millionaire?'.

Emily Bell said that when she and her fellow journalists are following breaking news, nine times out of 10, she switches onto Sky News.

2007

Also in 2006, Sky becomes the first major media company and the second FTSE 100 company to go carbon neutral.

Sky's See Speak Surf campaign is launched.

SONY®

Sony manufactures audio, visual, video, communications and information technology products for the global consumer and professional markets. With its music, pictures, game and online businesses, Sony is uniquely positioned to be one of the world's leading digital entertainment consumer brands. Sony's unique marriage of content and technology enables the company to understand consumer desires and the technologies which unite them.

Market

The UK market for consumer electronics comprises TVs, DVD players, audio products, computers, cameras and camcorders. Sony is the number one consumer electronics brand in the buoyant UK market with an overall AV/IT value share of 14.1 per cent, year ending March 2007 (Source: GfK).

Sony is a market leader in the march towards High Definition (HD). Having launched a raft of HD products over the past few years Sony is the only company that provides complete, end-to-end solutions from professional recording equipment to BRAVIA LCD TVs for today's HD World. Customers can create, edit, store and share in High Definition. In the UK, the HD-ready LCD TV market is worth £2 billion, with Sony, as market leader, taking a 24.3 per cent value share of this for the year ending March 2007 (Source: GfK). The HD camcorder market is also booming, with a market value of £12 million, and with Sony taking an 88.6 per cent value share for the year ending March 2007 (Source: GfK).

Achievements

The product that launched Sony as a consumer brand was the WALKMAN. Released in 1979, it quickly became Sony's most famous product. First described as a

'small stereo headphone cassette player', the WALKMAN introduced the concept of mobile entertainment. Sony sold 1.5 million WALKMAN players in its first two years on the market. The WALKMAN brand has evolved to offer a variety of hard disk drive and flash MP3 devices including the new WALKMAN Video player.

Product

Sony's consumer product portfolio includes more than 5,000 products, organised around a brand portfolio which includes WALKMAN personal audio, BRAVIA LCD televisions, VAIO notebook and desktop PCs, Handycam

camcorders and Cyber-shot digital cameras.

The launch of HD broadcast has been key for Sony's product portfolio, from the professional HD recording equipment, through to its BRAVIA HD-ready TVs, as consumers begin to realise the viewing benefits provided by High Definition. Sony has made two major developments in this area.

Sony entered an agreement with Sky to raise awareness of HD TV and to support Sky's launch package of HD channels, including sports, movies, entertainment, documentary and arts. The marketing campaign encompassed national advertising, direct marketing, experiential demonstrations

1946	1950	1968	1979	1990	1995
Tokyo Tsushin Kogyo K.K. – later to become Sony Corporation – is established with start-up capital of 190,000 yen.	Japan's first magnetic tape recorder, the 'G-Type', launches.	Sony launches the Trinitron colour TV.	The first personal headphone stereo – the 'WALKMAN' – is launched.	An HD-ready, widescreen, 36 inch television for home-use is launched.	Sony launches the Digital Handycam, the first consumer-use digital video camcorder.

and press and radio promotions. The two companies have promoted each other's products in their marketing activity and offered customers savings when they buy a Sony HD TV set and a Sky HD box together.

Sony's second major HD development is the addition of the Blu-ray format, set to become the storage medium for the High Definition era. Capable of storing 25GB on a single layer, one Blu-ray Disc can store the equivalent of five DVDs. Sony launched the world's first Blu-ray notebook under its VAIO brand in May 2006. Further Sony Blu-ray launches include DVD drives and DVD players. Elsewhere in the Sony Group of companies, PlayStation has bolstered the Blu-ray Disc message with the hugely successful launch of PlayStation 3 translating into one million Blu-ray players being installed in European households as of the first week of June.

Recent Developments

Responding to rapidly growing demand throughout Europe, March 2007 saw Sony reveal the latest addition to the Blu-ray Disc family, which previously included HD gaming and editing. Sony has now added the HD home theatre experience. Positioned as the ultimate cinema experience, the aluminium and glass BDP-S1E integrates with Sony's BRAVIA theatre concept and enables film lovers to watch films at 24 frames per second – just as the director first intended them.

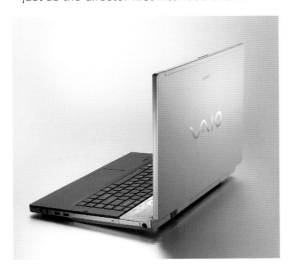

Also new for spring 2007 are additions to Sony's range of camcorders. Firstly, Sony's HDR-CX6EK, the world's lightest, smallest 1080i HD camcorder and Sony's first camcorder that harnesses the convenience of a removable Memory Stick for storing and sharing home movies. Secondly, available from June 2007 are the new AVCHD HDD Handycam models SR5E, SR7E and SR8E, offering up to 38 hours of recording time.

Promotion

In 2006 Sony became an official partner of the UEFA Champions League. This exclusive three year deal will make Sony the only consumer electronics and mobile hardware sponsor of the League. The aim is to create a link between the grandeur and excitement of the ultimate football club competition with the Sony brand. Comprehensive integrated marketing communications including advertising, public relations, promotions, online activity and in-store activity will support the sponsorship. This campaign will show how Sony products can enhance the entertainment experience of football.

In 2007 Sony Corporation announced the signing of a global partnership programme with FIFA from 2007 to 2014.

As a reflection of its BRAVIA TV's ability to recreate true-to-life colours, Sony built on its 2005 'Balls' launch campaign for its market-leading range of HD BRAVIA LCD TVs. The 'Paint' commercial, aired in 2006, used 70,000 litres of paint fired onto a disused tower block in Glasgow, Scotland, and was created by Jonathan Glazer, whose past credits include creating videos for bands such as Massive Attack and Radiohead and brands including Stella Artois and Guinness. Like the 'Balls' ad, the 'Paint' commercial was captured on screen to represent the strapline; 'Colour like no other'.

In the UK, Sony invests more than £40 million per year in the marketing support of its brands, using a mixture of television, cinema, specialist and consumer magazine press advertising, PR and sponsorship.

Brand Values

Sony designs its products with two goals in mind: to add spice to consumers' lives and to make their ecological footprint smaller. From manufacturing and product use to product recycling, environmental responsibility touches everything Sony does. It is committed to being a responsible organisation and has developed a worldwide strategy to reduce the ecological footprint created by the manufacture and use of its products. In February 2007 Sony was awarded a Sustainable Energy Europe Award; this is the first time a consumer electronics entertainment company has ever been given this prestigious recognition by the European Commission.

This ecological commitment is demonstrated in its latest range of devices, which are drastically reducing energy consumption thanks to several improvements in design, circuitry and components. The new DVD players, for example, now consume less than 0.1 watts in standby mode, whilst the latest BRAVIA models have some of the lowest energy consumption levels in standby mode on the market, below one watt with most being 0.3 watts.

www.sony.co.uk

Things you didn't know about Sony

The award-winning 2005 BRAVIA 'Balls' TV advert featured 250,000 multi-coloured balls bouncing down a San Francisco street. There were no computer graphics used to enhance this advert.

In December 2003, Sony successfully created QRIO – the world's first running humanoid robot.

The company name 'Sony' was created by combining two words: 'sonus', the Latin root of the words 'sound' and 'sonic'; and 'sonny', meaning little son. The words were used to show that 'Sony' represented a very small group of young people who had the energy and passion for unlimited creation.

Sony's first-ever product was a rice cooker.

2000

Sony launches the first 'CLIE' personal entertainment organiser.

2003

The first 'QUALIA' products are launched.

2006

Sony Corporation celebrates its 60th anniversary.

2007

Sony introduces a full line of Blu-ray Disc products to the European Market.

Specsavers Opticians is the largest privately owned opticians in the world and one of the UK's most successful retailers (Source: Retail Week 2005). Nearly one in three people who wear glasses in the UK buy them from Specsavers. Run by husband and wife founders Doug and Mary Perkins, Specsavers is also a success abroad, where it has 270 stores in Europe, plus a rapidly expanding supply chain in Australia.

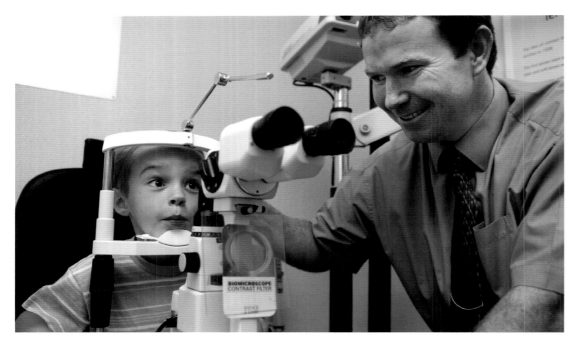

which were through the NHS. A further 252,000 eye examinations were conducted in Republic of Ireland stores and 14,000 in the Channel Islands where there is no NHS.

Much of Specsavers' success can be attributed to its joint venture concept. Stores are owned and run by more than 1,000 optician joint venture or franchise partners, while a full range of support services, from accounting to marketing, are provided by a team of professionals, freeing the optician to do what he does best – provide the highest quality customer service.

Achieving exacting standards in a high volume business requires state-of-the-art operations, so Specsavers has invested heavily in new systems and equipment to ensure that its supply chain partners attain world-class standards.

Market

The current UK market for eyecare products and services is estimated at more than £2 billion, with less than 40 per cent still being provided by small independent opticians (Source: Mintel February 2006). Specsavers currently has a 29 per cent share of the total market – three times that of its nearest competitor Dollond & Aitchison (Source: GfK December 2006).

While most opticians suffered a decline in turnover in 2005 as the number of eye examinations dropped and consumers deferred buying their glasses (Source: Mintel February 2006), this did not affect Specsavers, which continues to expand, celebrating

record like-for-like increases in 2007 and record sales of £16 million in one week.

Expansion in Europe, where Specsavers is one of the few British retail success stories, continues to be brisk with a move into Finland and more stores opening in Spain.

Achievements

Specsavers turnover reached a record £891 million in 2006/07 across all markets. In the UK, more than £8.1 million was invested in 25 new optical stores, creating 400 new jobs. Specsavers now employs nearly 16,000 people throughout the business.

The optical company performed 5.1 million eye tests in the UK in 2006, 65 per cent of

Product

Specsavers Opticians has maintained the Perkins' philosophy of providing affordable, fashionable eyecare for everyone. The company keeps its prices low but does not stint on quality, investing in new technology and continuing to scour the world for fashionable frames to suit all ages.

Specsavers offers the customer more than 2,000 styles to choose from, including several designer brand names, such as Tommy Hilfiger, fcuk, Red or Dead, Roxy, Quiksilver, Bench and its own best-selling designer range Osiris. Furthermore, it is soon to add an exclusive range by Jasper Conran to its collection.

1984	1997	1999	2002	2004	2007
Specsavers Optical Group is founded by Doug and Mary Perkins, who open the first Specsavers Opticians in Guernsey, Bristol, Bath, Plymouth and Swansea.	The first overseas Specsavers Opticians opens in Haarlem, Holland followed by Breda and Gouda in 1998.	With 350 UK stores, Specsavers opens its flagship store in London's Tottenham Court Road.	Specsavers expands into hearing, acquiring the Midlands based Hearcare chain.	Specsavers celebrates 20 years of business and record profits with expansions into Sweden, Norway and Denmark as well as the opening of the 500th store in the UK.	The retailer establishes a new product supply chain in Australia and expands into Finland while celebrating record sales with turnover of £891 million for the financial year 2006/07.

All Specsavers glasses now include Pentax lenses as standard and pricing is kept as simple and clear as possible so there are no hidden extras, proving that high quality and low price can go hand in hand. Specsavers also offers a store voucher for employers, meaning companies can now offer their staff more affordable corporate eyecare.

The largest retail provider of home delivery contact lenses in Europe and one of the top two retailers of continuous wear lenses in the world (Source: VisionTrak September 2005), Specsavers was one of the first optical retailers to introduce a direct debit scheme for contact lens wearers. Its own-brand easyvision lenses include daily disposables, monthly disposables and continuous wear lenses, which can be worn for up to 30 days and nights without removal.

Recent Developments

Specsavers is bringing its core offers to its rapidly expanding hearing service, which is now doing for hearing what the retailer has already achieved in optics – dramatically reducing prices and waiting times and making audiology services more accessible for everyone. Specsavers is already the largest retail dispenser of digital hearing aids in the UK and will offer a hearing service from more than 300 locations by the end of 2007. In 2006, the company won a Marketing Society Award for Marketing Excellence (in the Brand Extension category) for its hearing business.

The future continues to look bright for Specsavers' core optical business: a new store opens somewhere in the UK or Europe every week and turnover is anticipated to exceed a billion pounds well before the end of the decade, when the company expects to have more than 1,000 stores worldwide.

Promotion

Specsavers' marketing has helped to revolutionise the optical market with its Two for One promotion and Clear Price policy that other opticians have struggled to replicate.

Freedom to choose
Contact lens free trial

Indeed, Specsavers has been the largest advertiser in the optician sector for many years, with a total gross spend of more than £25 million to promote its special offers and build its brand.

The company's 'Should've gone to Specsavers' campaign was the first to win Retail Week's Marketing Campaign of the Year Award two years running and the phrase has been adopted by the nation. Its sponsorship of football and rugby referees has also attracted much support as it reflects a sense of humour appreciated by consumers.

Specsavers also runs an annual 'Spectacle Wearer of the Year' competition to find the UK's sexiest specs wearers and the nation's favourite specs-wearing celebrities.

The company also respects its duty of care to inform people when their next eye examination is due, which is done through more than 350,000 letters to customers each week.

Its in-store magazine View – published three times a year – is available free of charge in all stores and is mailed out to 600,000 customers.

Brand Values

Specsavers is still very much a family run business with family values to match, and over the past few years, the company has donated more than £1 million to various charities. Recipients include Guide Dogs, Deafness Research UK, Fight for Sight and Vision Aid Overseas, for whom stores collect and recycle unwanted glasses to send to the developing world.

Every two years the company also nominates a national eyecare charity to support – their current relationship is with Diabetes UK for whom they are raising £100,000 to fund vital research and raise awareness of diabetic retinopathy.

www.specsavers.com

Things you didn't know about Specsavers Opticians

Specsavers carries out more than five million eye examinations each year in the UK – more than a quarter of all the sight tests carried out in Britain (Source: Mintel).

7.4 million frames and 15 million Pentax branded lenses were sold during 2006.

Specsavers sells a pair of glasses every six seconds.

If all the glasses Specsavers have ever sold were laid end to end they would wrap around the world three times.

STANLEY®

MAKE SOMETHING GREAT™

The Stanley brand is well positioned to meet tomorrow's competitive challenges and is committed to being a leading worldwide manufacturer and marketer. The company's vision is to be the world's number one branded tool and tool storage supplier and to develop its high-growth security systems business. Stanley has moved effectively to expand its products into market areas such as the Far East and Eastern Europe.

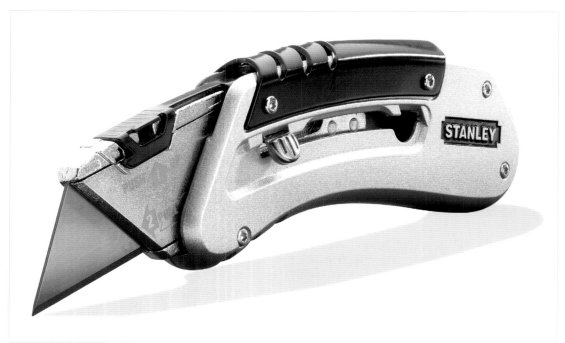

Market

Stanley is a worldwide manufacturer and marketer of tools, hardware and speciality hardware products for home improvement, consumer, industrial and professional use. The company still bears not only founder Frederick Stanley's name but also the spirit and passion which drove him to succeed where others have failed.

The brand name is known around the world as a reliable guarantee of quality and value. Stanley currently holds the number one brand position in hand tools with an estimated 27 per cent market share in the UK (Source: GfK).

Achievements

Stanley is one of the world's oldest tool manufacturers and has a history of receiving awards. For example, Stanley received what may have been the very first patent issued for ergonomic tools and since then has had numerous firsts, including various new product designs. In addition, in both 2000 and 2001 it gained the Prestigious Golden Hammer Award, presented for New Product Innovation.

In 2006, Stanley was awarded Product of the Year, for its Quickslide utility knife by members of the Hardware & Garden Retailers Association (HGRA) as well as 2006 Supplier

of the Year by leading industrial tool supplier, BuckHickman InOne. Furthermore, in 2007, Stanley won the competitive tool category in the 2007 CFJ/CFA Flooring Industry Awards.

Stanley and its employees support thousands of local and global causes and pledges to continue its legacy of charitable responsibility. For example, in the US Stanley has helped to build hundreds of affordable homes in partnership with Habitat for Humanity. In addition, Stanley has partnered with the US SkillsUSA organisation, instilling technical skills and leadership development in more than a quarter of a million high school and college students every year. For the past

1843

The Stanley works is founded by Frederick T Stanley as a bolt and door hardware manufacturing company in Connecticut, USA.

1857

Frederick's cousin, Henry Stanley, establishes The Stanley Rule and Level Company.

1902

Stanley makes its first exports.

1920s

The Rule and Level Company merges with The Stanley Works in 1920 and goes on to become its famous Hand Tools Division. In 1926 the first overseas location is established for Stanley in Germany.

two years, Stanley has been the single largest sponsor of SkillsUSA and has helped to develop new programmes to energize and excite the youth of America about their future.

Product

As a world leader in the design, development and delivery of tools, Stanley aims to bring to market the strongest and most innovative tools available. With thousands of products on the market and hundreds more introduced each year, Stanley aims to develop the tools people need to get the job done. Since 1857, Stanley has produced some of the most innovative tools ever made. Among these tools are the renowned Stanley knife, Powerlock tape rule, the Bailey plane, the Surform shaper and most recently the FatMax line of products including FatMax anti-vibe hammers.

In the autumn of 2006 Stanley introduced its most innovative tool range to date, FatMax XL. This product responds to the needs of professional users and the demands of today's construction methods and materials. As a result, these are not only the toughest, most durable hand tools available on the market today but they have also turned some traditional thinking on its head; for example, the FatMax XL screwdriver becomes a Demolition Driver, the FatMax XL tape reaches new levels of strength and stand out, whilst a new type of hand tool makes its debut – the Functional Utility Bar, or FuBar for short.

This investment in new product development will continue throughout 2007, with the introduction of over 350 new products

in all major hand tool categories, including wood chisels, clamping, screwdrivers and new introductions to the FatMax XL range.

Stanley's Industrial Tools Group also manufactures big tools for big jobs such as industrial hand tools, professional and industrial mechanics' tools, electronic diagnostic tools, pneumatic fastening tools and fasteners, hydraulic tools, shearers, breakers and crushers. Recognised as leaders in industrial tools, Stanley's products are used to build everything from cars and trucks to roofs and floors.

Recent Developments

In January 2006, Stanley announced that it had completed the acquisition of Facom and Britool from Fimalac for 410 million euros. The acquisition brings together two leading European suppliers of tools with complementary brands and products; Facom and Britool will strengthen Stanley's offerings of high-end industrial and automotive tools.

Promotion

Stanley Tools has committed to investing in a multi-million pound marketing campaign to support its new product ranges. In particular, emphasis will be placed on continuing to extensively support the launch of the new FatMax XL range.

The fully integrated media campaign will introduce a new harder hitting look and tone for the brand and will see Stanley back on TV screens for the first time in over 10 years, as well as advertising within key trade and

consumer media titles. A continuous programme of PR activity throughout the year will also be supported with a series of outdoor events, which will include on-site demonstrations, allowing customers to experience the benefits first hand, and a series of 'ambient' events scheduled throughout the summer of 2007.

Brand Values

Stanley tools are designed and built for the professional and those who think like professionals.

Innovation has always been important to Stanley ever since the company was founded over 160 years ago. Furthermore, the brand has gained a reputation for excellence and so continually tests, designs and improves its products to ensure quality and maximum functionality.

This is summed up in the brand's strapline; Stanley – make something great.

www.stanleyworks.co.uk

1937
Stanley enters the UK market via the acquisition of J A Chapman.

1966
Stanley is first listed on the New York Stock Exchange.

1980s/90s
Stanley acquires MAC Tools, Proto and Bostitch in the 1980s, followed by Goldblatt and ZAG Industries in the 1990s.

2006
After acquiring Blick and CST Berger in 2000, Stanley acquires Facom.

The Daily Telegraph

The Daily Telegraph, established in 1855, is the UK's biggest selling quality newspaper, with an audited circulation of circa 900,000 (Source: ABC, average daily circulation November 2006 – April 2007). Having maintained its broadsheet format, the newspaper offers home and international news coverage, a stand-alone business section which is highly respected in the city, and a compact daily sport section, full of world-class opinion.

Market

The UK's quality daily newspaper market comprises The Daily Telegraph, The Times, The Guardian and The Independent which together account for 2.1 million copies per day (Source: ABC Monday – Saturday average April 2007).

The Daily Telegraph is the market leader with 42 per cent share, 269,000 copies ahead of The Times.

Achievement

The Daily Telegraph has received many recent awards including Best Newspaper Sport Coverage from the Sports Industry Awards in March 2007; Jan Moir was awarded as Best Interviewer by the British Press Awards in 2007; while Matt Pritchett won Cartoonist of the Year for his 'Matt' cartoon at the What the Papers Say 50th Anniversary Awards in December 2006. Furthermore, The Daily Telegraph was found to be the leading newspaper for reporting wars around the world by the International Committee of the Red Cross in December 2006; The Daily Telegraph front page was voted front page of the century by viewers of Newsnight for coverage of the September 11th attacks as part of its 'Big-Read-All-About-It' initiative in May 2006.

Product

The Daily Telegraph is known for its outstanding line-up of distinguished journalists and columnists, who lend the paper its distinctive voice and personality. Delivering lively and challenging comment with wit, insight and rigour, The Daily Telegraph boasts such unique contributors as Boris Johnson, Craig Brown, and WF Deedes, columnist and former editor who first joined The Daily Telegraph in 1937. Its sport team includes the football writer Henry Winter, as well as numerous sporting luminaries such as Alan Hansen, Brian Moore, Zara Phillips and James Cracknell. The Daily Telegraph business section is famous for its accurate, bold and insightful coverage, provided by an award-winning team of journalists including the business editor-at-large Jeff Randall.

Fashion director, Hilary Alexander, is a stalwart of the front row and brings her flair and experience to the fashion pages both in the newspaper and now online at Telegraph.co.uk, where her video reports from fashion's most glamorous shows have become must-see viewing.

The Daily Telegraph has been home to the Matt cartoon since 1988, the creation of the award-winning cartoonist Matt Pritchett. One of the most popular features of the business section is its Alex cartoon. Held in great affection within the business community, Alex comments on the wheeling and dealing of the business world, winning awards and accolades for his creators.

September 2006 saw a design revamp of The Daily Telegraph on Saturday, including a new technology section, The Digital Life. Other sections include: Motoring, which features James May's column and advice from Honest John; Weekend, which features

1855

The first Daily Telegraph & Courier is published, having been founded as a vehicle for its proprietor, Colonel Sleigh, to wage a vendetta against the Duke of Cambridge and his conduct in the Crimea War.

1897

A young Winston Churchill reports from the North West Frontier for the Telegraph.

1987

The Telegraph moves from Fleet Street to the Isle of Dogs then moves to Canary Wharf five years later.

1994

The Electronic Telegraph becomes the first British paper to launch on the internet.

2004

The Barclay Brothers buy The Telegraph Group.

2006

The Group rebrands as Telegraph Media Group and moves from Canary Wharf into state-of-the-art offices on Buckingham Palace Road, London.

Graham Norton and Ruby Wax's outspoken advice column; and the award-winning Telegraph Magazine.

Recent Developments

In 2006, the Telegraph Media Group embarked on a momentous shift in the way news is published. Where previously stories were broken in the newspaper and subsequently posted online, stories are now reported as they happen and published across several platforms. In order to provide the state-of-the-art newsroom required for this new approach, the Telegraph moved to new offices in central London. It now occupies one of the biggest open office spaces in Europe, accommodating the new 'hub and spoke' editorial system.

This move also reflects the Telegraph's commitment to offering its customers quality news content when – and how – they want it. Since launching its daily podcast in November 2005 – the first newspaper to do so – the Telegraph has constantly innovated in bringing new features to its readers in the digital environment. Telegraph Talk and Telegraph TV provide quality broadcast content at Telegraph.co.uk, with recent highlights including Simon Hughes' video reports from the Ashes series in Australia, and Rory Bremner's 'Real Budget Speech', created to mark Gordon Brown's last Budget and exclusive to Telegraph TV.

Telegraph TV also produces 'The Business Show', a programme broadcast online at Telegraph.co.uk every weekday. Anchored by the Telegraph Business editors, this is a topical review of the day's business stories with comment, analysis and guest commentators.

As Telegraph.co.uk continues to bring new audiences to the Telegraph portfolio, so a

constant programme of product development is helping to build distinct communities of interest on the website.

May 2007 saw the launch of the brand's online channel dedicated to environmental issues – Telegraph.co.uk/earth. The channel aims to provide an informed view of key issues alongside tips and advice for readers on how to make environmentally sound life choices.

The new MyTelegraph online blogging community sees users of Telegraph.co.uk creating their own blogs, posting their views and contributing to a varied array of online discussions.

Meanwhile, TelegraphPM – a 10 page up-to-the-minute summary of the day's news, business and sport – was launched in Autumn 2006. It is published online at 4pm every day and can be read on-screen or printed off for the journey home.

Promotion

The brand positioning for The Daily Telegraph is Time:Better:Spent, which reflects the ambition of the Telegraph to offer rewarding experiences to its readers, however they consume its content. In today's busy world, time spent reading the Telegraph, visiting the website, participating in a promotion, or attending a reader event, is 'time better spent'.

The Daily Telegraph has initiated partnerships with many brands to provide rewarding experiences. Recent collaborations in the area of children's literature have produced highly successful cover-mount giveaways, including the works of Beatrix Potter, Roald Dahl and Dr Seuss. This commitment to children's reading is something the Telegraph continues to support; September sees The Daily Telegraph Bath Festival of Children's Literature staged for the first time.

The Daily Telegraph creates dedicated events for its customers, one highlight being a night of ballet at the Royal Opera House exclusively for Telegraph readers. Other events which the Telegraph has supported include Chelsea Flower Show, the BAFTA Awards, and the recent stage production of The Sound of Music.

The Daily Telegraph also has a long-established Junior Sports programme, which sees it supporting a variety of initiatives nationwide. In addition The Daily Telegraph is the official newspaper of the England cricket team, thanks to its partnership with the ECB, while each year thousands of readers and online users compete to manage the best team of the season in Telegraph Fantasy Football.

February 2007 saw a cross-platform advertising campaign to promote The Daily Telegraph's rugby coverage. Using the strapline 'We've got rugby's finest minds', the campaign featured three star writers – Brian Moore, Will Greenwood and Keith Wood – with their heads manipulated to resemble rugby balls. The campaign ran on

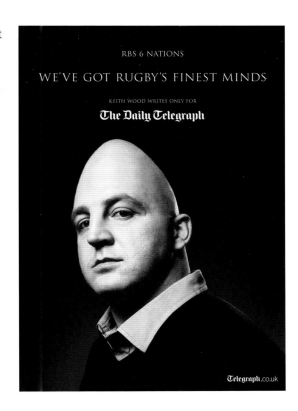

48 sheet poster sites and in pub washrooms within targeted areas.

In January 2007, Telegraph.co.uk ran its first stand-alone advertising campaign, announcing to consumers that it is 'Britain's No. 1 quality newspaper website', measured by the number of visits to the website. The campaign ran on 48 sheet posters on the rail network and escalator panels and tube card panels on London Underground.

In January 2007 The Daily Telegraph broke new ground by working with Google Maps to promote its Eat Out for £5 promotion. In March 2007, it ran an online campaign using rich media and video sharing sites such as YouTube to promote the exclusive 'Real Budget Speech' with Rory Bremner. Then in May 2007 it recreated The Daily Telegraph garden from the Chelsea Flower Show in the virtual world Second Life.

Brand Values

The Daily Telegraph brand values are defined as accuracy, honesty, integrity, quality and heritage.

www.telegraph.co.uk

Things you didn't know about The Daily Telegraph

In 1925 The Daily Telegraph became the first British newspaper to publish a daily crossword.

In 1887 The Telegraph hosted a party in Hyde Park for 30,000 school children to celebrate Queen Victoria's Golden Jubilee, which was attended by Her Majesty.

In 1899 a Telegraph Appeal for the Widows and Orphans Fund raised an astonishing £255,275.

Thomas Cook, named after its eponymous founder, first took Britons away from home in 1841 and invented the first-ever overseas package holiday in 1845. It has grown into one of the UK's best-known names in travel, operating 570 high street stores, a holidays division, TV channel and website plus Thomas Cook Airlines, Financial Services and Foreign Exchange. Three million people per year travel on a Thomas Cook holiday.

Market

The travel industry is a rapidly changing one. In the last 10 years tour operators have expanded into retail, retailers have expanded into tour operations and shopping online has come from nowhere to account for a quarter of all travel bookings.

There are four major tour operator companies in the UK – Thomas Cook, First Choice, Thomson and MyTravel. In addition there are the well-known online brands – lastminute.com, Expedia and Opodo as well as many other smaller retailers and tour operators.

The overall holiday market is growing, with the number of overseas holidays out of the UK reaching more than 50 million per year. Of these, package holidays make up around 20 million.

The travel industry is notoriously affected by many factors, from consumer debt and terrorism to weather conditions and sporting events. Thomas Cook, however, consistently outperforms the market during these difficult times and remains a much-trusted travel brand.

Achievements

Thomas Cook has proved itself to be a dynamic business in recent years. Since 2003 the company has annually reported record profits, with significant growth year-on-year. Since 2005 Thomas Cook has delivered a five per cent profit margin – considered the Holy Grail of the travel industry.

Thomas Cook was also named one of the '100 Best Companies to Work For' by The Sunday Times in 2006. Other accolades over the past 12 months include being voted Best Major Operator at the Travel Weekly Globe Awards, Leisure Travel Agent of the Year at the Agent Achievement Awards, Tour Operator of the Year at the British Travel Awards, Top Major Operator at the Travel Bulletin Awards and Peterborough's Business of the Year. In addition, Thomas Cook was recognised as Marketing magazine's Most Loved Travel Brand in May 2006.

The company takes very seriously its role as a responsible business. Thomas Cook raises money for Travel Foundation – the charity that establishes sustainable tourism projects around the world – and

contributes around £500,000 per year to the organisation.

In 2004 Thomas Cook selected the Variety Club Children's Charity as its corporate cause, based on a vote across all company employees. In total Thomas Cook has raised £1.9 million for the charity, through customer donations and company-wide initiatives as well as fundraising efforts from both teams and individuals.

In August 2005 the company pledged to raise the £2 million necessary to fund the Thomas Cook Critical Care Centre – a brand new ward for seriously ill children – at King's College Hospital. The campaign is well underway and building has already begun.

Product

Within its holiday products, Thomas Cook has focused heavily on taking package holidays to the next level. Far from a 'one size fits all' approach, Thomas Cook has reinvigorated its range over the last few years to offer everything from budget holidays to five star luxury, with special brochures now dedicated to spa and sports holidays,

1841
Thomas Cook's first excursion, a rail journey from Leicester to a temperance meeting in Loughborough, takes place.

1855
Thomas Cook personally leads the first continental tour from Harwich to Antwerp, then on to Brussels, Cologne, Frankfurt, Heidelberg, Strasbourg and Paris.

1872-73
Thomas guides the first around-the-world tour and is away from home for 222 days, covering more than 25,000 miles.

1939
Holidays by air on chartered aircraft are included in the summer brochure for the first time.

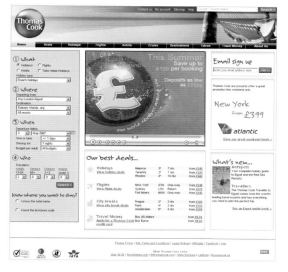

weddings and honeymoons, adult-exclusive holidays, family entertainment and more. Customers can even choose whether to fly with a charter airline or scheduled service.

While other travel companies have invested in specialist companies to diversify, Thomas Cook remains 100 per cent committed to the mass-market package holiday – but with options to help everyone find a holiday tailored to their preferences.

The company is constantly seeking new destinations and offers, the latest of which are Costa Rica, Kerala, Sardinia and the Istrian Riviera in Croatia for summer 2007. Over the last four years Thomas Cook has introduced Croatia, Morocco and Bulgaria, which are now strong and established destinations well received by customers.

In addition, Thomas Cook is currently working to expand its presence in long haul destinations and has overhauled its long haul flying to achieve this. As a result, the company introduced a brand new programme to Australia and New Zealand for 2007.

In terms of more tailored offerings, Thomas Cook last year launched its Spa & Sports brochure and introduced 'Thomas Cook Holiday Resorts' – a range of all-inclusive hotels designed to suit families or those seeking an active holiday with plenty of leisure facilities on offer.

Thomas Cook remains highly committed to its 'four ways to book' – stores, call centres, web and TV channel, Thomas Cook TV. The website has been greatly enhanced to increase its user-friendliness and holidays can now be booked in just four clicks – the shortest customer journey in the industry. In addition, ThomasCookinspires.com was launched in December 2006 to showcase thousands of videos of the company's destinations and hotels.

In addition to holidays and sales channels, Thomas Cook also has a strong presence in foreign exchange. Every Thomas Cook store offers a travel money bureau, stocked with all the leading currencies, travellers cheques and pre-loadable cards, together with expertise and competative rates. Millions of Britons rely on Thomas Cook to provide their holiday spending money every year.

Recent Developments

In addition to package holidays, Thomas Cook last year announced the introduction of two brand new business areas.

The first focuses on Independent Travel. Thomas Cook's stores, call centre and website already enable customers to build their own holidays using flights, car hire and accommodation, but this new business area will ensure that the best possible range and choice is on offer to customers, with all the protection and reassurance that customers expect from the Thomas Cook name.

The second is the new Financial Services arm. Thomas Cook's name is well recognised in connection with holiday money and travel insurance, which means that the brand is well placed to move further into this area. Thomas Cook has already launched a new credit card where cardholders gain travel pounds on all their spending, to use on travel products from holidays to theatre breaks. The company is also launching a range of new travel insurance products, tailored to customer needs.

Promotion

Thomas Cook employs an integrated through-the-line customer marcomms strategy, supporting its key categories – holidays, cruise, independent travel, foreign exchange and financial services – with its 'four ways to book' communications, driving customers to all channels: stores, sales centres, online and Thomas Cook TV.

On and offline media are planned together to provide greatest reach and to give customers a choice of information gathering and booking channels.

Marketing campaigns are focused around the key sales periods of post-Christmas and summer, and all marketing messages are communicated around the core value of 'Our World Revolves Around You', ensuring that every campaign is focused around customer benefits.

Other than standard online and traditional media choices such as TV, press, radio, outdoor and visual merchandising and a significant direct marketing programme maintaining contact with loyal customers, Thomas Cook also works with brand leading partners such as McDonald's, Nationwide, Disney and American Express to create innovative and topical promotions capturing consumers' imaginations.

Brand Values

Thomas Cook's commitment to customers is summarised in the strapline 'Our World Revolves Around You'. Thomas Cook's strategy is to put the customer first, and as a result has lower levels of complaints than its competitors.

Thomas Cook believes that its biggest differentiator is its people, and the 'Spirit of Thomas Cook'. Employees work for the brand with pride, and make it their personal mission to deliver the best possible service.

As one of the original travel companies, Thomas Cook remains one of the best-known names in travel, is well-trusted and seen to be pioneering. As a result it must continue to deliver exceptional holidays, new innovations, and excellent support for all its customers in every situation.

www.thomascook.com

1999

The merger of Thomas Cook and Carlson Leisure Group is approved by the European Commission.

In addition, JMC is formed by combining Sunworld, Sunset, Flying Colours, Inspirations and Caledonian Airways to become the UK's third largest tour operator.

2003

Thomas Cook rebrands its airline to Thomas Cook and launches a tour operating brand under the same name.

2007

Thomas Cook announces its intention to merge with fellow holiday company MyTravel.

Things you didn't know about Thomas Cook

Thomas Cook is the official travel partner for England football fans, Manchester City, Arsenal, Celtic, Chelsea and West Ham as well as the English Cricket Board.

Thomas Cook was the first UK company to introduce online holiday booking, in 1997.

Thomas Cook & Son transported the British Army relief force sent to rescue General Gordon from Khartoum in 1884.

The company was state owned under the British Transport Holding Company from 1948 to 1972.

It is the biggest seller of cruise holidays in the UK.

Tropicana

Tropicana is the leading juice brand in the UK, with sales topping £224 million in 2006 and a market share of 24 per cent, a growth of 88.5 per cent over the past five years (Source: ACNielsen). Tropicana offers a broad range of traditional fruit juices and fruit blends, and is well placed to capitalise on the wave of health awareness in the UK.

Market

Fruit juices have experienced a resurgence in recent years, with volume sales increasing by seven per cent in 2005 thanks to a greater consumer focus on wellbeing and natural products (Source: Zenith International).

Chilled juice has driven this growth, with its share increasing from 24 per cent in 2000 to 36 per cent in 2005, as a result of many consumers trading up from ambient juices to premium chilled juices such as Tropicana (Source: Zenith International).

The wave of 'functional' new products has also been a key factor in the growth of the market. For example, products containing ingredients with specific health benefits, now stand alongside those with added vitamins or minerals.

Most consumers now recognise the health benefits of drinking fruit juice, while the trend towards natural, healthy products in the UK is also helping to add value to the category. With drinks companies maintaining a high level of innovation, the fruit juice industry will be in a strong position to satisfy the demanding UK consumer. As such, the UK juice market is predicted to grow by 45 per cent between 2006 and 2011 to reach a value of £4.5 billion at current prices, according to Mintel.

Achievements

Launched in the UK in 1991, Tropicana Pure Premium has been the driving force in establishing the 'Not From Concentrate' juice market, and it has become a strong player in the sector.

As market leader, the brand takes its social responsibility very seriously and is committed to sustainable development and the use of materials from renewable resources. The Tropicana pack is made mostly from cardboard (around 79 per cent). This cardboard comes from trees, a renewable resource and its Nordic forests have an independent forestry management certification and promote a natural biodiversity.

Straight from the fruit

1947	1954	1965	1991	1995	1999
Tropicana is founded by Anthony Rossi as a Florida fruit packaging business.	Rossi pioneers a pasteurisation process for orange juice called flash pasteurisation.	The company receives its first international order (14,000 cases of Tropicana Pure Premium orange juice) at a European trade fair. Export of Tropicana juice begins, with the first shipment going to France.	Tropicana Pure Premium is launched into the UK, creating a new sector in the juice category – 'Not From Concentrate' juice.	Tropicana extends its core range to include new flavours including Ruby Breakfast, Sanguinello and Pink Grapefruit.	Tropicana Essentials range is launched which includes the Calcium, Multivitamins and Fibre variants.

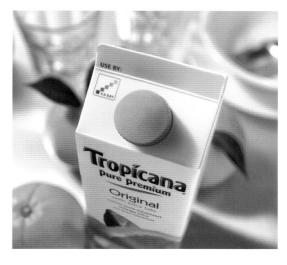

Product

Tropicana fruit is cultivated by experts and ripened by natural rainfall and the warmth of the sun. Tropicana Pure Premium is not produced from concentrate, and sugar and water are never added, resulting in 100 per cent pure squeezed juice straight from the fruit. Just 150ml of Tropicana Pure Premium equals one of the five daily portions of fruit and vegetables as recommended by health and medical experts.

Tropicana now offers 12 different flavours of juice under the Pure Premium range including, Raspberry Mandarin, Sanguinello and Super Fruit blends; Blueberry Blend, Cranberry Blend and Pomegranate Blend. The Essentials range includes: Multivitamins – a blend of 12 fruit juices with five extra vitamins for a healthy body; Calcium – orange juice with added calcium for healthy bones and teeth; and Fibre – four fruits and carrot juice with extra fibre for inner health.

Recent Developments

The Tropicana Pure Premium range has moved forward with the addition of the new Super Fruits range which launched in June 2007. The brand has also developed a new consumer website – www.tropicana.co.uk.

To help parents give their children the recommended five servings of fruit and vegetables per day, Tropicana moved into the children's market in 2006. The brand launched Tropicana Go! – a healthy fruit-juice drink for kids that is available in a 200ml sports-cap bottle, ideal for kids' lunchboxes. It contains 70 per cent juice, 30 per cent water which accounts for one portion of a child's recommended daily allowance of fruit and vegetables. Containing no added sugar, and free from artificial colours, preservatives, artificial flavours and sweeteners, it is available in three flavours: Orange and Pear; Apple and Blackcurrant; and Apple.

Promotion

Tropicana has put significant advertising support behind the premium chilled brand – £5.4 million in 2005. The year saw Tropicana launch its aspirational advertising campaign, 'Breakfast in New York', which was awarded an IPA effectiveness award in 2006. To support this activity an integrated campaign – The Tropicana Breakfast Club ran, which brought The Sunday Times and British Airways together to form an award-winning promotional campaign.

Building on this success, 2007 has seen the 'Fruit To The City' TV campaign brought to life through experiential installations in major UK cities. The installation comprised of a three metre high orange tree inside a clear Tropicana carton, with its own eco-system and orange aroma. The partnership with The Sunday Times was leveraged through a promotion whereby consumers can win a weekend break every 24 hours throughout September, supported on-pack, via direct marketing, radio and PR activity.

Brand Values

Tropicana believes that not all fruit is created equal and by only using the best fruit they

ensure that the product offers natural goodness and vitality, to create a superior and consistent taste and to achieve 'the best of what comes straight from the fruit' – for example its oranges are squeezed within 24 hours of picking.

www.tropicana.co.uk

Things you didn't know about Tropicana

A 250ml glass of Tropicana Orange Juice contains a full day's supply of Vitamin C, provides a good source of Folic Acid (33 per cent RDA) and is naturally cholesterol, sodium and fat free.

All Tropicana oranges are handpicked and squeezed within 24 hours.

Tropicana was the first bottled Florida juice to be sold overseas.

Tropicana gained one of its first corporate customers in 1954, the world famous Waldorf-Astoria Hotel in New York City which had a standing order for 1,000 gallons of juice and fruit jars each week.

2005

The award winning 'Breakfast in New York' TV ad and experiential activity is launched.

2006

Tropicana Go!, the all natural children's drink, is launched, while the core range is extended into Super Fruits and new Fruit Blends.

2007

A new TV Ad – 'Fruit To The City' – airs. Tropicana supports this by bringing fruit to the city with an innovative new sampling campaign.

Also in 2007, a new Tropicana UK website – www.tropicana.co.uk – is launched.

wagamama

wagamama has come a long way since opening its first restaurant in London's Bloomsbury in 1992. Its global expansion has seen restaurants appearing all over the globe with its most recent addition in Boston, USA. wagamama's philosophy is still just as important today as it was 15 years ago: 'to combine fresh and nutritious food in an elegant yet simple setting with helpful, friendly service and value for money.'

Market

wagamama is the most popular chain of Asian inspired noodle restaurants in the UK. Its competitors are extremely diverse ranging from lunchtime cafés to fast food establishments to formal restaurants. wagamama also has the advantage of appealing to a wide range of people – business professionals, backpackers, families, students and ladies who lunch to name but a few.

In the 15 years since wagamama was founded, more than 75 restaurants have opened firstly in the UK, then Europe, the Pacific Rim, the Middle East and the US. Throughout its expansion, whether in Manchester or Dubai, customers can expect the same wagamama experience.

Achievements

wagamama has received many awards since its launch, reflecting the enduring appeal of the brand. Recent accolades include being named Most Popular Restaurant by Zagat in 2006, Best London Restaurant at the Visit London Awards in 2006, Best Concept at the Retailers Awards in 2006 and Best Website at the Caterer Awards. It was also awarded

CoolBrand status continually between 2002-2006 by the Superbrands organisation.

wagamama also has two best selling cookbooks to its name – 'the wagamama cookbook' and 'ways with noodles', both written by acclaimed food writer Hugo Arnold.

Product

The wagamama concept is modelled on Japan's ramen shops, which have been popular for over two hundred years.

Things are a little different at this Asian inspired noodle restaurant. The seating is canteen style, with long benches that are frequently tightly packed with diners. In addition, all orders are entered on an electronic handheld PC by the waiters and sent straight through to the kitchen in order to speed up the ordering process.

Key to wagamama's menu is ramen – Chinese-style thread noodles, served in soups with toppings or griddle-cooked (teppan-fried) meat. This offers the perfect fast food; a nutritionally complete meal in a bowl. Other signature dishes include rice

1992	1995	1998	2000	2001	2003
wagamama opens its first restaurant in London's Bloomsbury.	After growing success, it opens its doors to its second restaurant, on Lexington Street in London's Soho.	The first international franchise is opened in Dublin.	The first out of London restaurant is opened in Manchester and the second international franchise is launched in Amsterdam.	wagamama moves into Leicester Square followed a year later by the first Australian restaurant in Sydney.	As wagamama expands in the UK, the 20th restaurant is opened in Canary Wharf.

based options as well as salads and desserts. These can be accompanied by freshly squeezed juices – a firm and healthy favourite – wine or Japanese beers. For the hungry, a variety of side dishes are available including meat and vegetable dumplings, skewered chicken, deep-fried prawns as well as raw salads.

wagamama also offers a children's menu with high chairs, kids chopsticks and colouring books adding to their visit. There is also a dedicated area for kids on the wagamama website.

For real wagamama addicts, a range of merchandise is available in restaurants including sauces, bowls, t-shirts and wagamama's books.

wagamama also offers a take away service in all but one of its UK restaurants where customers can ring in with an order then visit the restaurant to collect it.

Recent Developments

wagamama's first opening in the US was in central Boston in spring 2007. The historic Faneuil Hall, adjacent to Quincy Market, which is famous for shopping and dining, is wagamama's new home. Boston was selected for the first restaurant in the US as the demographics of the city suit the wagamama brand. In addition, thousands of American visitors to the UK confirmed Boston as ideal for the initial launch. Unlike all other non UK wagamama restaurants which operate under a franchise agreement, the restaurants in the US will remain wholly owned by the UK.

With its increasing success wagamama will open in Harvard Square, Massachusetts in summer of 2007 with other restaurants yet to be confirmed.

Promotion

wagamama utilises the full marketing mix when it comes to promoting its restaurants and brand values. Raising awareness of the brand and communicating what wagamama

is all about is achieved through national/local press. Outdoor advertising is used to direct customers to its restaurants and targeted media ensures that the right type of audience is being reached.

New media is used to a great extent, with the brand's fresh, vibrant website changing almost daily to communicate its latest offers, promotions and menu changes. Customers are encouraged to become online members so that alerts can be sent to them via email with news and rewards for their loyalty.

Partnerships have been developed with other brands with similar audiences such as Time Out, STA Travel, Handbag.com and Rough Guides, to reach other membership bases through joint promotions.

The wagamama message is also communicated in the restaurants themselves. All staff are trained to exude the brand's essence, and the design and ambience of the restaurants also supports this.

Brand Values

wagamama's ethos is Positive Eating + Positive Living. Its aim is for everyone who comes into contact with the brand to have a positive experience. This encompasses its food, people and restaurants. It works hard to be in tune with its customers' needs and aims to run its restaurants to the highest standards with energy, attitude and enthusiasm.

The wagamama brand stands for individuality with fresh and nutritious Asian inspired food served in a simple, well designed, quality environment. The brand aims to employ knowledgeable, helpful, friendly staff who love their jobs and can be themselves at work.

It also strives to offer value for money as well as 'experience for money', always questioning and challenging itself to be better at what the brand does.

www.wagamama.com

2004

wagamama opens in Dubai and the first award winning cookbook is launched – 'the wagamama cookbook'.

2006

The second cookbook – 'ways with noodles' – and wagamama sauces are launched.

2007

The first US restaurant opens in Faneuil Hall, Boston with another on the way in Harvard Square.

wagamama is due to open its 50th UK restaurant in Lakeside Shopping Centre. Restaurants are also planned in Egypt and Cyprus in the autumn.

Things you didn't know about wagamama

wagamama's top five selling dishes are Chicken Katsu Curry, Yaki Soba, Cha Han, Chicken Chilli Men and Chicken Ramen.

In total 130,000 people visit wagamama per week.

Twelve tonnes of noodles and 11,000 portions of edamame are served by wagamama each week.

There is no MSG in wagamama's food.

Local school children are regularly invited on educational visits to wagamama restaurants.

WEDGWOOD

Wedgwood has remained one of the globe's greatest luxury lifestyle brands for almost 250 years. Its fine ceramics and gifts effortlessly grace the tables of palaces, parliaments, leading hotels and homes the world over with modern classics and unsurpassed fashionable lifestyle accessories all encompassing the best of English heritage, quality, craftsmanship and international design.

Market

Wedgwood remains a market leader in luxury lifestyle within the ceramics industry. Part of the Waterford Wedgwood Group, it distributes to more than 90 countries worldwide providing premier fine bone china, earthenware and its unique Jasper stoneware, together with a range of silver and crystal accessories, textiles, gourmet foods, specialist teas and bespoke prestige items influenced by the company's unparalleled archive records.

Its key markets are the UK, North America, Western Europe and Japan, with a rapidly expanding operation both in China and Russia and a thriving corporate, sporting, hospitality and governmental portfolio.

Achievements

Wedgwood has almost two and a half centuries' experience of supplying beautiful giftware and stylish tabletop products to the luxury sector of the market. With its superlative standards of craftsmanship, quality, record of innovation and bespoke timeless design, it maintains a leading position in every one of its key markets.

With multi-million pound sales during 2006, it employs more than 2,000 people in its manufacturing, sales and distribution operations worldwide.

Holders of the Royal Warrant from Her Majesty Queen Elizabeth II, it includes among its past customers the White House, the Kremlin, the House of Lords and numerous other governments and Royal Houses.

Such is its popularity and heritage, this classic English brand attracts almost 100,000 visitors a year to its multi-million pound visitor centre in Staffordshire where people can immerse themselves in the history of the company while seeing for themselves exactly how products are crafted during unique factory tours.

A new £10 million museum is also due to open in 2008 at the company's greenfield headquarters on the rural outskirts of Stoke-on-Trent. The museum, being built by the independent Wedgwood Museum Trust, will house thousands of priceless artefacts from the last 250 years of the company's history. In total, the new galleries will house in the region of 6,000 Wedgwood pottery artifacts, 75,000 manuscripts and 680 pattern books – alongside the results of 10,000 trials conducted by a young Josiah to develop 'new' ceramics, such as the now world-famous Jasper. The museum will also house a host of other exhibits, from the portraits of Josiah and his wife Sarah by Sir Joshua Reynolds and paintings by George Stubbs, through to a fire engine used at Wedgwood's original Etruria Works.

1759	1773	1774	1789	1902	1940
The Wedgwood Company is founded by Josiah Wedgwood.	Empress Catherine the Great of Russia commissions a 952-piece dinner service, known as the Frog Service, for her imperial palace. It is now a Russian national treasure.	After thousands of experiments Josiah Wedgwood perfects the world famous Jasper ceramic.	Wedgwood successfully reproduces in Jasper, the now iconic Portland Vase, a copy of the ancient Barberini Vase currently housed in the British Museum.	President Theodore Roosevelt orders a 1,282-piece fine bone china banqueting service for the White House.	The Wedgwood factory moves from Etruria in Stoke-on-Trent to a new 300 acre greenfield estate at Barlaston. The factory remains the company's headquarters.

Product

Wedgwood's product range has grown significantly in recent years. Beyond its designer tableware, it encompasses a nursery collection, cutlery, crystal glassware and jewellery as well as a comprehensive collection of gifts providing a diverse portfolio of lifestyle items such as clocks, photo frames and table accessories.

Throughout its history Wedgwood has pioneered innovation in the ceramics industry. The founder, Josiah Wedgwood, was given the title of Potter to Her Majesty in the 1760s after he developed cream coloured earthenware and provided a service for Queen Charlotte, wife of King George III. After thousands of experiments he also developed the now iconic Jasper, along with a Black Basalt body. Innovation continued with the development of the pyrometer – the first time the temperature in kilns could be accurately measured. But it is not just technical innovation that Wedgwood is famous for – design is also central to the brand.

Wedgwood seamlessly blends its own design expertise with that of international designers to provide a constant flow of contemporary classics. In recent years, American bridal designer Vera Wang, clothing designer Jasper Conran and interior designers Barbara Barry and Kelly Hoppen have each in their own unique way partnered with Wedgwood to create fashionably relevant products for the modern consumer.

Recent Developments

Innovation plays a key role in the development of Wedgwood's product. Wedgwood has experimented with clays from as far away as China, the Cherokee (Ayoree) Lands in America and Australia to find the perfect recipe for its diverse portfolio. Most modern clays, however, continue to be drawn from high quality deposits in Devon and Cornwall.

Recently, contemporary colours including delicate taupe and romantic chocolate have been created for the company's iconic Jasper ware, as well as a unique lead free lustre glaze which adds both glamour and sophistication to its already opulent armoury of products.

Independent compression tests show the strength of Wedgwood fine bone china is already among the strongest ceramic in the world, with an average of 17,597 pounds per square inch needed to break it.

Promotion

The company's marketing dates back to the early days of the company with the introduction of the first money back guarantees in the early 1770s, pre-dating John Wanamaker, who is normally given credit for this concept, by nearly a century.

Recently the speed of innovation has not lessened. The company is forging sales opportunities by partnering new distribution channels and new agreements with key retail partners to develop the width and scope of its appeal while maintaining its classic modern brand heritage. It is also contemporising its

product portfolio to ensure continued relevance to today's discerning customers.

Very astute in its self promotion, the company targets its key knowledgeable audience through top magazines and newspapers, with the majority of its promotion through careful product placement in films and magazines.

In addition, Wedgwood sponsors premier fashion events and sporting competitions such as the World Golf Championships, the World Sailing Championships, horse racing, tennis and selected charitable events.

Brand Values

Wedgwood has a reputation for timeless luxury developed through its high standards of authenticity, quality, heritage, innovation, design, craftsmanship and customer service

www.wedgwood.com

Things you didn't know about Wedgwood

Wedgwood fine bone china was first introduced in 1812 with the famous Chinese Dragons pattern.

Josiah Wedgwood's son, John, (1766-1884) was one of the founders of what was to become the Royal Horticultural Society. He suggested the idea to the King's gardener William Forsyth in 1801.

In 2006 Wedgwood used 260 kilos of 22 carat gold and platinum at its factory in Staffordshire to decorate its products.

A vase with decoration designed by the Prince of Monaco and manufactured by Wedgwood's special skills department at Barlaston, Staffordshire, raised £400,000 at an auction for children's charities in 2006.

1953
A 1,200-piece dinner service in Wedgwood Persephone is chosen as the tableware for the coronation banquet for Her Majesty the Queen.

1986
Wedgwood merges with Irish crystal producer Waterford to form the luxury Waterford Wedgwood Group.

1994
The Russian Government orders a 47,000-piece fine bone china service, believed to be the largest banqueting service ever produced, manufactured for use in the Kremlin.

2009
Wedgwood will mark its 250th anniversary with global celebrations.

which?

For 50 years the Which? brand has existed to tackle the issues that matter to all consumers. Which? campaigns for a fairer deal for all and publishes expert, unbiased information and advice to help consumers make the right choice, whatever they're buying. Today, Which? is the largest consumer organisation in the UK, with more than 650,000 members.

Market

Since Which? was founded in 1957 consumers have experienced unprecedented improvement and opportunity. The entire shopping experience has changed, with today's 24/7 mentality and level of choice far removed from the days of even 30 years ago. In the last decade, linked to the time pressure that many consumers are under, home delivery and online shopping have grown exponentially.

Alongside the dramatic change in the shopping experience consumers now have even more ways of paying for their goods; the variety of charge cards, credit cards and loans is broader than ever before with immediate access to money often provided at point of purchase.

Today's consumers are also bombarded with more advertising, information and advice than ever before via newspapers, magazines, TV, radio and the internet. Many organisations are providing this content without charge as a means of creating and enhancing consumer relationships.

But trust is at a premium and consumers are still keen to retain their links with those brands who they believe in and who represent their interests, so that even in today's market, no other 'paid-for' factual publications outsell Which? and Which? Online in the UK, except for three that carry TV listings.

Achievements

Which? has a proven track record over the last 50 years of executing targeted campaigns which deliver a better deal for consumers in everything from financial and

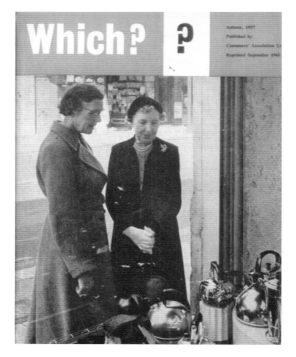

legal services, to food, estate agents and health issues. Which? has also helped to create an environment whereby high-level consumer involvement has become essential across a range of government agencies, regulators and standard-makers.

In financial services, Which? has put the spotlight on government and industry over the endowment mortgages miss-selling scandal and helped hundreds of thousands of people get compensation via its endowment action campaign. Most recently, Which? has kept up the pressure on banks and regulators over the high charges for unauthorised overdrafts which are now the subject of an inquiry by the Office of Fair Trading.

From the aftermath of the BSE crisis, Which? championed the need for the consumer interest to be at the heart of future decision making on food issues. Its lobbying came to fruition in 2000 with the creation of the Food Standards Agency – its primary aim to protect the interests of consumers. Which?'s campaign for better labelling of food products to help people make more informed choices has also seen great success in the form of EU wide legislation.

In addition, Which? took the car prices campaign to the European Commission, resulting in an end to the 'block exemption' which saw UK consumers paying higher prices for their cars.

1957	**1964**	**1970s**	**1980s**	**1996**	**2006**
The first Which? magazine is published by a volunteer group from a converted garage in Bethnal Green, London.	Which? pioneers the concept of 'mystery shopping' with 34 members signing up for a marriage bureaux.	Which? introduces the use of large scale surveys to provide brand information on product reliability and service quality.	Expansion into free-standing magazine products is consolidated by the launch of Gardening Which? followed by other titles like Health Which?.	Early adoption by Which? of internet services leads to the launch of Which? Online.	The Prize Draw mechanic is replaced with a highly successful integrated brand approach that reverses years of decline in sales of Which? magazine.

Which? also put its legal range of powers to work to expose markets which are not working in the consumer interest. This has led to 'supercomplaints' on Northern Ireland banking and competition in legal services in Scotland. Which? is also the first organisation to test new powers to get people their money back from JJB Sports for over-inflated football shirt prices during certain periods in 2000 and 2001.

Product

Which? is much more than just a magazine; it is the leading independent consumer champion in the UK, researching more products, more comprehensively, than anyone else in the world. In 2006, Which? tested over 3,000 products and services in around 80 categories.

The operating framework for Which? has remained much the same since its beginning. It has always been a not-for-personal-profit organisation supervised by a Council (board), which since the first few years has been elected by members.

The Which? magazine offers reviews of products and services, providing advice on what to buy and how to obtain best value. This advice is truly independent and impartial and is provided in a straightforward and easy to understand way; Which? takes no advertising or government money and all product reviews are based on rigorous research.

Such has been the success of its flagship magazine that Which? has been able to develop a range of other products: Which? Online, Gardening Which?, Computing Which? and Holiday Which?. A number of books are also published by Which?, including the market leading 'Good Food Guide'.

Recent Developments

Always at the forefront of innovation, Which? has maintained its relevance to consumers by keeping pace with their lives.

For most of its 50 years, the organisation had a 'split personality' in the outside world – using the name Which? where magazine content was discussed, and Consumers' Association for policy and campaigning. In 2004 the persona for all purposes became Which?, the more consumer friendly brand.

In 1996 – before even Google existed – Which? Online was up and running and now membership for this alone stands at 165,000, making it one of the biggest online subscription services in the UK. Recently

another online product, Which? Local, has been added providing local recommendations on everything from plumbers to hairdressers.

The Which? product range of magazines, online offerings and book titles never stands still, and has been developed further in 2007 with a new personal finance magazine – Which? Money.

Promotion

Which? grew very rapidly in its early months as a result of press coverage and word-of-mouth recommendation, but by the 1960s a dedicated marketing department was set up, developing the art of direct-mail promotion. Prize draw became the central marketing technique in August 1982, remaining a crucial marketing tool for more than 20 years until its declining effectiveness in the 21st century led to its replacement in 2006.

The new successful marketing approaches work by combining an advertising led campaign, to help consumers appreciate the diversity of the products researched and tested by Which?, alongside a direct marketing lead generation approach to engage people with information from Which?.

Consumers are offered free guides with mass appeal on topics such as the internet, PCs and broadband and then once the benefits and quality of information from Which? has been appreciated, are given the opportunity to become members.

Since the introduction of this brand led marketing activity in 2006, Which? has distributed over a million free guides and has reversed years of decline in sales of the flagship product, Which? magazine.

Brand Values

Which? exists to make individuals as powerful as the organisations they have to deal with in their daily lives by delivering

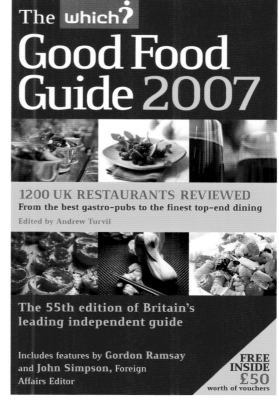

independent advice, active support and ending unfairness in the way some markets are structured and operate.

The key principles that bind the brand together are:

Independent – the brand's unique core, Which? takes no advertising or government money and is totally unbiased, unlike almost every other source of information and advice.

Rigorous – at its heart Which? is rigorous in its product testing and evaluation and for many consumers the end result of this, the Which? Best Buy, acts as a kite mark for quality.

Energetic & Passionate – the heritage of Which? shows an energy and passion to ensure that consumer wrongs could and should be righted. While the issues may be different in today's more complex world, the approach is the same.

www.which.co.uk

Things you didn't know about Which?

Between 1988 and 2007 the Consumers' Association was mentioned on average once every three days when Parliament was sitting.

In 1963 Which? tests exposed 52 potentially dangerous products.

Never heard of the Moskovich? That's because Which? testing reported that the brakes were dangerous and following this the car disappeared from the market, never to be seen in the UK again.

Which? was instrumental in setting up the Food Standards Agency.

In less than 17 years, Whirlpool has risen to become the number one household appliances brand in Europe. The strategic investments it has made in innovation, design, manufacturing, and the community are at the heart of its commitment to maintaining the loyalty of its customers and its leadership position within the industry.

Market

Whirlpool is a leading producer of major home appliances in North America and Latin America and has a significant presence in markets throughout India, China and Europe, where it is outpacing industry growth.

Indeed, Whirlpool Europe's net sales for 2006 increased by seven per cent to a record US$3.4 billion. These strong results were driven by gains in market share, new product introductions and a widened mix of products on offer, particularly from the Whirlpool brand's expansion of its built-in appliances range.

Whirlpool Europe became the wholly owned subsidiary of Whirlpool Corporation in July 1991. This followed Whirlpool's purchase of the remaining share of its 1989 joint venture with Philips of the Netherlands.

Achievements

Whirlpool markets its products in 170 countries and manufactures in 13 countries across four continents, employing 73,000 people worldwide and operating 73 manufacturing and technology research centres around the world. Whirlpool Corporation achieved record annual sales in 2006 of US$18.1 billion, a 26 per cent increase on the previous year.

Whirlpool's success is born out of relentless innovation. During 2006, Whirlpool brought a record number of new products to the marketplace globally, and a record US$1.6 billion of its worldwide revenue came from innovative products and services.

Whirlpool's disciplined and structured design and innovation process, coupled with its employees' dedication, led it to be named one of the world's 100 most innovative companies by Business Week magazine and to be listed in the Ocean Tomo 300 patent index, the first equity index based on the value of corporate intellectual property.

Overall, Whirlpool's growth strategy over recent years has been to introduce innovative new products, increase customer loyalty for its brands, enhance management of its trade customers and to make strategic acquisitions. This included the completion in March 2006 of the acquisition of MAYTAG, which is expected to bring future growth opportunities.

Product

Whirlpool Europe manufactures and markets home appliances such as ovens, dishwashers, tumble dryers, freezers, microwave ovens, refrigerators and washing machines. Within this marketplace, Whirlpool consistently produces industry leading design and innovative technological solutions to better meet consumer needs.

The turn of the century saw Whirlpool launch a series of design innovation concept projects: 'mAcrowave – new frontiers for the modern microwave' featured at the Milan Triennale and The Louvre; Project F, a concept design project looking at the future of laundry; and in 2004, In.Kitchen, a visionary design project on the future of kitchen space and appliances, became the third installment of the biennial research and design initiative by Whirlpool's global product design studio.

In.Kitchen is Whirlpool's vision for highly integrated built-in kitchens. Although not

1911

Upton Machine Corporation is founded in St. Joseph, Michigan, to produce electric motor-driven wringer washers. It subsequently merges with the Nineteen Hundred Washer Co. in 1929.

1919

Gottlob Bauknecht starts a small electric workshop in Taillfingen, Germany, eventually establishing his first factory in 1933. Philips acquires the Bauknecht business in 1982.

1950

Nineteen Hundred Corporation changes its name to the Whirlpool Corporation.

1989

Whirlpool Corporation and Philips form a European joint venture. Whirlpool Corporation becomes the sole owner in 1991.

2006

In March Whirlpool completes the acquisition of MAYTAG.

2007

Whirlpool launches the Essence and Gallery built-in collections across Europe.

available to buy, these are not-too-distant product hopes: glimpses of product experiences that could be achieved in the very near future.

Its ability to look ahead is a cornerstone of the Whirlpool brand. Among Whirlpool's recent innovations is Pret-a-Porter, a fabric freshener that revitalises clothes using steam; and Origami, the first cooking hob with a complete set of accessories.

In 2006 Whirlpool launched 24 major product innovations and also presented In.Home, the fourth biennial conceptual research and design project. The project focused on the product-user interface and interprets the domestic environment as constantly evolving and adapting to different situations and moods throughout the day. In.Home products include the LivingCube, a modernised coffee table with advanced technology to heat and cool food, the Lighthood, a hanging multicolour lamp and air purifier as well as the Laundry Wall, a fully integrated wardrobe system that brings washing and clothing maintenance to a walk-in closet.

Recent Developments

Whirlpool's commitment to innovation and design enables the company to stretch its thinking, allowing it to take risks and develop solutions that break through boundaries. Its range of built-in products plays a vital role in its growth strategy. The built-in segment is a growing business and an area to which Whirlpool is dedicating significant focus and resources. Three years ago, Whirlpool set out on a built-in development strategy and has since seen an annual growth rate of nearly 20 per cent.

Characterised by elegant ergonomic design and high-quality materials, the range of built-in products offers a variety of shapes, sizes and aesthetics, all containing intelligent functionality, including innovations such as text-assisted displays and Whirlpool's patented 6th Sense technology.

The 6th Sense intelligent sensor control technology which senses, adapts and controls, is applied to many Whirlpool products. This encompases a multi-function oven with two sensors that are able to sense the weight of the food that is being cooked and the precise temperature inside the oven, adapting the cooking time and controlling the cooking process accordingly, while giving regular feedback on cooking time.

For 2007, Whirlpool revealed the Essence and Gallery ranges of built-in products. These highly designed anti-fingerprint stainless steel ovens, wine cellars, coffee machines, extractor fans and under-counter cooling drawers are all made to fit precisely into kitchen units, and are designed to create time and space in the kitchen.

Promotion

Whirlpool's award winning consumer campaign, which has been running for a number of years, is unique within the market. It is based on a goddess theme and spans print, outdoor and online.

Whirlpool pursues its business objectives while contributing to improve the lives of people in the communities where it operates. The most important corporate social responsibility project supported by Whirlpool is its partnership with Habitat for Humanity, which is committed to providing simple, decent, affordable houses for families in need, in more than a hundred countries. By the end of 2005, more than one million people were living in Habitat homes.

Whirlpool has supported this global, non-profit organisation, dedicated to eliminating poverty housing worldwide, in many ways over a number of years; not only providing products, to date more than 3,500 employees have volunteered to build homes.

In 2001, the charity recognised Whirlpool Corporation for its commitment as the largest corporate donor to the project. Since the beginning

of the programme, Whirlpool has supported Habitat for Humanity with an investment of more than US$25 million and donated 62,000 appliances.

Three years later, Whirlpool announced the extension of its collaboration with Habitat for Humanity in Europe, and created a three-way partnership, whereby tennis player Amélie Mauresmo represents the Whirlpool-sponsored Women's Tennis Association (WTA) as official ambassador for Habitat for Humanity in Europe.

In 2005, Whirlpool launched a series of initiatives including 'Aces for homes', the Whirlpool 'Love food' cookbook and the Whirlpool 'Players Painting' to raise further funds and awareness of the work done by Habitat for Humanity.

Brand Values

Whirlpool strives to make intelligent appliances that make people's lives more efficient and pleasurable. The Whirlpool brand is about relentless inquiry and innovation, consistently producing industry-leading design and technological solutions to better meet consumers' needs. New design trends, technological advances, evolutions in society and changes in domestic behaviour have all aided the development of its innovations.

www.whirlpool.co.uk

Things you didn't know about Whirlpool

One of Whirlpool's latest innovations – the Side by Side – is a fridge-freezer with a built-in coffee machine.

Whirlpool operates three of Europe's seven largest factories.

Whirlpool products can be found in more than 200 million households worldwide.

Whirlpool has been a specialist in home appliances for 96 years.

Yellow Pages has been putting buyers in touch with sellers for more than 40 years and is published by Yell, a leading international directories business whose UK brands also include Yell.com and 118 24 7. There are some two million businesses listed in Yellow Pages and last year 28 million copies were delivered to homes and businesses across the UK, helping to make Yellow Pages the UK's most used classified directory (Source: Saville Rossiter Base 2005/06).

Here's to the people behind the numbers™
Chengy Muchemey, Soft Play Supervisor, Essex

Market

Yell is the biggest player in the £4.1 billion UK classified advertising market (Source: The Advertising Association 2006). The highly competitive market consists of a range of media, including other printed directories and local and national newspapers.

Achievements

Since Yellow Pages was first published in the UK in 1966, the directory has become a part of everyday life, delivering results for consumers and advertisers alike.

Yell is very aware of environmental and social issues and its impact on the wider community. This affects the way all parts of its business and operations are managed. In April 2007, Yell won a second Queens Award for Enterprise,

which recognises it as a benchmark for sustainable development.

In winning this award, Yell demonstrated a sustainable approach that lies at the heart of all its business activities. Special mention in the official award summary was given to the Yellow Woods Challenge, Yell's flagship environmental campaign for schools which is run in partnership with the Woodland Trust and local authorities across the UK.

The past year has been hugely significant for the campaign as it smashed its target to involve one million schoolchildren and recycle one million directories. The secret of the campaign's success? A simple concept: pupils recycle old Yellow Pages directories and compete against local schools whilst learning about the environment.

Another Yellow Pages schools programme which has seen massive success this year is Mini Pots of Care.

Run in partnership with Marie Curie Cancer Care as part of Yellow Pages' lead sponsorship of the charity's Great Daffodil Appeal, Mini Pots of Care saw nearly a quarter of a million school children get involved to raise funds for Marie Curie nurses.

Yellow Pages has helped Marie Curie raise more than £20 million since the sponsorship first launched in 1999.

Product

Yellow Pages is the UK's most used classified advertising directory with more than one billion uses last year (Source: Saville Rossiter-Base 2005/06). In 2006, 104 editions were printed across the UK, ensuring that 96 per cent of UK adults have a Yellow Pages directory at home with 84 per cent of UK adults using the directory (Source: Saville Rossiter-Base 2005/06).

From Alexander Technique teachers and Cake Makers to Tree Surgeons and Vets, the

1966
The UK's first Yellow Pages directory appears.

1970s
Yellow Pages is rolled out across the UK in 1973, becoming a registered trademark in 1979.

1993
Talking Pages is launched.

2000
Yell.com is launched, replacing Yell.co.uk, which began in 1996.

2001
Full colour advertising is launched nationally in Yellow Pages. In addition, Yellow Pages Insurance Guide is launched.

2,300 classifications ensure users can find the person they want easily. This is demonstrated by seven out of every 10 'look-ups' resulting in a business being contacted and more than half (57 per cent) of contacts resulting in a purchase (Source: Saville Rossiter-Base 2005/06).

The breadth and depth of enterprises within Yellow Pages is due to Yell's commitment to offer value for money advertising that delivers leads time and time again. On average, Yellow Pages helped advertisers generate over £25 worth of new business for every pound spent on advertising (Source: Saville Rossiter-Base 2005/06).

Yellow Pages' telephone information service – 118 24 7 – is also going from strength to strength with its firm emphasis on quality of service leading to a significant growth in call volumes. The service offers a classified business directory service, as well as opening hours, store locations, cinema times and train times. 2007 sees the expansion of the service with the opening of a new call centre in Wales, helping to ensure continued delivery of the award winning personal quality service with which 118 24 7 has become synonymous.

Recent Developments
In 2007 a significant new brand positioning for Yellow Pages was launched which builds on the modernity and relevance of the book and focuses on its enterprising advertisers at work.

The new integrated campaign has resulted in a total review of activities including a refreshed logo, front cover, above and below-the-line advertising campaign, sponsorship deal and website, all supported by an integrated PR campaign and a commitment to champion enterprising people across the UK.

For the first time, the cover of Yellow Pages moves away from a graphics-led 'yellow' design, instead featuring real advertisers using the tools of their trade. The clean and refreshed look has a magazine lifestyle feel with headlines highlighting the extensive content within the pages. The new covers will be rolled out from July with the first featuring Wendy Bose, a cake maker from London, decorating a wedding cake.

Promotion
Yellow Pages is renowned for its award winning advertising, which in the past has focused on personality and character-led advertising campaigns on one business classification that have positioned Yellow Pages as the answer to a problem or need.

The new brand positioning has seen a radical departure from this approach, with the focus on the enterprising people that can be found within Yellow Pages as Yell believes they are the best advert for the brand.

A new integrated campaign – people behind the numbers – supports the brand mission to champion and celebrate the enterprising people whose skills, ingenuity and passion make up businesses, both big and small, across the UK.

The launch TV ad sets the scene and stars include: Chengteai Muchmeyi, a play assistant in Essex; Barry Parker and Adrian Blake, roofers from Newcastle; Denis Maloney, a plasterer from Edinburgh and Ruth Greidinger, an Alexander Technique teacher from Edgware in London. The TV ad voiceover – an ode to enterprising people – was read by Barry Marsh, a pest controller from County Down.

The new campaign also features a series of TV and radio ads, posters, direct mail, public relations, a high profile sponsorship and a supporting website, www.peoplebehindthenumbers.com.

The stars of the ads each had a local premiere, complete with yellow carpet. They have become local heroes, gaining intense media interest and have been enjoying their new found star status; Graham Barnard, a rabbit hutch maker from Hull who appeared in posters and his own 30 second TV ad, even has an area dedicated to Yellow Pages on his website.

Yell has also secured one of the most prestigious TV sponsorship opportunities, available for the first time in 10 years – network film on Channel 4 – under its Yellow Pages and 118 24 7 brands. The multi million pound deal includes films across Channel 4, E4, More4, Film4, online and Movie Rush.

The creative trails for the sponsorship will feature real advertisers introducing the film, with the first films being introduced by the Taxi Drivers of Sunderland, the Kennel Owners of Norwich and the Beauticians from Hull.

Brand Values
The Yellow Pages brand is built on its reputation for accessibility, trustworthiness and warmth, underpinned with a firm commitment to champion the enterprising 'people behind the numbers'.

www.yellgroup.com

Things you didn't know about Yellow Pages

New classification headings in 2007 include Garage Conversions, Paving & Driveways and Irrigation Design & Installation.

Yellow Pages can be recycled into animal bedding, stuffing for jiffy bags, egg boxes, newsprint and cardboard.

In 2006, Yellow Pages appeared 41 times on The Apprentice, made 117 appearances on Emmerdale and was on screen for 357 seconds in Eastenders.

Kirk – the mascot of Yellow Woods Challenge – secured a bronze medal in the Great North Mascot Steeplechase.

2003
Yellow Pages 118 24 7 is launched.

2006
Yellow Pages 118 24 7 wins five of the International Directory Assistance Awards – including 'Best UK 118 Service' for the third year running.

Also in 2006, TFL travel guide launches across London Yellow Pages directories.

2007
A new brand mission to celebrate the 'people behind the numbers' is launched.

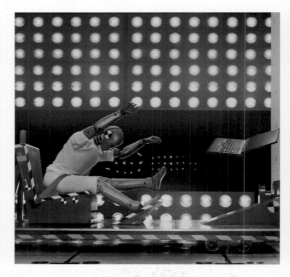

Brands to watch

On the pages that follow you will find brands that the Superbrands Council 2007/08 has rated as:

"Brands that have, through exceptional marketing and communication strategies, positioned themselves as significant challengers to established rivals. These brands are expected to grow market share and have the potential to develop into Superbrands of the future. They are either new or rejuvenated brands, whose reputation and brand strength make them an emerging force in the market. These brands have been tipped as the 'ones to watch'."

It is Amarula's unusual marula fruit spirit base which differentiates it from the plethora of other cream liqueur brands on the market. With its roots in Africa, the brand conjures up a sense of exotic adventure and captures the spirit of Africa. Amarula has grown to become the second largest volume selling cream liqueur globally and is available in 150 countries worldwide.

Brand Overview

Amarula Cream was first launched in South Africa in 1989. The fruit of the native marula tree, which only grows in Southern Africa, is the key ingredient and lies at the heart of Amarula's individual and distinctive personality.

Marula trees can be found on the African plains and hold a position of importance both in the animal kingdom and in human legend and ritual. Known as 'the marriage tree' due to its fruit – which locals believe has aphrodisiac properties – it is also commonly referred to as 'the elephant tree' because local wildlife (including elephants) are attracted by the scent of the ripening fruit. The trees themselves cannot be cultivated, so the fruit must be harvested in the wild, where it stands ripening under the African sun. As it ripens, the skin becomes a light yellow, encasing white flesh around a large nut. Every year local people harvest the fruit, which is fermented and then distilled into marula spirit using traditional copper pot stills. Ageing of the young marula spirit then follows for two years in oak barrels before being finally blended with fresh cream. This is the essence of Amarula Cream Liqueur.

The heart of the marula growing region is Phalaborwa, which lies at the extreme north eastern reaches of South Africa in the

Limpopo province. The livelihood of local residents is closely tied to the marula tree and it is estimated that close to 60,000 people are supported through the harvesting of the fruit alone. However, the harvesting season lasts for about 10 weeks only, and the local residents who collect and sell the fruit are without incomes for the greater part of the year.

Through a consultative process with tribal chiefs, Amarula has helped to introduce a range of sustainable economic development programmes to ensure that the locals have alternative incomes for the remainder of the year. Programmes are centred on the small towns and villages surrounding Phalaborwa and include wire fence making projects, training in basic business skills, and secondary processing of the oil-rich marula nuts, which are now being used for a range of products. Amarula's involvement in the local community is not just window-dressing – Amarula has also built the community a clinic, a crèche and a community hall.

Amarula is also committed to preserving its most important brand icon – the elephant. The Amarula Elephant Research Programme, based in the school of Biological and Conservation Sciences at the University of KwaZulu-Natal, Durban, is an initiative aimed at conserving, protecting and managing the African elephant and its environment.

Amarula is delicate, indulgent and smooth. From its pale but rich colour, fresh clean nose, and essences of fruit with hints of butterscotch and toffee, Amarula is an indulgent taste to savour.

Amarula is best served chilled or over ice, but is also extremely versatile. Consumers are encouraged to sip an indulgent Amarula Coffee, or experiment and discover the countless cocktail recipes for which Amarula is a key ingredient, including the Springbokkie, Elephant's Mudbath and White Nile Martini.

Marketing and Communication

In the UK, Amarula invests heavily in consumer sampling. Recent activity includes comprehensive in-store and experiential sampling campaigns, as well as attendance at consumer sampling events such as the Ideal Home Show, the BBC Good Food Show and the National Wedding Shows.

Amarula has carried out TV advertising, but now focuses on print press campaigns. Magazine advertorials in consumer lifestyle magazines and retail titles are also used to increase awareness of the brand.

PR activity is focused on the theme of exotic indulgence. Link ups to date include Time Out magazine's film website, various press activities as well as third party associations, the latest of which creates an exclusive association with a boutique jewellery designer to create 'The Amarula Tusk' pendant.

www.amarula.com

Future Plans

To consolidate the brand's current strong market position by continuing to communicate Amarula's highly differentiated essence as the spirit of Africa.

To continue to implement a heavyweight consumer PR programme to drive consumer engagement further.

To continue to focus on consumer sampling campaigns to introduce new consumers to the brand.

To continue to educate consumers on new ideas and serving suggestions.

ghd
a new religion · for hair

In January 2001 ghd was born. Girls gasped and A-listers praised. Word spread rapidly and demand soared. From this day, ghd transformed the understanding of hair and beauty and brought belief, guidance and miracles to a new generation of women. Adored by millions and worshipped the world over, ghd is 'a new religion for hair'.

Brand Overview

Despite its success, ghd is still a young brand, established in 2001 when a small business in Ilkley, West Yorkshire, discovered ceramic hair styling technology. ghd styling irons were so effective that despite supply difficulties and with virtually no marketing, they became an immediate viral success and initiated a cult following.

In the early days, women who discovered ghd couldn't keep it a secret; as the word spread demand increased, with some women travelling the length of the country to find ghd styling irons and snapping up as many as they could for family and friends. Once supply issues were resolved, ghd achieved second-year revenues of £12 million.

Following ghd's initial success, it continued to lead the sector, primarily through word-of-mouth promotion. In 2003, ghd launched a series of hair beauty products to complement its range of three styling irons. A hero product quickly emerged – 'iron oil', a thermal protector to use with ghd irons. In 2006 this range was updated to 'ghd thermodynamics™' – a complete collection of products to protect hair from heat. UV protection is also built into every step so 'urban angels' (ghd's name for their brand evangelists) are protected from the sun's damaging rays.

ghd has now enhanced its cult classic with a range of new features to make versatile styling accessible to all. The new ghd styler makes it even easier to create curls and waves, while retaining its unrivalled ability for achieving straight and sleek hair.

As well as improved temperature control to maintain the heat during styling, the new styler also boasts intelligent technology that incorporates a sleep mode whereby the styler switches itself off if not used for 30 minutes.

Showcased backstage at London Fashion Week, the new ghd styler achieved impressive results – so it comes as no surprise that there was a waiting list when the product launched.

The face behind the brand is managing director and co-founder Martin Penny, who in 2005 won Ernst & Young's Northern Entrepreneur of the Year, going on to win their national title for consumer products.

Marketing and Communication

A key decision in the brand's history was to make the products only available through salons. ghd was the first salon-only brand to advertise on TV and the first to advertise in top fashion glossies including Vogue, Elle and Marie Claire. The objective of the campaigns was to create consumer demand that could only be satisfied in salons.

Based on consumer faith in ghd's products, 'belief' became ghd's brand essence; with the cult expanding into a bigger belief system coined 'a new religion for hair'. Since 2002, religious connotation has continued to drive the brand's marketing, focusing on its magical, almost supernatural ability to transform the looks and confidence of girls and women the world over.

The brand's first campaign to focus on the religious angle, 'accidental halo' placed consumers styled by ghd in front of everyday circular objects to create a halo effect. The idea being that whatever nature has given you ghd can improve upon it.

It is widely acknowledged that women can view hair as essential to how they look; a fantastic outfit does little to compensate for a bad hair day. ghd has used this intrinsic link between hair and fashion to its advantage by sponsoring catwalk collection launches by celebrity fashion designers including Jenny Packham and Frost French, in addition to styling models for the catwalk shows of fashion designers (including the likes of Matthew Williamson, Zac Posen and Stella McCartney) at Fashion Weeks around the world.

www.ghdhair.com

Photograph courtesy of Bob Carlos Clarke

Future Plans

To roll out the brand globally; already in 17 countries, ghd plans to enter Japan, China, The Middle East, Canada and South America in 2007.

To launch its Spa products division and flagship retail sites around the country, starting in Leeds at the end of 2007.

Glasses Direct breaks the mould of the optical industry, asking customers to make a huge and innovative behavioural change. Today Glasses Direct is the largest direct seller of glasses in the world, selling a pair every seven minutes around the clock, with a multi-million pound turnover and the company is forecasting sales north of £10 million by 2008.

Brand Overview

On 1st July 2004, at the age of 21, while still at university and with no formal business training, James Murray Wells launched glassesdirect.co.uk, a website that would deliver low cost prescription glasses to consumers in an industry dominated by four major optical chains. Now glassesdirect.co.uk is the largest direct seller of prescription glasses in the world, selling a pair every few minutes over the internet, with sales growing at over 6.5 per cent per month.

James initially came up with the idea for the business at university when he had to pay £150 for a pair of reading glasses. When he tried to research the actual cost of making glasses he was met with a wall of silence from everyone across the optical industry. On the brink of giving up on the idea, he called one final laboratory – and got the information he needed. James uncovered that the costs involved were just £5 - £7 per pair. Glassesdirect.co.uk was born. From the outset the company challenged the traditional notion of buying glasses from the

high street, offering consumers a new media alternative. Just a few months after launching, with more than 8,000 orders to the company's name, James realised that what had started as a sideline had the potential to completely revolutionise the market. Glassesdirect.co.uk boasts a database size of 150,000 – growing at the rate of 91 per cent per annum – and has received over 10 million hits to the site.

Marketing and Communication

Glasses Direct's initial marketing activity consisted of two girls handing out flyers in the centre of Bristol, which secured one or two orders each day. Word spread and within two months of trading, the phone was ringing and regular orders were coming in. Glasses Direct now actively drives word of mouth referrals using a variety of marketing mechanisms from social web features to member-get-member incentivisation; even through sending out eyeball gobstoppers with every order, to get people talking.

PR has been a massive contributor to the company's dramatic growth. An external agency positioned the founder, 21-year old James Murray Wells as a young and inspirational entrepreneur, and he was soon winning many awards including the Shell LiveWire Young Entrepreneur of the Year. A celebrity auction was organised by Glasses Direct in March 2006, featuring the glasses of the celebrities Ant & Dec, Trevor Macdonald and Alex Ferguson to name but a few. The auction raised money for Great Ormond Street hospital and the event was covered in both the regional and national press. It was also the first time Glasses Direct involved celebrities with the brand.

The company's marketing efforts always support this 'David versus the Goliath' of the optical giants positioning. Glasses Direct aims to be the consumer's champion,

which is reflected in the brand's heavy hitting controversial guerrilla marketing campaigns, which target radio, print, tube carriages, billboard, direct mail and internet advertising. Glasses Direct's first television advertising campaign is currently in the planning stages and will be launched later this year.

www.glassesdirect.co.uk

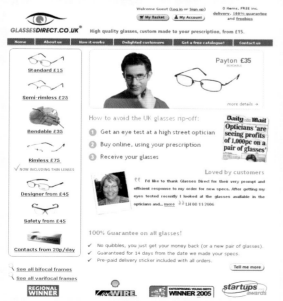

lenovo™

It's no accident that 'New World, New Thinking' is the Lenovo brand signature. In just four words, it sums up both the company's strategic business approach and its branding strategy. Created in May 2005 when China's Lenovo Group acquired the IBM Personal Computer Division, Lenovo is a new kind of global company, forging a 21st century approach to the personal computer business.

Brand Overview

Today, under the umbrella of the Lenovo brand, the company offers two families of products: the Think family and the 3000 family. The Think family, including the legendary range of ThinkPad notebooks which celebrate their 15th anniversary in 2007, stands for products offering industry-leading capabilities that improve productivity and reduce the total cost of owning a PC, while maintaining stability and manageability.

The Lenovo 3000 family, designed specifically with the needs of the SME market in mind, aims to provide worry free computing in every price class.

Upon its creation in 2005, Lenovo instantly became the world's third-largest PC manufacturer. It benefited from a market-leading position in China, the world's fastest growing PC market, and strong positions elsewhere thanks to the international scale and scope of the IBM PC Division, from which it inherited the ThinkPad brand.

One of the major challenges facing the new organisation was to develop a branding strategy that would enable it to leverage the strength of the ThinkPad name and continue to outgrow the market in Asia, while building visibility and equity around the Lenovo brand across the world.

In light of the company's ambitious global objectives, it became clear right from the start that Lenovo would need to build a global brand. Marketing experts at the new

company mapped out a phased approach; the idea was to gradually establish Lenovo as the master brand, while growing brand equity of the Think family.

During the initial months, high priority was given to reassuring customers about the highly esteemed ThinkPad name for notebook computers. The initial phase proved a success, as new ThinkPad products continued to win wide acclaim, customer satisfaction soared and sales remained strong. The next – and most essential – phase of the plan was to introduce the Lenovo master brand.

Marketing and Communication

In order to get the Lenovo brand name into the spotlight, the company launched a new line of Lenovo-branded notebook and desktop PCs at the 2006 Olympic Winter Games in Turin, Italy. As a truly worldwide event the Games provided an ideal opportunity to position Lenovo as a global brand, while giving the company a chance to demonstrate the quality and reliability of its products. Lenovo was not only a sponsor, but also played a key role in providing computers and support. More than 5,000 Lenovo desktop PCs, 800 notebooks and 350 servers were used in nearly every aspect of the IT infrastructure, supporting accurate and rapid collection, distribution and storage of competition results. Lenovo's error-free performance was publicly recognised by the International Olympic Committee.

Lenovo will once again rise to the challenge in 2008 as the official computing equipment provider to the Olympic Games in China. As a TOP sponsor, Lenovo aims to demonstrate its commitment to global excellence, providing PCs, servers, and printers for the 2008 Games.

The company is now entering the third phase of its branding programme. Designed to accelerate the visibility of the Lenovo brand, while continuing to build equity in

ThinkPad, the latest initiatives focus both on corporate and product aspects, using advertising and web-based programmes through to corporate philanthropy and viral marketing to achieve maximum impact.

Lenovo has begun to underline the quality and innovation of its portfolio by positioning its products as 'the best engineered PCs.' The 'Why Choose Lenovo?' advertising campaign, for example, focuses on the company's technical expertise and leadership. Applied to the Lenovo product range, the emphasis is on the worry-free, stylish design and value for money customer benefits. Applied to the ThinkPad line, Lenovo is emphasising solidity, low cost of ownership and thoughtful design.

While the Lenovo brand may not yet be on everyone's lips worldwide, it has achieved much progress during its first two years.

www.lenovo.co.uk

Future Plans

To work with the new brand signature – 'New World, New Thinking'. In just four words, it sums up both the company's strategic business approach and its branding strategy.

To achieve global brand awareness, by building visibility and equity around the Lenovo brand.

To improve the overall experience of PC ownership by addressing the total cost involved.

To provide seamless execution of computing equipment, for the Olympic Games in Beijing in 2008.

"Old Speckled Hen" is an ale with unusual origins. Named after a paint-spattered car used by workers assembling classic British sports cars, its taste is equally distinctive; described as a combination of malt loaf and toffee, it blends bitterness with sweetness alongside a rich, fruity aroma with malty undertones. Confident and quirky, it is reinvigorating traditional ale drinking.

Brand Overview

"Old Speckled Hen" was launched in 1979 and has since made its mark recruiting a new breed of younger drinkers to real ale and cementing its position as number one premium ale in supermarkets and number four in the on trade (Source: Off trade ACNielsen Scantrack March 2007, On trade ACNielsen January 2007).

Hens drinkers, are described as style conscious, independent, 30 something's who want to indulge in a drink that reflects their individuality. Fans – including Brit Art's enfant terrible Tracey Emin – have helped in securing a 60 per cent growth for the brand over the past five years.

The beer was originally brewed to mark the 50th anniversary of the MG motor plant in Abingdon, Oxfordshire. To celebrate this birthday the beer was named after an old MG car which workers used to get around the plant. They would park the old MG Featherweight Fabric Saloon outside the paint shop where it would normally get spattered in paint and so it became known as the 'Owld Speckl'd Un'. This turned into "Old Speckled Hen" when the beer was unveiled.

Since then this finely balanced ale with a distinctive rich malty taste and a fruity aroma has become the bestselling premium ale in UK supermarkets with annual sales of more than 12 million bottles.

In October 2006, the ABV of the beer was reduced from 5.2 per cent to 4.5 per cent in cask and keg format, but remains at 5.2 per cent in bottles and cans. As a result, distribution in pubs and bars increased by an impressive 60 per cent (Source: ACNielsen January 2007), making "Old Speckled Hen" more accessible to more pub-goers.

The success is not limited to the UK. Currently exported to over 40 countries, "Old Speckled Hen" has become famous the world over. Furthermore, one English pub in Singapore sells more than 200 pints of the smooth brew every day. Even New York's bright young things are adopting it as their own with movers and shakers in the music and arts scene regularly pictured with a bottle of "Old Speckled Hen" in their hands at premieres and parties.

Marketing and Communication

"Old Speckled Hen" has always been a bit different in its marketing. Traditional Punch-style cartoon advertising featuring a gentleman fox on the hunt for a 'hen' broke new ground when it was launched 12 years ago – reflecting the eccentric and quirky personality of the beer. With the beer appealing to 'those in the know' quality daily media was used to build the brand and encourage those in search of something different to give it a try.

Premium packaging and a wide choice of formats have continued to boost sales. From casks and kegs in pubs and bars – the kegged version of the beer has alone seen 50 per cent growth in recent years – to a range of multipacks encased in premium packaging in-store. Indeed, all formats of this premium positioned ale are in strong growth.

www.oldspeckledhen.co.uk

Future Plans

To communicate "Old Speckled Hen's" unique confident and quirky image through further advertising, and maintain the high standards on which the brand was built.

To stage marketing campaigns in both the UK and the US, to encourage younger drinkers to think differently about drinking real ale.

To continue to help re-invigorate traditional ale drinking across not only the UK but the globe.

The birth of uSwitch signalled a revolution in consumer choice. With a strong consumer focus, it pioneered quick and easy online switching of energy providers. Its success with this market paved the way for uSwitch to branch out into other areas: firstly home phones, then personal finance including loans and credit cards and most recently mobile phones and car insurance.

Brand Overview

uSwitch was formed in early 2000 when a group of visionary internet entrepreneurs had the idea of developing a website that allowed British consumers to find a better deal on their gas and electricity bills, with the facility to switch suppliers online.

uSwitch's free, impartial online and phone-based comparison service has since expanded to include other products. In addition to gas and electricity, it now helps consumers compare prices on home telephone, broadband, mobiles, digital television, heating cover, water services, credit cards, loans, car insurance and current accounts.

Its aim is to help customers take advantage of the best tariffs and services on offer from every supplier. The company has developed a set of proprietary calculators that evaluate a number of factors, including price, location, service and payment method, to advise customers on the best deal to suit their individual needs.

The uSwitch core values are to provide consumers with choice based on simple, impartial, comprehensive and accurate information. Indeed, one of uSwitch's unique features is its independence and impartiality. It has the ability to offer its consumers complete information on all available suppliers in the market, regardless of whether a commercial relationship exists.

The UK website currently has a 24 per cent market share of the UK's utility website visitors and is the UK's biggest and fastest-growing comparison and switching company, ranked number one in the Business and Finance - Utilities sector (Source: Hitwise UK Top 10 Awards Programme January 2007).

The company attributes much of its success to its focus on customer experience, ensuring its site is easy to use and helpful. uSwitch is dedicated to ensuring the best possible user journey, reflected in the redesign of its site, which was launched in October 2006.

Marketing and Communication

uSwitch aims to be perceived as a consumer champion that acts as a one-stop-shop for financial information, providing education, tools and advice to empower consumers and help them reach a decision.

uSwitch regularly sets the news agenda highlighting issues and lobbying for fairer deals for the consumer and recently launched a multi-million pound brand marketing campaign.

First aired on Boxing Day 2006, featuring a gospel choir singing 'U gotta switch', the campaign included a mix of TV, radio, print and outdoor advertising. It aimed to increase brand awareness and drive traffic to the website and call centre in order to generate switches. The first wave of advertising in December featured a 40-second TV advert to raise awareness. This was followed by shorter TV adverts for specific products airing throughout 2007 to drive cost effective response.

The drive heralded a move away from the previous strategy of targeting ABC1 adults in order to reach a wider, mass-market audience and make uSwitch.com a household name. The advertising was designed to make people sit up and think about how much they could save by switching. The uSwitch campaign generated a 'surround sound' effect, which reached consumers across several touchpoints. For instance, on the radio in the morning, on a backlit poster on their way to work, in the paper at lunchtime and on the TV when they arrived home. The main aims of this brand push were to boost awareness, create excitement, challenge consumer apathy and put switching on people's radar.

www.uswitch.com

Want to win a year's free gas and electricity?

Want a year free from worrying about your gas and electricity bills? Go straight to **www.uSwitch.com/freeenergy** and enter our free prize draw to win a year's free energy courtesy of uSwitch.com*

*Terms and conditions apply

Future Plans

To open a US operation, based in New York.

To empower consumers to take advantage of the best prices and services on offer from major, national, regional and local suppliers for a range of utility and financial products.

To establish itself in the long term as a trusted link between customers and suppliers, over a range of different products and services.

Charities supported by the Superbrands

On the pages that follow you will find details of some of the charities supported by the Superbrands featured in this publication.

BBC Children in Need
www.bbc.co.uk/pudsey
Freephone: 0845 733 2233
Registered charity no: 802052

BBC Children in Need helps disadvantaged children and young people in the UK.

Some have experienced domestic violence, neglect, homelessness or sexual abuse, and others have suffered from chronic illness, or have had to learn to deal with profound disabilities from a very young age.

Many organisations supported by the charity aim to create a lasting impact on children's lives. Some offer low achieving children from areas of deprivation a chance to develop their educational skills and ambitions and others create opportunities for young people who are homeless or socially excluded, to enable them to move forward and secure a fulfilling future.

The charity offers grants to voluntary groups, community groups and registered charities around the UK that focus on improving children's lives. Grants are targeted on the areas of greatest need and money is allocated geographically to ensure that children in all corners of the UK receive a fair share of what is raised.

Supported by: BBC, Boots The Chemist, BT

BEN
www.ben.org.uk
Tel: 01344 620191
Registered charity no: 297877

BEN is the automotive and related industries' own charity. BEN provides care and support for anyone who works or has worked in these industries and this provision also extends to dependants. This charity provides friendship, advice, emotional support and financial assistance to thousands of people living in their own homes throughout the UK and Ireland. BEN also runs four nursing and residential centres across the country, providing a home to more than 350 people of different ages and needs.

BEN is not cause specific, which means its only guiding principle is to care for colleagues who have found themselves in need. The work which its dedicated welfare and care staff undertake is truly diverse.

BEN requires £11 million each year to maintain the services it provides, and more than half of this comes from individual and corporate support.

Supported by: AA, RAC

Breast Cancer Campaign
www.breastcancercampaign.org
Tel: 020 7749 3700
Registered charity no: 299758

Breast Cancer Campaign is the only charity that specialises in funding independent research throughout the UK.

Medicine has taken giant steps forward in our lifetimes, yet one woman in nine will still develop breast cancer. Although survival rates are improving, too many women will die from the disease.

It is still not known what causes breast cancer and how it develops and progresses. Established in 1988, Breast Cancer Campaign aims to find the cure by funding research which looks at improving diagnosis and treatment of breast cancer, better understanding how it develops and ultimately either curing the disease or preventing it.

Supported by: Royal Doulton

Breast Cancer Care
www.breastcancercare.org.uk
Helpline: 0808 800 6000
Registered charity no: 299758

Every day 120 people discover they have breast cancer. Breast Cancer Care is there for every one of them, 24 hours a day, seven days a week. Through our helpline, website forums and face-to-face activities we offer the chance to talk to someone who has 'been there' and has experienced breast cancer themselves.

We respond to over two million requests for support and information about breast cancer or breast health concerns each year. In addition, our highly specialised team provides all the latest knowledge and information through our website, helpline, booklets and fact sheets, helping people understand their diagnosis and the choices they have.

Breast Cancer Care is committed to campaigning for better treatment and support for people with breast cancer and their families.

Supported by: Boots The Chemist, Highland Spring, Royal Doulton, Wedgwood

British Lung Foundation
www.lunguk.org
Tel: 08458 50 50 20
Registered charity no: 326730

The British Lung Foundation is the only UK charity working for everyone affected by lung disease. The charity focuses its resources on providing support for people affected by lung disease today as well as working in a variety of ways to bring about positive change, to improve treatment, care and support for people affected by lung disease in the future.

One person in seven in the UK is affected by a lung disease. Whether it's mild asthma or lung cancer, the British Lung Foundation is here for every one of them.

We support people affected by lung disease through the individual challenges they will face. Support is the focus of many of our activities, including Breathe Easy, our nationwide support network. We help people to understand their condition. We do this by providing comprehensive and clear information on paper, on the web and by telephone. We work for positive change in lung health. We do this by campaigning, raising awareness and funding world-class research.

Supported by: AA

Cancer Research UK
www.cancerresearchuk.org
Tel: 020 7242 0200
Registered charity no: 1089464

Cancer Research UK is the world's leading independent organisation dedicated to cancer research. We carry out scientific research to help prevent, diagnose and treat cancer, and we ensure that our findings are used to improve the lives of all cancer patients.

We have discovered new ways of treating cancer that together have saved hundreds of thousands of lives across the world and we work in partnership with others to achieve the greatest impact in the global fight against cancer.

We help people to understand cancer by providing life-changing information to patients, their families and friends, and we run cancer awareness campaigns to help people reduce their risk of the disease.

One in three of us will get cancer at some point in our lives. Our ground-breaking work, funded almost entirely by the general public, will ensure that millions more people survive.

Supported by: Superbrands (UK) Ltd

Caudwell Children
www.caudwellchildren.com
Tel: 01782 600812
Registered charity no: 1079770

Caudwell Children is one of the nation's fastest growing children's charities to make direct donations to children with special needs throughout the UK. They provide: funding for children with disabilities who require specialised equipment to provide independence and enhance lives; pioneering treatments; therapies (e.g. for autism); and dying wish holidays – giving families desperately needed magical memories. Since the Charity was registered in 2000 it has provided £4 million worth of practical support and has been formally acknowledged as the third largest provider of specialist equipment across the UK.

All Caudwell Children applications are turned around within one month and donations are organised from beginning to end, alleviating the stress from the parents.

Caudwell Children is unique in that all the management and administration costs are covered by the founder, businessman John Caudwell, meaning that every single penny donated goes directly to the children.

Supported by: Wedgwood

Comic Relief
www.comicrelief.com
Tel: 020 7820 5555
Registered charity no: 326568

Comic Relief was launched from the Safawa refugee camp in Sudan, on Christmas Day 1985, in response to crippling famine in Africa. The aim was to take a fresh and fun approach to fundraising and, through events like Red Nose Day, inspire those who hadn't previously been interested in charity, to get involved. Red Nose Day is a UK-wide fundraising event organised by Comic Relief every two years. Sport Relief, in association with BBC Sport, brings the worlds of sport and entertainment together.

Comic Relief has worked with some of the biggest names in entertainment, sport and business and tackles some of the biggest issues facing people across the world. Their work ranges from supporting projects that help children who are living rough in India to community programmes helping the elderly across the UK. A number of high profile partnerships have brought in millions of pounds to help reach these aims but the biggest group of supporters remains schools.

Supported by: BBC, BT

Costa Foundation
www.thecostafoundation.org
Tel: 07747 767029
Registered charity no: 327489

We set up the Costa Foundation in 2006 to give something back to the communities within the countries from which we source Costa's coffee beans. Each year the Foundation will implement programmes to improve their social and economic welfare.

In 2007, education will be a key focus of the Foundation. We plan to build, improve and maintain schools within three coffee-growing communities in Colombia, Ethiopia and Uganda. This will make a big difference in regions where children have a three hour walk to school, or have no access to clean water.

We'll also be investing in a nutrition programme to develop land for crop growing. This programme will help educate the farmers and their families about better nutrition, and provide them with food.

We are also researching future projects in Guatemala, Honduras, Costa Rica, India, Kenya and Vietnam.

Supported by: Costa

Diabetes UK
www.diabetes.org.uk
Tel: 020 7424 1000
Careline: 0845 120 2960
Registered charity no: 215199

Diabetes UK is the largest organisation in the UK working for people with diabetes, funding research, campaigning and helping people to live with the condition.

There are over two million people in the UK living with diabetes and up to 750,000 who have the condition but don't know it. If not managed effectively diabetes can lead to complications including blindness, kidney failure and heart disease.

Diabetes UK's mission is to improve the lives of people with the condition by providing practical support, information and safety-net services to help people manage their diabetes; the work of Diabetes UK is vital.

Supported by: Specsavers Opticians

Habitat for Humanity
www.habitatforhumanity.org.uk
Tel: 01295 264240
Registered charity no: XR18070

Habitat for Humanity builds and renovates simple, decent and affordable homes with the help of volunteer labour and donations of money and materials.

We build a new home every 24 minutes. Habitat homes are sold to low-income families at no profit and financed through affordable, no-interest loans. Future homeowners also help to build their own home and the homes of others.

Every day Habitat for Humanity turns hope into homes for families living in poverty housing. We work in partnership with Whirlpool, who help through supplying products and manpower and by raising both awareness and funds.

Supported by: Whirlpool

Hearing Dogs for Deaf People
www.hearingdogs.org.uk
Tel: 01844 348100
Registered charity no: 293358

Hearing Dogs for Deaf People selects and trains dogs to respond to everyday household sounds such as the alarm clock, doorbell, telephone, cooker timer, baby cry and smoke alarm.

The dogs alert the deaf person by touch, using a paw to gain attention and then lead them back to the sound source. For sounds such as the smoke alarm and fire alarm, the dogs will lie down to indicate danger.

Most dogs are chosen from rescue centres, giving unwanted dogs useful and happy lives to the benefit of deaf people – the size and breed of dog is usually unimportant.

The practical value is obvious, but the therapeutic value should not be underestimated. Many recipients find their increased confidence and independence encourages them to go out and participate in activities which they previously avoided.

The charity celebrates its 25th anniversary in 2007 and has placed more than 1,300 hearing dogs since its inception in 1982.

Supported by: Specsavers Opticians

John Muir Trust
www.jmt.org
Tel: 0131 554 0114
Scottish charity no: SC002061

The John Muir Trust (JMT) is the UK's leading wild land conservation charity. Through conserving, campaigning and inspiring people, we seek to ensure that wild land is protected and that wild places are valued by all members of society. Established in 1983 the JMT owns and manages estates on Skye, Knoydart and Assynt. The iconic peaks of Ben Nevis and Schiehallion and many of the southern Cuillins of Skye are protected by the Trust. We also assist communities in wild places to take ownership and control of their natural environment. We influence the Government and national bodies on wild land issues and oppose industrial developments which threaten wild land. The John Muir Award is our environmental award scheme that encourages awareness and responsibility for wild places. It is open to all, inspiring people to enjoy and care for the environment. We also run varied conservation activities throughout our properties – from tree planting to path repairs and litter collections. The Trust depends on members and supporters to carry out its work.

Supported by: Berghaus

Life Routes
www.liferoutes.org.uk
Tel: 020 7843 6000
Registered charity no: 258825

Life Routes' work began in 2000 with Nokia funding as part of a global youth development initiative devised by Nokia and the International Youth Foundation. Since then, the programme has directly impacted the lives of hundreds of thousands of young people in over 25 countries around the world. The UK programme, which is managed by the National Children's Bureau (NCB), works in school and community settings to help young people develop the skills and confidence they need to ensure they keep healthy, stay safe, enjoy and achieve, make a positive contribution and enjoy economic wellbeing as outlined in the Government's Every Child Matters strategy.
    Learning skills such as communication, setting and achieving goals and managing emotions is important for all of us and by helping young people to develop life skills, we help them to feel empowered, resist negative influences and have the confidence to make informed choices and participate actively in shaping their lives and their community.

Supported by: Nokia

Marie Curie Cancer Care
www.mariecurie.org.uk
Tel: 020 7599 7777
Registered charity no: 207994

Marie Curie Cancer Care provides free high quality nursing to give terminally ill people the choice of dying at home, supported by their families. Every day 410 people will die of cancer in the UK. Most want to be cared for in their own homes, close to the people and things they love. This year Marie Curie nurses will make this possible for more than 18,000 cancer patients. But for every family that we help there are always others that we can't. We want to reach all of these families – making choice a reality for them all.

Supported by: Yellow Pages

missing people

Missing People
www.missingpeople.org.uk
Helpline: 0500 700 700
Tel: 020 8392 4524
Registered charity no: 1020419

Missing People is the UK's only charity that works with young runaways, missing and unidentified people, their families and others who care for them. As well as actively searching for missing people and supporting those who are trying to find them, Missing People offers three other services: Runaway Helpline, Message Home and Identification.
    Runaway Helpline is a 24 hour confidential helpline for runaways, offering help and advice to young people who have run away from home or care, or who have been forced to leave. Runaway Helpline offers a Freefone number and email service for young people seeking confidential help and advice. Message Home is a unique confidential service offering help, advice and support to adults who are missing – a 24 hour Freefone service that helps people contact their family or carers via a message or three-way call. Identification is a specialist service to support police, coroners, hospitals and social services to resolve cases of unidentified people (alive or dead).

Supported by: National Express

Naomi House Children's Hospice
www.naomihouse.org.uk
Tel: 01962 843513
Registered charity no: 1002832

Naomi House is a purpose-built children's hospice that provides a homely environment for children and young people with life-limiting conditions that mean that they will not live to become adults.
    Situated just north of Winchester in Hampshire, we offer one-to-one palliative care that includes respite, terminal and bereavement care and support to children and their families in central southern England. We are available 24 hours a day, 365 days of the year and it costs around £2.5 million every year to keep this service running.
    With just 10 per cent of our income coming from the Government, Naomi House relies on the generosity of people in the community to continue its work. Their help and time allows us to provide these crucial care services, free of charge, to children and their families.

Supported by: AA

NSPCC
Cruelty to children must stop. FULL STOP.

NSPCC
www.nspcc.org.uk
NSPCC Helpline: 0808 800 5000
ChildLine Helpline: 0800 1111
Registered charity no: 216401
Scottish registered charity no: SC037717

The National Society for the Prevention of Cruelty to Children (NSPCC) is the UK's leading charity specialising in child protection and the prevention of cruelty to children. The Society has been protecting children from cruelty since 1884, when it was founded by Benjamin Waugh. It is the only children's charity with statutory powers enabling it to act to safeguard children at risk. It has 180 teams and projects around the UK as well as five Divisional Offices, a National Centre (Weston House) in London and the NSPCC Training and Consultancy Centre in Leicester.
    The NSPCC provides an independent campaigning voice for children. It works to influence the Government on legislation and policy that affect the lives of children and families, and runs public education campaigns to raise awareness of, and encourage action to prevent, child abuse.
    ChildLine is a service provided by the NSPCC.

Supported by: AA, BT, Wedgwood

Ronald McDonald House Charities (RMHC)
www.rmhc.org.uk
Tel: 0844 840 0844
Registered charity no: 802047

RMHC was established in the UK in 1989 as an independent registered charity and is the leading charity provider of accommodation for families with children receiving in-patient care in hospitals and hospices across the UK.

When a child is admitted to hospital time pressures and cost of travelling to and fro can be very stressful for the whole family. RMHC support families by providing them with a place to stay near the hospital, which is available without charge. Our Houses and Family Rooms can be found in over 38 hospitals across the UK providing over 300 bedrooms a night for families to stay in. Each House and Family Room provides families with a place to get some crucial rest, gain some sense of normality and support from other families in similar situations. Where possible every bedroom has a telephone directly linked to the hospital ward.

The need for the service we provide continues to grow and RMHC has committed to support and provide an additional 400 bedrooms in the next five years at a combined cost of over £33 million.

Supported by: McDonald's

The Donna Louise Trust
www.donnalouisetrust.org
Tel: 01782 654440
Registered charity no: 1075597

The Donna Louise Trust cares for children, who, due to illness or accident, are not expected to reach adulthood.

We give physical and emotional support to both the child and their family. Respite and end of life care is provided at our hospice, Treetops, and in the family home. We also provide ongoing bereavement counselling for the whole family, including for siblings who are left behind.

Providing this service for Staffordshire and South Cheshire costs £1.5 million. The Trust does not receive any statutory funding, relying entirely on the generosity of donations from both the local community and companies.

Supported by: Wedgwood

The Eve Appeal
www.eveappeal.org.uk
Tel: 020 7380 6900
Registered charity no: 1091708

Each year, around one million women are diagnosed with gynaecological cancers worldwide. The Eve Appeal was set up to save women's lives by funding groundbreaking research into these cancers.

We are the only UK charity dedicated to funding research into all four gynaecological cancers. In the UK, however, ovarian cancer is the most common and fatal gynaecological cancer, which is why it is the focus of our current fundraising campaign.

Every year over 7,000 women across the UK are diagnosed with ovarian cancer. 5,000 of them will die. That's a death rate of over 70 per cent – similar to the survival rate for breast cancer.

Our current and most urgent aim is to raise the last £5 million required to complete a world-class research programme at University College London, which aims to find techniques that will halve the death rates from ovarian cancer within 10 years. The programme includes the largest ovarian screening trial in the world.

Supported by: Boots The Chemist

The National Autistic Society
www.autism.org.uk
Tel: 020 7833 2299
Helpline: 0845 070 4004
Registered charity no: 269425

The National Autistic Society (NAS) champions the rights and interests of all people with autism including Asperger syndrome, as well as providing a range of direct services and support appropriate to their needs. We do this by working with local and central Government bodies, as well as raising public awareness of autism and the issues facing those affected.

To continue providing its diverse array of services each year, the NAS relies on a wide range of funders and donors. We encourage support for our work through volunteering, fundraising and campaigning initiatives.

Help from the NAS is available across the UK. Our team – including many volunteers – works tirelessly to provide: local advice and support for families affected by autism, practical and emotional support, care and education for adults and children with autism, employment training and support, training for parents, carers and professionals, lobbying and campaigning, information and increased awareness and understanding of the needs of people with autism, their families and carers.

Supported by: LEGO®

THE OUTWARD BOUND TRUST

The Outward Bound Trust
www.outwardbound.org.uk
Tel: 0870 513 4227
Registered charity no: 313645

The Outward Bound Trust is the originator and leading facilitator of experiential learning in the outdoors. Established 65 years ago to boost personal learning and development through a programme of challenging activities in the outdoors known as Outward Bound®, today we work predominantly with young people aged nine to 24, including apprentices, through their schools and colleges.

Outward Bound® aims to inspire young people to fulfil their potential through experiences in the outdoors which help them overcome their fears, raise their self-esteem and prepare them to face whatever life throws at them with confidence, respect and compassion. We show them the meaning of "I can", and we help generate memories and experiences that last a lifetime, changing the way young people approach and view their life choices and helping them take full responsibility for them.

Supported by: Berghaus

The Travel Foundation
www.thetravelfoundation.org.uk
Tel: 0117 9273049
Registered charity no: 1065924

The Travel Foundation develops solutions to help protect holiday destinations – helping tourism to make a positive contribution, this is called sustainable tourism. It works in partnership with the UK tourism industry to encourage widespread action at favourite destinations across the world.

The Travel Foundation works by helping to protect local culture and tradition; encouraging best practice in tourism; creating new excursions to support the local economy; helping suppliers produce local fresh food for the tourism industry; supporting local crafts; and protecting the environment and wildlife.

Supported by: Thomas Cook

Variety Club Children's Charity
www.varietyclub.org.uk
Tel: 020 7428 8100
Registered charity no: 209259

For more than 50 years Variety Club
Children's Charity has been helping sick,
disabled and disadvantaged children.
The Charity provides direct support and
assistance to children and young people
up to the age of 19.

We are best known for our Sunshine
Coaches but the Variety Club helps children
in many different ways: it equips children's
hospitals, takes children on very special
outings, and, through our EasyRider
programme, provides the latest electric
wheelchairs.

This is made possible because volunteers
from many walks of life give generously of
their time and money, supported by a galaxy
of celebrities from show business and sport.
Our volunteers' hard work ensures that for
every pound raised a remarkably high
percentage goes straight to the children.

So, when you support Variety, you can
be sure that your contribution is making a
real difference.

Supported by: Thomas Cook

Victim Support
www.victimsupport.org
Helpline: 0845 30 30 900
Registered charity no: 298028

Victim Support is the national independent
charity for people affected by crime. It
provides a free and confidential service,
whether or not a crime has been reported
and regardless of when it happened. Trained
staff and volunteers offer information,
support and practical help to victims,
witnesses, their families and friends via a
network of local branches.

Victim Support provides the Witness
Service, based in every criminal court in
England and Wales, to offer assistance
before, during and after a trial.

The national helpline, Victim Supportline,
provides information, support and referral
to local services.

Victim Support works to increase
awareness of the effects of crime and to
achieve greater recognition of victims' and
witnesses' rights. The organisation receives
funding from the Ministry of Justice and
welcomes corporate donations and
sponsorship.

Supported by: Autoglass®

Vision Aid Overseas

Vision Aid Overseas
www.vao.org.uk
Tel: 01293 535016
Registered charity no: 1081695

Vision Aid Overseas (VAO) is a charity
dedicated to helping people in the developing
world whose lives are blighted by poor
eyesight, particularly where spectacles
can help. Over 300 million people in the
developing world need spectacles to live
an ordinary life due to poverty, lack of
facilities and long distances between optical
service providers.

VAO works by sending abroad teams of
volunteer optometrists and dispensing
opticians who set up clinics, screen large
numbers of patients and provide appropriate
spectacles. In addition, it establishes
workshops and trains nurses in eye testing
skills with the aim of developing long term
optical services in its target countries.
Founded in 1985, Vision Aid Overseas has
provided 600,000 eye tests and given over
300,000 people the ability to see with a pair
of spectacles. Its work continues to have a
life changing effect on its patients.

Supported by: Specsavers Opticians

Wallace and Gromit's Grand Appeal
www.grandappeal.org.uk
Tel: 0800 919 649
Registered charity no: 1043603

Wallace and Gromit's Grand Appeal was
established in 1995 to support the rebuild
of Bristol Children's Hospital and donated
£12 million to the project. Since the hospital
opened in April 2001, The Grand Appeal
has continued as a revenue appeal to
support and enhance the Bristol Children's
Hospital by providing much needed
additional facilities, comforts and equipment
for patients and families, which are not
funded by the NHS.

Supported by: AA

WOODLAND
TRUST

Woodland Trust
www.woodland-trust.org.uk
Tel: 01476 581111
Registered charity no: 294344

The Woodland Trust is the UK's leading
woodland conservation charity, owning
more than 1,200 woods which are open free
of charge for the public to enjoy. Our vision
is to protect what we have, restore what has
been spoilt and create new woods for the
future, to make our countryside friendlier for
people and wildlife.

The UK has only 12 per cent woodland
cover compared to a European average of
44 per cent. To tackle this, the charity works
with communities to plant millions of trees
throughout the UK. It also campaigns for
better protection of ancient woodland which
is the UK's most precious wildlife habitat and
home to threatened species such as the
dormouse and red squirrel. Trees and forests
also stabilise the soil, generate oxygen, store
carbon, transform landscapes and provide
one of the richest habitats for flora and fauna.

Supported by: Yellow Pages

Peter Fisk
Founder and CEO
The Genius Works
www.TheGeniusWorks.com

Peter Fisk is an experienced strategist and marketer, a leading business advisor, and inspirational speaker and coach. He spent many years working with the likes of British Airways and Coca-Cola, Marks & Spencer and Microsoft®, Virgin and Vodafone.

He is author of the best-selling books Marketing Genius and The Complete CEO, and is described by Business Strategy Review as "one of the best new business thinkers". His new books on accelerating growth, innovation, and green business will be published in 2008.

He is founder of The Genius Works, recently launched The Marketing Fast Track and will host CNBC's The Marketing Show later this year. He was previously CEO of the world's largest marketing organisation, The Chartered Institute of Marketing, partner of strategic innovation firm, The Foundation, managing director of brand effectiveness firm, Brand Finance, and global leader for strategic marketing at PA Consulting Group.

He is an accomplished international speaker on all aspects of marketing, customers and brands, strategy and innovation. He is thoughtful and considered, provocative and entertaining – capturing what's hot, what works, and what's next. He defines the emerging agenda for customers, explores emerging practices around the world, and how to make the best ideas happen practically and successfully.

Einstein and Picasso Brands:
The genius of brands that deliver extraordinary results

By Peter Fisk
Author of 'Marketing Genius' and founder of The Genius Works

Next generation brands will combine the talents of Einstein and Picasso, the ambitions of customers and business, the opportunities of today and tomorrow.

They will fuse like yin and yang, connecting affinity and difference, aligning love and value. The best brands will do more for consumers, engage them more deeply, drive more sustainable growth, and superior economic value.

From the vision of Apple to the insight of Zara, the passion of Nike and irreverence of Jones Soda, the entrepreneurship of JetBlue and thrill of Agent Provocateur, the greening of GE to the viral impact of MySpace, the new brand leaders think and act differently.

World changing
The big issues of individuality, connectivity and sustainability will challenge and transform the way brands will evolve in coming years:

Consumer power: the fundamental shift in power from business to consumer, and diverse individuality of consumers,

where people don't buy standard products generically pushed at them. Instead there is a new world of conversations and co-creation, doing business on consumers' terms.

Connected world: the connectivity of new technologies removes the old market inefficiencies that were the source of many companies' revenues, the limits of geography and scale. Instead, we now live in an always-on world of unlimited opportunity and self-forming communities.

Global impact: The rapid rise of our ethical and environmental conscience, only amplifies the consumer's lack of trust and engagement in companies and brands. This is not about charity, it is about embracing green issues at the heart of your business model, to be different, make money, and do the right thing.

Amidst all of this complexity, consumer expectations continue to grow, competition becomes more intense, and

cycle times continue to shrink, capital is increasingly scarce, and shareholders will not rest for anything less than sustained, profitable growth.

Thinking different
This calls for something extra: a richer fusion of ideas and approaches that have more impact competitively and commercially.

Genius = intelligence + imagination = extraordinary results

'Genius' addresses these challenges with a more integrated and inspired approach to doing business – describing how to bring together consumers and business with more intelligence and imagination to achieve high performance.

Outside in: How to do business from the outside in, rather than the inside out. How to make consumers and markets, rather products and capabilities your starting point. How to do business on customer terms rather than your own.

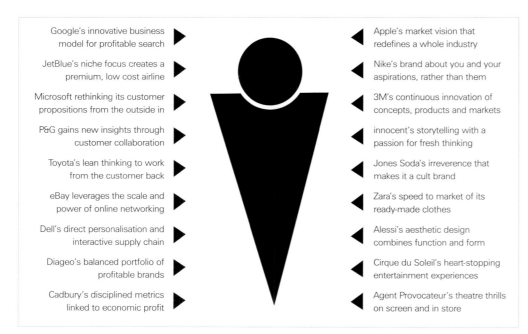

Google's innovative business model for profitable search ▶	◀ Apple's market vision that redefines a whole industry
JetBlue's niche focus creates a premium, low cost airline ▶	◀ Nike's brand about you and your aspirations, rather than them
Microsoft rethinking its customer propositions from the outside in ▶	◀ 3M's continuous innovation of concepts, products and markets
P&G gains new insights through customer collaboration ▶	◀ innocent's storytelling with a passion for fresh thinking
Toyota's lean thinking to work from the customer back ▶	◀ Jones Soda's irreverence that makes it a cult brand
eBay leverages the scale and power of online networking ▶	◀ Zara's speed to market of its ready-made clothes
Dell's direct personalisation and interactive supply chain ▶	◀ Alessi's aesthetic design combines function and form
Diageo's balanced portfolio of profitable brands ▶	◀ Cirque du Soleil's heart-stopping entertainment experiences
Cadbury's disciplined metrics linked to economic profit ▶	◀ Agent Provocateur's theatre thrills on screen and in store

Right brain and left brain: How to take a more thoughtful, creative and holistic approach to your challenges. How to embrace new ideas, rather than be a slave to numbers. How to free your creative side, to focus your imagination in a more intelligent way on what matters most.

Future back: How to create tomorrow whilst also delivering today. How to seize the best market opportunities, unlimited by real and perceived conventions of your business or market. How to start from what is possible and then turn the radical ideas into practical action.

Rule Breakers

Einstein and Picasso both had the imagination and intelligence to fundamentally challenge the rules of their worlds – to see things from a different perspective, the courage to think differently, and to deliver extraordinary results.

It is little more than 10 years ago since we wrote letters rather than emails, browsed CDs in the music store rather downloaded our favourite tracks, and relied upon a small number of media channels, retail outlets and brand owners to run our lives.

We now live and work in flux – markets come and go, converge and fragment at unbelievable speed, and in unpredictable ways; Kodak used to be a market leader and now doesn't have a market, Google went from zero to corporate hero in a few years, Apple reinvented the world of music, and YouTube became our favourite place to watch movies within months.

Satisfaction and improvement, derivatives and incentives are not enough. Incremental brand management can be the quickest way to a painful death.

Just meeting existing consumer needs, or being a little better than existing competitors is not a recipe for success. Stretching, refreshing and exploiting the brand as no more than a name and logo, putting an advertising gloss on commoditised products, thinking that consumer brands will always win over 'inferior' retail brands, or resorting to price competition is a not even a recipe for survival. We need to do more.

Broader vision

Branding today requires 'heads up' rather than 'heads down' thinking.

So what can marketers learn from Einstein and Picasso? Einstein, who we think of as a scientist and mathematician, made his breakthroughs through his creativity – walking in his nearby Swiss Alps, imagining new patterns, hypothesising new possibilities, then proving them. Heads up. Making the creative leap, then focusing his effort.

In this complex, unlimited world, intelligent disciplined analytics are crucial – the ability to identify and ruthlessly manage and focus product and customer portfolios in real time. But it's the imagination to see these opportunities first and differently from others that really matters – helping the customer to achieve their ambitions through a novel application of your product, rather than just selling it to them.

Innovating the market and applications, the purpose and meaning of the brand – rather than just reinventing the business model internally, or the features of the product.

Picasso, who we think of a crazy guy for his art and lifestyle, committed himself to the conventions – gaining respect by learning the rules first, training with the Impressionists in Paris – and then challenging them with his new genres, constantly evolving from Cubism to sculpture, using his ruler and protractor, and then adding creative intuition.

'Intelligent imagination' – focusing the creativity where it will have most impact.

Brands and their managers need more innovation – faster, more stretching, and more effective. They need to engage their logical left-brains and radical right-brains to focus their effort and stretch their creativity. The focus comes by understanding the market best – which is why business needs marketers to drive strategy and priorities from the outside in. The creativity is needed to shape markets in your own vision, rather than live by that of others.

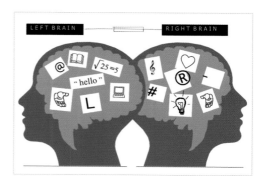

Starting point

We are all consumers in our everyday lives, yet when we go to work we put these incredibly narrow blinkers on. We limit ourselves in so many ways – to our own definitions of the markets in which we compete, to all the real and perceived conventions of the market, to our narrow functional roles, to the products we sell and the short term priorities we set ourselves for results.

This is not how consumers think. Consumers have a much larger and more interesting view of the world, unlimited by definitions of "what sector are you in?", or the rules, or functions, or time. You might sell them a drink, but they want to party, to meet people, to celebrate a birthday, or whatever. You might sell them a loan to buy a new car, but what they really want is to treat themselves, to look the cool cat amongst their mates, or go on a family holiday with enough space to breathe.

In these bigger, broader consumer contexts, brand choices are based on a different set of alternatives from your own defined competitors – how else can they party, or transform their image – and their perceived value of this could be completely different from a product-based price. Changing the context gives you an incredibly simple opportunity to do more, to better meet needs and wants – and at the same time, sell more, charge more, sell other things – and drive profitable growth.

Outside in

'Outside in' rather than 'inside out' thinking starts with opportunities rather than capabilities – finding the best markets, then developing the capabilities to win in them; finding the best customers, then bringing together the right products and solutions that enable them to achieve their goals.

It applies to every aspect of marketing – what, when, where and how consumers, rather than you, want. In an age of surplus supply rather than surplus demand, consumers call the shots. Power has fundamentally shifted.

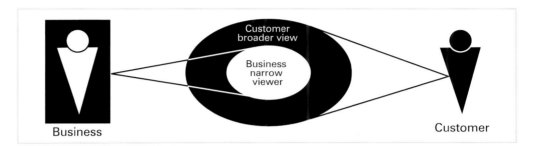

- Does your brand define your target consumers and their ambitions – or arrogantly talk about your business or product and what it does?

- Is your research still centred on average statistics or existing prejudices – or does it listen to and explore more deeply the real needs and wants of individuals?

- Do you still subject all consumers to blanket communication campaigns – trying to sell what you want, when and how you choose?

- Are your distribution channels chosen for your convenience and efficiency, rather than who and where your consumers want?

- Does your pricing model play at the margins of your direct competitors, rather than based on the perceived value relative to the consumer's view of their alternatives?

- Do you still try to persuade consumers to have 'relationships' with your company, when they'd thank you much more for connecting them with other people like them?

- Are you brave enough to take a lead in your market, take risks and set new rules, to shape your own destiny, or are you happy to live by that of others?

Stepping up

As I travel around the world I come across amazing new brands – new ideas, new ways to engage people, new business models to deliver them effectively, and truly inspirational people who develop brands with incredible vision and purpose.

From the tech entrepreneurs of Latvia and Estonia to the funky water and fabulous wines of Serbia and Montenegro, the limitless possibilities of companies like China's Li and Fung and Yue Yeun, the funky finance of Umpqua in Oregon and personalisation of Geranti in Turkey, the deep conscience of (Product) RED mixed with the irreverence of the Jones Soda crew.

The best brands are built on a passion – like the one that burns brightly at innocent's Fruit Towers, or in the labs of Cuppercino, or in the gym at the heart of Nike Global Campus.

The genius of Einstein and Picasso, of Steve Jobs and Phil Knight, of Philippe Starck and Renzo Rosso is that they see things from a different point of view. This liberates and stimulates them to think differently, and because it is real and human, then they fundamentally believe a different, better way is possible.

Brands require new thinking for a new world. A world that has changed – where great brand owners no longer have power, but intelligent, self organising, powerful consumers do; where causes such as poverty and climate change engage people more than the latest fashions and celebrity; and where market share and channel relationships matter less, but trust and advocacy matter more.

See things differently. Think different things.

Go for walks in the mountains like Einstein and make new connections, or disrupt conventional thinking like Picasso, and have the confidence to do what nobody has done before. You and your brands have the potential to deliver extraordinary results.

Cheryl Giovannoni
Managing Director
Landor Associates, London
www.landor.com

One of the world's leading strategic brand and design consultancies, Landor Associates has been Packaging Agency of the Year for an unprecedented two years running (GRAMIA Awards) and twice named Design Agency of the Year (Marketing). Founded by Walter Landor in 1941, Landor pioneered many of the research, design and consulting methods that are now standard in the branding industry.

Partnering with clients, Landor drives business transformation and performance by creating brands that are more innovative, progressive and dynamic than their competitors.

Landor's holistic approach to branding is a balance of rigorous, business-driven thinking and exceptional creativity. Its work spans branding services including brand research and valuation, brand positioning and architecture, naming and writing, corporate identity and consumer packaging design, branded environments, brand engagement and digital branding.

With 22 offices in 17 countries, some of Landor's current and past clients include Ariel, BP, Citi, E45, Ernst & Young, Gulf Air, Heinz Baked Beanz, Lenor, Morrisons, Nokia, PJ Smoothies, Quaker, Smirnoff, Tropicana and Walkers.

Landor is part of WPP, one of the world's largest global communications services companies.

Power shift:
Thinking differently about consumers

By Cheryl Giovannoni
Managing Director
Landor Associates, London

There was a time when managing brands wasn't so complex. With varying degrees of simplicity brands such as Kellogg's, Coca-Cola and Heinz acquired dominance by creating identities that were easy to understand, resonated with consumers and then they 'spoke to' consumers through a finite number of channels.

Skip 50 years, add to the mix a competitive marketplace, channel proliferation rising exponentially and power to the people that couldn't have been envisaged. The once restful world of a brand owner has been turned on its head.

Before going any further, it's important to clarify one thing. That's the distinction between the words brand and branding. They're often used interchangeably, and incorrectly so.

A brand is something that exists in your head. It's an image or a feeling. It's based on associations that are conjured when a brand's name is mentioned. The 'ing' part – branding – is the signals or expressions of the brand that generate those images and feelings. Branding signals can include advertising and

package design, of course, but also product design and functionality, retail environments, online experiences, public relations, and human behaviour. Branding is the process by which images of the brand get into your head.

Lipstick on the gorilla won't wash
Consumers have become too 'brand savvy' to be fooled by a simple makeover and because of this the need for things like a redesigned logo is diminishing. This isn't to say that a powerful brand image is no longer a necessary part of the brand mix but

other ways in which customers experience brands are taking increasing precedence.

Take for instance Virgin Media – a current example of how a new logo is simply not enough to shift perceptions and associations of the brand, but where branding, especially around human behaviour, may be the key to success.

ntl consumers remember their experience of that brand long before brand gurus introduced a fancy new Virgin Media logo. Consumers went so far as to create ntl:hell, an independent online consumer lobby group designed in 2002 to discuss issues and create a community where people submitted their own views of the company, and how to make products or services better. The forum also contained a high number of ntl employees who regularly helped out customers and provided a source of official information.

Given ntl's historical reputation for poor customer service, a fresh start under the Virgin Media name can only be a good thing – especially since Virgin has a strong pre-existing reputation for innovation and customer focus.

For Virgin, this is a tale of risk and reward. The rebrand as Virgin Media is a promise that the ntl customer experience will be transformed. If it doesn't, then that promise will be broken and Virgin may have another Virgin Trains on its hands.

This rebrand will create excitement amongst customers – but also a great sense of expectation. The potential reward is sufficiently great that you can see why Virgin has been tempted. If they really can deliver a great product combined with a great service, then it could be the brand that wins in the race for the much-coveted quadruple play convergence.

It's too early to tell how this will all play out, but the proof of Virgin Media's success will ultimately be in the delivery of the customer experience, not in a new logo.

Power to the people
There is too much power wielded by consumers today for them and their feelings to be ignored by brand owners. Social networking, blogging and the impact of arenas like Second Life give a greater democracy to the way brands are perceived and ultimately greatly influence how brands are created, take themselves to market and eventually evolve.

They enable consumers to become self-appointed ambassadors or critics of brands, offering powerful cut-through voices in this world of cluttered media and messages. Brands need to welcome, encourage and nurture them.

Many brand owners now invite their most loyal customers to engage with the brands they know and love. They are moving away from the historical norm of

'speaking to' customers and entering a new era of dialogue and conversations.

Sony and Nokia have websites dedicated to capturing the very best ideas to fill their innovation pipelines. JetBlue engages its fans to help redefine the flying experience with them, always looking for new ideas to surprise and delight, and to create viral stories around the brand.

Such is the power of consumers today that many would argue they can make or break a brand. Take Coca-Cola's entry into the UK water market with Dasani. The soft drinks giant launched Dasani in February 2004, backed by a £7 million marketing campaign. However, the drink was beset by problems from the outset. First, and despite retailing at 95p for a small bottle, the water was found to be purified tap water. Next, the drink was revealed to contain potential cancer causing chemicals.

With a little media help, a consumer backlash ensued and just two months after launch the product was withdrawn from the shelves.

People co-creating brands
This power is leading towards an increasing trend in consumers co-creating brands, be it by creating advertising content, telling companies what new products they'd like to see on shelf, advising on how to improve customer

services, or anything else. Consumers have found their voice and aren't afraid to share it with the brands they know and love. Equally, consumers are becoming increasingly vocal when they are let down and when companies fail to deliver on their promises. And many brands are now encouraging consumers to create these shared brand experiences.

Frito Lay's Doritos brand, did exactly that in early 2007. It skipped on the traditional big name celebrity for its Super Bowl television ad spot, instead inviting consumers to create and shoot their own ads. The ads of five finalists were then voted on by the public, with the winner's effort shown during the Super Bowl ad break.

In today's increasingly reality-driven world, people are looking for new ways to interact with, shape and even personalise the brands that are important to them. By allowing consumers to make their own ads and to vote online, Doritos empowered them and created a new memorable branded experience.

Delivering a brand promise
If you were to ask people how successful brands get built, many would say it starts with the branding. This is not the case. Building a successful brand starts with establishing a differentiated meaning for your brand,

then working out if this difference will actually matter to anyone. It's only after this has been done that you can begin to think about the branding and what channels will create the most engaging experiences for your customers.

Defining the brand promise, then empowering employees to understand how they deliver that promise at each and every moment, is critical when considering how consumers will get a brand-differentiated experience. It's your people who deliver your brand's promise to customers, so any serious branding initiative worth its salt must also engage employees. Ultimately this is about putting the brand at the centre of your business then ensuring everything you do and say delivers on it, always keeping your customers at the forefront of your decisions.

Can allowing the consumers to be part of a brand's evolution allow it to truly deliver on its promises?

Chevrolet had its fingers burnt in 2006 after it allowed its website visitors to piece together images and text to create a commercial for its Chevy Tahoe sports utility vehicle. Anti-SUV activists quickly seized on the opportunity to make videos condemning the environmentally unfriendly elements of the Tahoe, and though Chevrolet claimed that much of the content generated was positive, it was the negative responses that circulated most rapidly around the internet.

Beauty brand Dove realised that consumers' idea of beauty had become hugely distorted. Its global 'Campaign for Real Beauty' aims to change the

status quo and offers in its place a broader, healthier, more democratic view of beauty. It created a community site with content created by the women who visited it.

The creation of an online forum for women to participate in a dialogue and debate about the definition and standards of beauty in society hit the right note and that campaign, supported by impactful advertising featuring women of all shapes and sizes has been a resounding success. So successful that in the USA in December 2006 Dove launched a competition inviting women to create their own 30-second commercial to launch the new Dove Cream Oil Body Wash Collection. The ad that Dove felt best captured the essence of the new products and the brand's philosophy

was premiered in a commercial break during coverage of the Oscars ceremony on US television network ABC in February 2007.

Power shift

The days where brands fully control their customer's experience are over. The power is shifting. The customer is now a collaborator in the development of the brand, for better or for worse. Those brands that embrace and act on this shift will likely be the winners.

There has never been a greater need for brands to define then, deliver on relevantly differentiated promises, to be scrupulously honest and transparent, to fix problems quickly and with integrity when they do arise, and most of all, to work with, not against, their customers in creating branded experiences.

**Paul Kemp-Robertson
Co-Founder
& Editorial Director
Contagious**

CONTAGIOUS

The relationship between brands and consumers has shifted. The media landscape has fragmented. The transmission of ideas is more rapid and more viral than ever. Technological revolution accelerates these changes. It means the challenge facing brands – how to stand out and be heard amongst the din – is more acute than ever.

Contagious recognises that strategic creativity remains the last legal way to gain an unfair advantage over the competition. Incorporating a quarterly magazine and DVD, a weekly newsletter, a bespoke information feed, an events organiser and a consultancy, Contagious analyses the creativity and the strategies behind the brand ideas that work.

Branded Utility: A Crash Course in Giving Something Back

By Paul Kemp-Robertson
Co-Founder & Editorial Director
Contagious

When we launched Contagious in 2004, we recognised that the traditional 'push' model of advertising had been knocked sideways as consumers – liberated by technology – began enacting a zero tolerance policy towards unimaginative brands. The plates had shifted, weaning advertisers away from the traditional USP towards a less rational approach. Advertising used to be about 'things'. Now it was all about 'relationships'.

In our first issue we ran an article called 'What's In It For Me?' in which we suggested that in order to engage this empowered audience, brands needed to provide spaces; to build communities, to create new ways to entertain.

In other words, to become more like 'benefactors' than salesmen.

The changes were fuelled by sheer fatigue at the volume and homogeneity of commercial messages. People are bored with much – but not all – of the traditional advertising they are being exposed to.

Think about the growth of websites like Digg, Del.icio.us, MySpace, MetaCafe, YouTube and so on. People are delighting in creating, tagging and discovering interesting content. The good news for the ad industry is that people are happy for commercial content to be part of this new world – but on their terms. The Sony BRAVIA 'Balls' commercial from Fallon/London went on to win dozens of awards around the world, but the first time I encountered this visual extravaganza was via some snaps of the shoot uploaded onto photo-sharing site Flickr by curious local residents in San Francisco!

Tagging makes it easier to circumvent traditional sources of news and entertainment, allowing people to find exactly what they want very quickly. This has huge implications for advertising. In this age of instant search, how old fashioned does a commercial break look to the 'Create, Share & Delete' generation?

McDonald's, P&G, GM and Unilever have all slashed their TV budgets by as much as 25 per cent and diverted dollars into alternative forms of marketing. An example? Cathy's Book: an interactive novel that P&G helped to fund; linking directly to its Cover Girl cosmetics brand and its teenage website, being-girl.com via the book's editorial.

Is this advertising? Branded Content? PR? Sponsorship? Who cares. Labels are so 20th century. Award shows take note! When you have P&G's CEO AG Laffley urging marketers to 'Let Go!', you know the game played by the old rules is well and truly up.

So, traditional ads may be becoming an old and inefficient way to communicate, but on the positive side, if the conventional ways aren't working as well as they used to, then marketers can always try some new ones. People still happily enjoy relationships with brands – especially those that provide entertainment, information and a social conscience in exchange for their custom. Today's successful brands are evolving their relationships by reinventing what it means to get close to consumers.

The overarching development is the desire to be seen to be more than just an advertiser – and actually to become a friend or advisor.

The Patron

There is a general move away from brands, especially youth brands, saying 'We understand you' ('We talk your language') towards saying 'Time to give you a voice'.

This is the brand as Medici, patron of expression and creativity, providing a canvas that the grateful individual is invited to fill.

It is almost as though the brands have tired of trying to entertain (or just plain inform) the consumer: time now for the consumer to entertain and inform the brand.

We've seen this recently – with two very different brands throwing down the gauntlet.

Both Doritos and Dove invited US consumers to create their own commercials, to be aired during the Super Bowl and the Oscars. Interestingly, the winning 'citizen media' commercial actually topped a public poll conducted by IAG as the 'most liked' spot of the entire event. Madison Avenue take note!

The Emperor

As the Roman tyrant would hand power over the gladiator's life to the crowd, so canny brands now hand key elements of decision-making over to consumers – or appear to. The online environment is especially good at cultivating this kind of relationship.

Kellogg's allowed young fans of their Fruitwinders snack to determine which flavour would be next to go into production. The unlucky fruit would then be squashed on live TV in a commercial campaign. More than a million votes were cast online – and sure enough poor Mr Strawberry was duly flattened.

And – the godfather of the emperor phenomenon – the cult appeal of Burger King's Subservient Chicken website came from the illusion that the brand was literally dancing to the consumer's tune.

YouTube is a natural extension of the Emperor strategy. It is the ultimate meritocracy, where brands sink or swim based on the quality of their content. Think of it as the Colosseum in which

brands can battle their way to glory before the eyes of the crowd – or be fed to the lions if their content isn't up to scratch.

Unilever's Dove 'Evolution' spot showing the retouching of a model to 'perfection' has been viewed more than two million times on the site, as has VW's UnPimp My Ride series from Crispin Porter.

The Philanthropist

People like to think they are getting something for nothing.

Younger consumers have been conditioned by their use of file-sharing sites like Napster, Bit-Torrent and Limewire to regard 'free stuff' as a right. Marketers are therefore getting sharper at tailoring their freebies towards the most receptive target groups.

In the US, Ford ran a series of 'flash' concerts to promote its Fusion model – advertised via SMS to a select group of buyers and prospects only hours beforehand. Vodafone UK ran a similar programme, called TBA – which was also turned into a branded TV show.

As part of its 'Coke Side of Life' platform in the Netherlands, Coca-Cola brought some winter sunshine to a popular park in Amsterdam. People could hang out in deckchairs underneath a huge artificial sun – a lighting balloon which rose in the morning and set at 11 o'clock at night.

Branded philanthropy is evolving. It's not all about free stuff. As brands occupy a larger space in popular culture, they also assume a responsibility towards that culture. This is a transparent world in which corporate ethics are becoming as important and influential as marketing messages. In Spain, Heineken funded a social programme called Green Space. This is a brand that has walked away from commercials altogether in the UK.

With Green Space, the brand pays to renovate a building in a neglected city neighbourhood, which then plays host to an arts/music festival before the space is handed back to the community for sustained future use. This is a 'hearts &

minds' approach – providing something of value in exchange for a voice.

Network BBDO in Johannesburg built a solar billboard that will generate enough power to provide over 1,000 children in the neighbouring school with the one hot meal they get each day. Part of the brand's 'Make Things Happen' push, the billboard is a tangible demonstration of the bank's commitment to environmental and educational initiatives.

Contagious is advising brands to really see what they can do in the 'Philanthropy' space. The door is very much open.

The Entertainer

Unsurprisingly, this is the biggest category resided in by brands. For many marketers, the Holy Grail now is to make the leap from marketing to entertainment – or to further elide the difference between the two. Brands are welcome if they can make a genuine difference.

The proliferation of digital TV channels means that many brands can explore new possibilities. In the UK Audi and Honda are now funding their own digital TV channels. Tired of clutter, brands are less willing to pay media owners for the right to interrupt the audience that the media owner has aggregated and have instead started to act as curators of content; with the eye of a talent agent and the bank balance of a movie studio. Online, Budweiser has introduced Bud.TV – a series of channels hosting popular and original entertainment content – an original approach that diverts media dollars away from TV. With the right content and the right approach, brands know they can create their own audience – where quality is much more important than quantity.

Branded Utility

Against this backdrop, TV is increasingly being used as a complementary, rather than a cornerstone medium. Now that people have been allowed to participate and collaborate with the brands they consume, they won't tolerate advertisers shouting at them from a distance.

Consequently, brands as diverse as AmEx, Hersheys and Volvo have used commercials simply as teasers to attract 'eyeballs' to longer branded films on the web.

The future has to be collaborative and open source. Customisation and targeting are key. Brands will be expected to provide services, not messages. To spark conversations and provide invitations.

The Brand Benefactor trend has flourished and developed into something more personalised and proactive – something that has now been termed 'branded utility' – the evolution of 'what's in it for me?'

A long-standing example is mobile operator Orange's 'Orange Wednesday' promotion. A simple text message gets Orange customers two for one cinema tickets on Wednesday nights and has helped to cement Orange's long standing association with film.

Brand alliances are very much at home within the branded utility trend. Strategic, tactical and complimentary joint ventures; the amplification of shared expertise are a definite growth area. Think of the tie-in between iPod and Nike. Nike+ provides detailed training and workout information, plus an online community to put you through your paces. UK magazine publisher NatMags is offering women a branded, personalised diet plan in conjunction with Tesco. The service – based around a social network – monitors calorie intake and allows participants to build an online shopping list.

Electronics brand Philips' 'Sense and Simplicity' positioning has sparked a series of initiatives designed to purge ad clutter and improve the consumer experience. Recent examples include buying adspace at the front of magazines like TIME and Fortune, so that readers can get straight to the list of contents. The campaign extends to experiential efforts allowing customers in 10 countries to feel the benefits of simplicity in action. 'Simplify New York' provides universal access to the New

Image: Al Murphy/Pocko People

York Times' online service, whereas in Brazil Philips is creating a bespoke online resource for the inhabitants of São Paulo and Rio de Janeiro. Loyal to the shift toward consumer generated content, Philips invites people to share their thoughts at Livesimplicity.net.

If the consumer has taken control, then permission-based marketing is paramount. This is a great way to show your consumers that you care what they think. Smart marketers are starting to see that Branded Utility really comes to life on the web.

Nokia's Nseries, for example, has launched a Music Recommenders service that navigates the overcrowded online music scene by tapping into the brains of the world's best independent record shops – aligning perfectly with the brand's 'See new, Hear new, Feel new' strapline.

Or imagine if all those people who wear Nike branded clothes could add a Nike branded 'badge' to their MySpace page showing clips of their favourite moments in sport. They get content, the brand gets back to basics visibility through a 21st century version of the testimonial format. Advertising then becomes less about screaming 'SNEAKERS ARE GREAT!' and more about finding '50 ways to get the most out of your sneakers'.

That's why Contagious predicts that Branded Utility is the future – where brands will only earn a place at the centre of people's lives if they provide a useful service or a helpful application – without demanding an immediate return.

So, place a bet on benevolence. Provide services not messages. Ask not what's in it for you, but what's in it for them.

Superbrands Selection Process

 ## By Stephen Cheliotis, Chairman, Superbrands Councils (UK)

As the chairman of the Superbrands Council (UK) my role is to oversee the judging panel and the selection process that determines which brands are ultimately awarded Superbrand status.

I am very proud of the process we undertake, especially as unlike other 'award' schemes in the industry, brands do not apply to be considered by submitting an entry. Instead, we simply survey the entire market regardless of whether brands are actively promoting themselves or not. By doing so we know that the results will be both comprehensive and accurately reflect the experts' and public's opinion.

We consider brands based on merit and it is important to me that no commercial considerations can impact on the process. As such, both the creation of the list and the rating of the brands is left to the independent researchers, council and public, without the influence of the Superbrands organisation.

Interestingly, and probably to the annoyance of the Superbrands commercial team, every year brands wanting to be involved in the related publication and membership programme have to be turned down simply because they did not score highly enough in the award scheme. Even long term supporters, who enjoy a strong relationship with Superbrands, be they Shell or Specsavers, have to go through the same process each year and if they fail to make the grade they will not be

eligible to participate in Superbrands activities. This maintains the elite proposition of Superbrands, which is fundamental to its offering.

To generate the initial 'population list' a number of independent researchers are employed; they have the large undertaking of analysing databases, research reports, media titles (both consumer and trade) and other sources of information to find suitable brands. They look at sectors as diverse as airlines to cleaning products and do this throughout the year.

Agencies and brands can, and do, call on occasions to suggest a brand for consideration; I welcome this but in reality nine out of 10 times the brand will already be featured on the register. In fact the population list usually features between 5,000 – 10,000 brands so it is practically impossible to miss any brand due to the depth and breadth of the list. The range of brands and sectors considered is reviewed with every new programme.

The next job is to turn the population list into a short list, a more manageable sized selection for consideration by the Superbrands council. This is generated using the information provided by the researchers. This year the short list featured 1,450 brands. Any brand considered a genuine contender is included; when there is debate about its credentials, a brand is given the benefit of the doubt so that the council can decide

its fate. As a final check any council member can request that we include a brand they feel has been omitted.

The 'short' list is then sent to each independent and voluntary council member. We continue to grow the size of the council from 14 members in 2005 to 17 in 2006/07 and 19 in 2007/08 – the current programme – to give us as wide a view of experts as possible and ensure a diverse collection of perspectives and experiences.

The big change in the council this year is that we no longer have individuals from the marketing departments of brands that could feasible qualify for that given programme. This is simply to avoid the possibility that people might assume that they could have influence over their own brands performance – of course they were never allowed to vote for their own brand. Council members are now either senior figures from marketing services agencies, across different disciplines, or from media and/or trade bodies and associations. The council consists of a combination of new and existing members from the previous year; this ensures a balance between consistency and comparability with keeping things fresh and up-to-date.

Council members score each brand on the presented short list in their own time, giving each a rating from 1-10. Council members are asked to score each brand instinctively, presenting a rating that illustrates their overall impression of the brand's strength. Individuals do not research the brands or think too long about each entity.

Council members only consider a brand's status within the UK, although international strength may constitute part of a brand's make-up and improve its image. Individuals cannot score brands that they are involved with, i.e. clients of their company. In addition, competitor brands cannot be scored. Equally, council members are asked not to score a brand that they are not familiar with – we do not want them to deduce a ranking based on a glance at the brand's website or through second-hand opinion. In these instances Superbrands applies an average score to that brand based upon the ratings of the other council members.

Whilst council members are asked to consider their overall perception of each brand, we do request that council members consider three factors and keep these in mind when allocating their scores. They are:

Quality – does the brand represent quality products and services?

Reliability – can you trust the brand to deliver consistently against its promises and maintain product and service standards at all customer touch points?

Distinction – is it well known in its sector? Is the brand suitably differentiated from its competitors? Does it have a personality and values that make it unique within its market place?

We believe that all three qualities are essential ingredients in a Superbrand. In addition all highly rated brands must be able to stand up against the following definition:

"A Superbrand has established the finest reputation in its field. It offers customers significant emotional and tangible advantages over other brands, which (consciously or sub-consciously) consumers want and recognise."

Council members score the brands in the context of the entire list, so there is no weighting by sector and they can allocate their scores as they choose. My commercial involvement with Superbrands is merely part-time, however, I do not score the brands personally to avoid any 'commercial influence' claims.

The returned scores are collated and a league table is presented to the council who have the opportunity to review and discuss it at a council meeting. This is the final opportunity they have to add any missing brands,

note any mistakes, examine the definition and the methodology and provide opinion on the next and final stage of the process, which is the consumer vote.

The 725 most highly rated brands according to the council's scores, i.e. the top 50 per cent, were put forward to the consumer vote which was managed by the research agency YouGov. A total of 3,265 people took part in the online polls. A new league table based on the consumer vote was created with the top 500 considered to be the Superbrands – this table is published in the national press, as well as being listed alphabetically at the back of this book so that all the brands are suitably acknowledged. The top 500 brands are also invited to take up membership with Superbrands, giving them marketing and networking opportunities through its campaigns, events, publications, online networking tools and so forth.

Now that Superbrands in the UK is an independent franchise – it effectively split from the parent group in 2006 – its ability to make swift changes has been enhanced. If you have any questions, comments or thoughts on the programme and the process please do contact me on: stephen.cheliotis@superbrands.uk.com

The myth	The truth
Brands pay to be considered for the Superbrands programme.	All brands with the potential to succeed are considered. There is no cost to the brands.
Brands pay to be a Superbrand.	All brands in the top 500 are Superbrands regardless of any wider involvement with the Superbrands organisation. Their achievement is acknowledged by publishing the full list of 500 in the national press, in the Superbrands book, and at www.superbrands.uk.com.
The Council determine which brands are Superbrands.	The Council plays an important role by approving and ranking the initial short list. However, the final top 500 is determined by a nationally representative poll of consumers, surveyed by YouGov plc.
If you are a member of the current programme you automatically qualify for next year's programme.	Each year the process starts afresh and brands are considered by the council and the UK public. Only brands highly rated that year can take up membership and feature in the Superbrands publication. Qualification one year is no guarantee of qualification the following year.

Superbrands
Council 2007/08

Howard Beale
Founder &
Managing Director
The Fish Can Sing

Howard is an entrepreneur with a passion for building successful marketing services businesses.

He is the founder and managing director of The Fish Can Sing (TFCS), a marketing company with offices in London and New York. TFCS sells high level creative ideas to major global brands. The company's blue chip client list includes Nike, Motorola, Johnnie Walker, BMW, and the world's leading eyewear group, Luxottica.

He is committed to delivering innovative and commercially-effective marketing solutions. He believes brands must do more to engage consumers by ensuring brand messages are of real interest and relevance in whatever medium they are delivered.

Prior to TFCS, he co-founded BlueberryFrog, the sister company of StrawberryFrog, an international advertising agency. He also worked for Hill and Knowlton (WPP), and as a journalist and staff writer at The Sunday Telegraph.

He graduated from London University (School of Oriental and African Studies) with a BA (Hons) in History.

Drayton Bird
Chairman
Drayton Bird
Associates

Four years ago Drayton was named by The Chartered Institute of Marketing as one of the 50 living individuals who have shaped modern marketing. Other names mentioned were Kotler, Levitt and Peters.

He has written three widely admired marketing books, over 1,000 articles for various magazines, spoken or trained in 40 countries on the subject and was on the worldwide board of the Ogilvy Group.

He has worked with some of the world's most recognised firms, including Procter & Gamble, Unilever, Visa, American Express, BT, Toyota, Mercedes, Volkswagen, IBM, McKinsey, Microsoft® and many others. Drayton is the chairman of five firms involved in various aspects of marketing, from direct marketing to event management. He writes copy, trains, runs seminars and is consulted by a wide range of firms in a number of countries.

Leslie de Chernatony
Professor, Brand
Marketing & Director,
Centre for Research in
Brand Marketing
Birmingham University
Business School

With a doctorate in brand marketing, Leslie has written extensively for American and European journals and is a regular presenter at international conferences. He has written several books on brand marketing, the two most recent being Creating Powerful Brands and From Brand Vision to Brand Evaluation.

A winner of several research grants, his two most recent have supported research into factors associated with high performance brands and research into services branding. He has been the Visiting Professor at Madrid Business School and is currently visiting professor at Thammasat University, Bangkok and University of Lugano, Switzerland. Leslie is a Fellow of the Chartered Institute of Marketing and Fellow of the Market Research Society. He acts as an international consultant to organisations seeking more effective brand strategies and has run acclaimed branding seminars throughout Europe, Asia, America and the Far East. He is also an experienced expert witness in legal cases involving branding issues in commercial and competition cases.

Mark Cridge
Chief Executive
glue London

Mark has worked in interactive since 1994 when he left the world of Architecture realising that it just wasn't his cup of tea. Previously a senior creative at Modem Media in London, in 1999 he left to establish glue London to inject some much needed creativity and more rigorous thinking into the UK's digital advertising scene.

Mark has been cited by Campaign magazine as a 'Face to Watch', has featured in the FT Creative Business 50, picked up the inaugural Digital Achiever of the Year gong at the 2005 Campaign Digital Awards and was hilariously even voted as the most influential person in new media by his peers in New Media Age. He is a regular speaker at industry events and is often called upon to sit on award juries, most recently chairing the digital panels at the Asian Advertising Awards and D&AD.

glue has grown quickly to over 120 people with an enviable client list including: Virgin, Coca-Cola, adidas, Sky, Nokia, the COI, Eurostar, RAC and MINI.

Tim Duffy
Chief Executive
M&C Saatchi

Tim graduated from King's College, Cambridge and in 1986 joined Saatchi & Saatchi, as a strategic planner. There he worked on major projects for clients including IBM, British Airways, Procter & Gamble and the launch of the National Lottery.

In 1995 he was one of the founders of M&C Saatchi, helping it become a top 10 agency in five years. It now has 20 offices across 15 countries worldwide. In the UK, the agency works for a wide variety of clients including Fosters, Transport for London, ITV, Lucozade, Ribena, Halfords, the COI, Royal Bank of Scotland, Australia Tourism, Curry's and PC World.

He was appointed managing director in 1997 and chief executive of the London Agency in 2004.

Vanessa Eke
Managing Director
Language Line
Services Ltd

Vanessa joined Language Line Services, the world's leading provider of interpreting services, as managing director in 2006.

Building further on the global media expertise gained during her tenure as managing director of Nielsen Media Research and AdEx International, she is now developing new products and services for both the private and public sector. Enabling organisations to actively engage with limited English speakers to improve both access to services and commercial opportunity is a key driver for the business.

Underpinned by her early career at KPMG and further senior management positions she brings a good deal of insight and expertise relating to 'Superbrands' at home and abroad.

This now extends to an insight into the response of ethnic communities to companies and their services, representing an enormous potential growth market for a wide range of organisations.

Peter Fisk
Founder
Genius Works

Peter is an inspirational author, speaker and coach – described as "one of the best new business thinkers" by Business Strategy Review. His best-selling book, Marketing Genius, explores how to combine a more intelligent and imaginative approach to customers and business in order to deliver extraordinary results. It has been translated into 20 languages.

Peter has managed or advised many of the world's leading brands including American Express and British Airways, Coca-Cola and Marks & Spencer, Microsoft® and Vodafone, and was also CEO of The Chartered Institute of Marketing. He created the Genius Works (www.thegeniusworks.com) to bring together the latest ideas and best practices in strategy and marketing, innovation and brands as leading-edge thinking (his new books Customer Genius, Business Genius and Creative Genius will be published in Spring 2008), inspirational events (including The Genius Lab and The Marketing Fast Track), and innovative solutions (strategic consulting and new ventures).

Winston Fletcher
Chairman
Advertising Standards
Board of Finance

Winston is chairman of the Advertising Standards Board of Finance, the Royal Institution, the Knightsbridge Association, and Barnardo's in London and the South East. He is also vice president of the History of Advertising Trust and on the Advisory Council of the Barbican.

His career appointments include being founder chairman, Fletcher Shelton Delaney; chairman and CEO, Ted Bates UK Group; and chairman and CEO, Delaney Fletcher Bozell.

Winston is the only person to have been chairman of the Advertising Association and president of the IPA, as well as a council member of the ASA, and founder chairman of the World Advertising Research Center.

He has also published 12 books and over 3,000 articles. Winston is a visiting professor at Westminster University Business School and lectures at the London Business School, and City University. He is currently writing The History Of British Advertising 1951 – 2001, for publication by the Oxford University Press next year.

Cheryl Giovannoni
Managing Director
Landor Associates,
London

Cheryl joined Landor as managing director of the flagship London office in October 2005. She is passionate about the pivotal role that branding and design play in the health and long term growth of brands.

South African born, Cheryl moved to London in 1993 to join ad agency Ogilvy, working with Unilever, Mattel, SmithKline Beecham and BUPA, before moving to Lowe Howard-Spink to run the global Braun account.

In 2001 Cheryl changed direction to join brand design agency Coley Porter Bell as CEO, also leading the agency's accounts with Nestlé, GlaxoSmithKline and GE. She was also a member of the Ogilvy UK Group Board.

Landor was twice named Design Agency of the Year (Marketing, 2001/2005) and has been Packaging Agency of the Year for an unprecedented two consecutive years (GRAMIA Awards, 2005/2006). Landor's clients include BP, Citigroup, Diageo, Ernst & Young, Jet Airways, Kraft Foods, Morrisons, Nokia, Procter & Gamble, PepsiCo and Traidcraft.

David Haigh
Chief Executive
Brand Finance

David qualified as a chartered accountant with PricewaterhouseCoopers LLP in London. He worked in international financial management before moving into the marketing services sector, firstly as financial director of The Creative Business and then as financial director of WCRS & Partners.

He then left to set up a financial marketing consultancy, which was later acquired by Publicis, the pan European marketing services group, where he worked as a director for five years. David moved to Interbrand as director of brand valuation in its London based global brand valuation practice, leaving in 1996 to launch Brand Finance.

David is a fellow of the UK Chartered Institute of Marketing. He is the author of Brand Valuation (FT – Retail and Consumer Publishing, 1998), Brand Valuation – a review of current practice (IPA, 1996), Strategic Control of Marketing Finance (FT/Pitman Publishing, 1994) and Marca Valor do Intangível (Editora Atlas, August 2003).

Graham Hiscott
Consumer Editor
Daily Express

Graham has been a qualified journalist for 12 years, six of those specialising in consumer affairs. His career started with a degree in journalism at the University of Central Lancashire in Preston. After graduating he landed a job as a reporter on the Cambridge Evening News.

Eighteen months later Graham left to become a reporter at a press agency in Birmingham, News Team International. His career continued to progress 18 months later with a move to the Press Association as a regional reporter covering the East Midlands. It was here Graham developed his interest as a consumer affairs correspondent, which led to another move to the Press Association's HQ in London. From there he was appointed consumer editor of the Daily Express, in March 2005.

Graham was runner-up at the London Press Club Awards 2005 and 2006, for Consumer Journalist of the Year. Among the reasons for his nominations were breaking the Dasani bottled water story and a series of stories about soaring energy bills.

Paul Kemp-Robertson
Editorial Director &
Co-Founder
Contagious

Paul started his career at corporate communications firm Maritz before helping to launch shots magazine in 1990. After a spell in commercials production, he returned to shots, becoming editor in 1994. Subscriptions trebled under his tenure.

In 1998 he succeeded Donald Gunn as Leo Burnett's worldwide director of creative resources in Chicago. Paul was responsible for the agency's Great Commercials intranet site and its quarterly creative councils, known as the Global Product Committee.

Paul left Leo Burnett in 2004 to co-found Contagious – a quarterly magazine and DVD reporting on future trends and non-invasive marketing techniques. A joint venture with Xtreme Information in London, Contagious sees Paul reunited with shots founder Gee Thomson.

Paul has written numerous articles for publications including Business 2.0, The Guardian, Hollywood Reporter and M&M Europe, as well as co-editing D&AD's The Commercials Book. He has appeared on BBC Radio 4's The Today Programme and Five Live's Wake Up To Money.

David Magliano
Ex Director of
Marketing
London 2012

David was director of marketing for London 2012. He was responsible for building UK public support as well as presenting London's bid to the International Olympic Committee.

Before London 2012, David was sales and marketing director of two low-cost airlines – Go (of which he was a founder) and easyJet. David is the only person to have been named UK Marketer of the Year twice (1999 and 2005). In September 2006 Advertising Age named David Global CMO of the Year. He was awarded an MBE in 2006.

Mandy Pooler
Director
Kantar

After reading English at Jesus College Oxford, Mandy had a rush of numbers to the head during two years spent in the marketing department of the International Thomson Organisation. In 1982 she joined Ogilvy & Mather as a media planner, becoming media director in 1991 and managing director of O&M Media in 1994. Mandy was a founder of The Network, which launched Ogilvy's 26 media operations into a single European media organisation.

In 1998 she became the first CEO of MindShare UK and after three turbulent but rewarding years changed direction to launch another new venture. The Channel is a knowledge centre around media and communications and a focus for collaboration for the WPP Group and its clients. In July 2006 she became director for development at Kantar, the holding group for the research and consultancy businesses owned by WPP.

She is chairman of AGB Nielsen in the UK, a fellow of the IPA and a former Advertising Woman of the Year.

Chris Powell
Co-Founder
BMP

Chris was a co-founder of the advertising agency BMP, which went on to build the strongest creative and planning reputation in the world and became the second largest UK agency, working on well loved brands such as Cadbury's, Smash, John Smith's Bitter and Walkers crisps.

He now chairs the National Endowment for Science, Technology and the Arts (NESTA) that fosters innovation and business start-ups, the Institute of Public Policy Research (IPPR) – the UK's largest Think Tank – and is vice chair of the Public Diplomacy Board. He is a member of the Board of Doctor Foster and Media Metrica and of the corporate advisory Board of PricewaterhouseCoopers LLP.

Anna Ronay
Editor
Ethos

Anna was editor of the marketer, the monthly member magazine for members of The Chartered Institute of Marketing, for over three years. She launched the title in April 2004 and collected a series of industry awards, including Most Effective Membership Magazine at the Association of Publishing Agencies Awards in November 2005. Anna recently took up editorship of a new magazine called Ethos, created by Sunday Publishing on behalf of Serco. The first issue was launched in March 2007.

Anna has also edited Marketing Business magazine, Critical Marketing – a quarterly journal for senior marketers – and titles for financial services provider Alliance & Leicester and law firm Davies Lavery. Prior to this she worked for Lafferty Group, writing and reporting on the global financial services industry.

Tim Sutton
Chairman
Weber Shandwick,
Europe

Tim is one of the European PR industry's most respected practitioners. He is also European chairman of the Constituency Management Group of the Interpublic Group of Companies, including its businesses in the areas of public relations, events management and corporate & brand identity.

Educated at Magdalen College, Oxford, he is a renowned corporate PR professional having directed corporate programmes and campaigns for some of Europe's top companies and industries. He has a particularly strong track record in reputation strategy, brand development and public issues campaigning, which has won him significant industry recognition. His long term programme for bmi british midland remains the only European PR campaign to have won both of the industry's top awards: the PR Week Grand Prix and the IPR Sword of Excellence.

Tim has advised numerous other companies on communications strategy and is a recognised authority on crisis management, brand strategy and employee communications.

Suki Thompson
Founding Partner
The Haystack Group

Haystack works with clients to help them evaluate, search and select agencies across all disciplines. Since its launch in 2001, the company has grown to become one of the leading intermediaries globally, placing approximately £500 million of communications budgets annually and running both search, audits and training for companies on a global basis. Clients include the Post Office, Sainsbury's, Camelot, Honda, Nationwide, NSPCC and Volvo.

Prior to Haystack, Suki set up Kendall Tarrant in Asia and in the UK was an experienced agency director, managing business development for London agencies, WWAV Rapp Collins, FCA! and TBWA, as well as running a variety of accounts including M&SFS, Debenhams, Lever Brothers and British Tourist Association.

Suki is a frequent contributor to the national and marketing press and a regular speaker at industry conferences. She is a board director of The Marketing Society and has devised and chaired events that look at client/agency relationships.

Mark Waugh
Deputy Managing
Director
ZenithOptimedia

When Mark joined the UK media planning fraternity from Oxford University, media was seen as a trading-based discipline that followed the strategic lead offered by the advertising agency. In the intervening 17 years Mark has been a key player in driving the strategic importance of media planning in the industry, at the age of 28 he became the youngest ever managing partner of Optimedia. Mark joined market leader ZenithOptimedia as deputy managing director in 2003.

In his career Mark has amassed experience across almost every market category, from motors to luxury goods and financial services to FMCG. This, coupled with his agency's £700 million UK spend, allows him a uniquely scaled perspective on the behaviour of some of Britain's biggest brands. In 2007 Mark launched newcast, ZenithOptimedia's integrated communications unit, which develops and executes everything from experiential marketing to digital branded content. If anyone has an holistic approach to building Superbrand fame it should be Mark.

Stephen Cheliotis
Chairman
Superbrands
Councils (UK)

Stephen attained a degree in PR & Marketing before joining global brand valuation and strategy consultancy, Brand Finance, where he helped to advise brands on maximising shareholder value through effective brand management. In addition he produced a range of significant reports, including comprehensive studies of global intangible assets. His annual study of City Analysts, which explored the City's need for marketing information, was vital in understanding the importance of marketing metrics in appreciating and forecasting companies' performance.

In 2001 Stephen joined Superbrands UK, becoming UK managing director in 2003 and overseeing two years of significant growth. Given a European role in 2005, his expertise was used across 20 countries. In 2006 he set up his own business providing PR and marketing advice to companies.

Stephen chairs the three independent Superbrands Councils in the UK. He speaks at conferences on branding and is a regular commentator for international media on the subject. He is a frequent guest on CNN, the BBC and Sky amongst others.

Panos Manolopoulos
Managing Director
YouGov
www.yougov.com

About YouGov

By Panos Manolopoulos
Managing Director

"The poll I rely on most, because of its methodology and track record, is YouGov."

William Rees-Mogg, former editor of The Times

YouGov is a full service online research agency, collecting high quality in-depth data for marketing research and opinion polling. YouGov operates a diverse panel of over 160,000 UK residents with similar operations in America and the Middle East.

Based on its recent records YouGov is the UK's most accurate public opinion pollster and dominates Britain's media polling today through the publication of its work in the media. Based on its work in the consumer research and opinion polling sector, the agency has one of the fastest growth rates in the industry. YouGov is a pioneer of online research and e-consultation, using its strong market research skill set and industry expertise to support its clients. The agency's full service work extends across industry sectors including consumer, financial, healthcare, media, new media and technology. A range of different research types and data collection methods are used in survey designs tailored to individual client requirements. YouGov offers innovative and tailored market research solutions, quality of service and insight that allow its clients to make effective decisions about their business.

YouGov offers a wide range of market research services designed around our clients' needs first. Based on traditional market research skills, YouGov demonstrates industry leading expertise in opinion polling and online research methods and techniques.

YouGov services include omnibus, syndicated, continuous and tracking research and bespoke research solutions. The agency also specialises in creating and managing specialist audience and client-branded proprietary panels. Examples include senior level professionals from the private and public sectors, health professionals, hospital patients, local authority residents, utility customers and global news consumers.

The scope of its research solutions include Consumer Research, Daily Omnibus, Opinion Polling, Usage & Attitude Studies, Advertising Research, Brand Research, B2B, Children/Youth and Family Research, Concept Testing, Customer Satisfaction, Employee Research, Multi-Country Studies, New Product Development Testing, Packaging/Design, Product Testing, Segmentation Research, Syndicated Research, Tracking Studies.

Detailed demographic, marketing and other lifestyle profiling information is collected for panel members. This enables YouGov to select a national sample representative of the elector or adult universe. YouGov also selects samples for marketing research from the panel based on individual survey selection quota and profiling requirements.

Respondents are then emailed an invitation to complete a survey online. Alternative data collection techniques are also used where appropriate. Raw data for national opinion surveys can be weighted post-field to ensure it is still representative of the target sample. During the panel registration process, YouGov collects a vast amount of information on each panellist and can therefore design almost any sample. This registration information is regularly checked and updated. For quantitative research, YouGov generally provides larger samples and delivers data at a greater speed than other research methods.

Response rates of at least 40 per cent are normally achieved within 24 hours and 60 per cent within 72 hours. Little difference has been detected between early and later responses, once the data has been weighted to demographic and attitudinal variables, including past vote and newspaper readership.

YouGov is a member of the Market Research Society and of the British Polling Council. YouGov is also registered with the Information Commissioner.

AA
Abbey
Absolut
Actimel
Adidas
Adobe
After Eight
Aga Rayburn
Airmiles
Alfa Romeo
Alka-Seltzer
Alton Towers
Amazon
Ambre Solaire
American Express
Anadin
Anchor
Andrex
AOL
Apple
Argos
Ariel
Arsenal FC
Asda
Audi
Autoglass
Avis
A-Z Maps
B&Q
Bacardi
Baileys
Bang & Olufsen
Barbie
Barclaycard
Barclays
Bassett's
BBC
Beck's
Beechams
Bell's
Ben & Jerry's
Benylin
Berghaus
BIC
Birds
Birds Eye
Bisto
Black & Decker
Blaupunkt
Blu-Tack
BMW
Bold
Bombay Sapphire
Bonjela
Boots The Chemist
Bosch
Bounty
BP
Branston
Brillo
British Airways
British Airways London Eye
British Gas

Britvic
BT
Budweiser
BUPA
Burberry
Burger King
Cadbury
Cadbury Creme Egg
Cadbury Crunchie
Cadbury Dairy Milk
Cadbury Flake
Caffè Nero
Calpol
Calvin Klein
Campbell's
Canon
Carling
Carlsberg
Carte D'Or
Castrol
Cathay Pacific
Center Parcs
Chanel
Channel 4
Chelsea FC
Cif
Clarins
Clarks
Clinique
CNN
Coca-Cola
Colgate
Colman's
Comfort
Cosmopolitan
Costa
Courvoisier
Cow & Gate
Crayola
Crown
D&G
Danone
Daz
Deep Heat
Dell
Dettol
Dettox
Diesel
Diet Coke
Dior
Disneyland Resort Paris
DKNY
Dolmio
Dom Perignon
Domestos
Domino's
Douwe Egberts
Dove
Dr Martens
Drambuie
Dulux
Dunlop
Duracell

Durex
Dyson
Early Learning Centre
Ebay
Eden Project
Elastoplast
Elizabeth Arden
EMI
Emirates
Emporio Armani
Esso
Estée Lauder
Eurostar
Eurotunnel
Evian
Fairtrade
Fairy
Famous Grouse
Fanta
Ferrero Rocher
Filofax
Finish
First Choice
Fisher-Price
Flash
Flora
Flymo
Foster's
Friends Reunited
FT
Fuji
Galaxy
Gap
Garnier
Gaviscon
Gillette
Giorgio Armani
Givenchy
Glenfiddich
Goodyear
Google
Gordon's
Gossard
Grand Marnier
Green & Black's
Grolsch
Guardian
Guinness
Häagen-Dazs
Habitat
Halfords
Halifax
Hamleys
Harley-Davidson
Harrods
Harvey Nichols
Head & Shoulders
Heineken
Heinz
Hellmann's
Hennessy
Hertz
Hewlett-Packard

Highland Spring
Hilton
HMV
Holiday Inn
Holland & Barrett
Homepride
Hoover
Horlicks
Hornby
Hotmail
Hotpoint
House of Fraser
Hovis
HP
HSBC
Huggies
Hugo Boss
IBM
Ikea
Imperial Leather
Intel
Interflora
IPod
ITV
J₂O
Jack Daniel's
Jacob's Creek
Jaeger
Jaffa Cakes
Jaguar
Jameson
JCB
Jean Paul Gaultier
John Lewis
John Smith's
Johnnie Walker
Johnson's
JVC
Kellogg's
Kellogg's Corn Flakes
Kellogg's Special K
Kenco
Kenwood
Kingsmill
KitKat
Kleenex
KLM
Kodak
Kraft
Kronenbourg 1664
Kuoni
Kwik-Fit
Ladbrokes
Lancôme
Land Rover
Le Creuset
Lea & Perrins
Lego
Legoland
Lemsip
Lenor
Levi's
Lexus

Lindt
Liquorice Allsorts
Liverpool FC
Lloyds TSB
L'Oréal Paris
Lotus
Lucozade
Lufthansa
Lurpak
M&M's
Maclaren
Madame Tussauds
Magnum
Maltesers
Manchester United FC
Marks & Spencer
Marmite
Marriott
Mars
Martini
Mastercard
Mattel
Max Factor
McCain
McDonald's
McVitie's
Mercedes-Benz
Michelin
Michelin Guides
Microsoft
Miele
Moët & Chandon
Monopoly
Monsoon
Morphy Richards
Mothercare
Motorola
Mr Kipling
Mr Muscle
Mr Sheen
MSN
MTV
Müller
National Express
National Geographic
Nationwide
Natwest
Nescafé
Nestlé
Newcastle Brown Ale
New Covent Garden Food Co
Nicorette
Night Nurse
Nike
Nikon
Nintendo
Nivea
Nokia
Norwich Union
Nurofen
O2
Odeon
Olay

Olympus
Omega
Optrex
Orange
Ordnance Survey
Ovaltine
P&O Ferries
Pampers
Panadol
Panasonic
Parker
PayPal
PC World
Pedigree
Pentax
Pepsi
Pepsi Max
Perrier
Persil
PG Tips
Philadelphia
Philips
Pimm's
Pioneer
Pirelli
Pizza Express
Playstation
Pledge
Polaroid
Polyfilla
Porsche
Post Office
Post-It
Pret A Manger
Pringles
Puma
Quaker Oats
Qantas
RAC
Radio Times
Radisson
Raleigh
Ralph Lauren
Ray-Ban
Red Bull
Reebok
Remy Martin
Rennie
Reuters
Ribena
Ritz Carlton
Robertson's
Robinsons
Rolo
Ronseal
Rotary Watches
Royal Albert Hall
Royal Bank of Scotland
Royal Doulton
Royal Mail
Royal Worcester
Russell Hobbs
Ryvita

Saab
Sainsbury's
Samsonite
Samsung
Sanatogen
Savlon
Scalextric
Scholl
Schweppes
Scottish Widows
Scrabble
Selfridges & Co
Sellotape
Seven Seas
Sharwood's
Shell
Sheraton Hotels & Resorts
Shredded Wheat
Silent Night
Silver Cross
Singapore Airlines
Sky
Slazenger
Slumberland
Smarties
Smeg
Smirnoff
Snickers
Sony
Sony Ericsson
Southern Comfort
Specsavers Opticians
Speedo
Sprite
Stanley
Starbucks
Stella Artois
Strepsils
Strongbow
Swarovski
Swatch
Swiss Army
Tag Heuer
Tampax
Tate & Lyle
Tate Galleries
TCP
Technics
Tefal
Tesco
Tetley
The Body Shop
The Daily Telegraph
The Economist
The National Lottery
The Observer
The Sunday Telegraph
The Sunday Times
The Times
The Tussauds Group
Thermos
Thomas Cook
Thomson Holidays

Thorntons
Tiffany & Co
Timberland
Tipp-Ex
T-Mobile
Toblerone
Toilet Duck
Tommy Hilfiger
Toshiba
Travelodge
Trivial Pursuit
Tropicana
Tunes
Tupperware
Twinings
Twix
Ty.phoo
Umbro
Uncle Ben's
Vanish
Vaseline
Vicks
Virgin Atlantic
Virgin Holidays
Virgin Megastores
Virgin Mobile
Virgin Trains
Visa
Vodafone
Vogue
Volkswagen
Volvic
Volvo
Wagamama
Waitrose
Walkers
Wall's Ice Cream
Waterford Crystal
Waterstone's
Wedgwood
Weetabix
Weight Watchers
Wembley Stadium
Werther's Original
Which?
Whirlpool
Whiskas
WHSmith
William Hill
Wonderbra
Wrigley's
Xbox
Xerox
Yahoo!
Yakult
Yellow Pages
Yorkie
Zanussi
Zippo

QUALITY RELIABILITY DISTINCTION